A STONEY ROAD

Patrick Coyle

To Nuala

Patricia Coyle

Dedication

To our eight delightful grandchildren:
Philip, Patrick, Sean, Colin, Cliona, Alex, Sinead & Aoife

The moving finger writes; and, having writ,
Moves on: nor all thy piety nor wit
Shall lure it back to cancel half a line,
Nor all thy tears wash out a word of it.

Omar Khayyam

Contents

Foreword

It's 2013 and as this little tale begins it's hard to believe how the world has changed since my childhood. Imagine a world without electricity or mechanical power. No radio, telephone or television. Your only contact with the outside world was an occasional religious magazine or a newspaper. A world of so few cars that roads were a favoured place for meetings, recreation and games such as skittles, bowls, marbles, not to mention dancing. All the work on the land and most of the transport was still done by horses. To do anything or to go anywhere, just preparing the horse was not a quick or simple job. Harnessing involves a lot of strapping and buckling and then you were always exposed to the elements. Today, you can be in your warm car in seconds, listening to a perfect reproduction of the 1812 Overture as you speed away in armchair comfort while rain and snow lash down.

On the small farm where I was born, self- reliance was almost total. We grew all our own food, once a year we killed and butchered a pig for bacon, churned milk for butter and ground the corn for flour. Shopping was a rare exercise: paraffin for oil lamps, candles, tea and sugar and tobacco for my father's pipe. Seldom did we bring money to pay for our shopping. Instead, we carried a small wicker basket with perhaps a dozen or more loose eggs. If we didn't have enough eggs to pay for all our shopping then we dropped items from this meagre list.

Shercock was the name of our nearest village. Travelling there involved crossing the fields because it was a much shorter distance than going by road, but getting through hedges and ditches while cradling a small basket of loose eggs with the neighbour's angry dogs snapping at your legs could be hazardous.

Think of homes without water and all that goes with this, including and especially toilet facilities. Our main water source was rain off the roof collected in a barrel, or in summer, a well in a neighbour's field. With all today's modern comforts you may feel we had a fairly grim existence. We did. But not because of the reasons mentioned. It was a grim, brutal time because as a community and a nation, we were in the blinding grip of total denial about ourselves and our failures. And a degree of openness and honesty which would allow us to deal with them did not exist. Our independence was recently won and we were all members of the one true faith. How could we possibly be wrong about anything? As a society we were flawless and I read at the time that we were indeed 'a light onto other nations'. Anyone who held up a mirror or raised a tiny voice telling us the truth was demonised. Books and plays letting in a little light were banned and their authors banished.

Yet ironically, as individuals we were told repeatedly how sinful we were. Satan's hordes assailed us from all sides, so mamma responded by organising battalions of saints to keep us safe. At the heart of our outer defensive shield was the child of Prague. There she sat in our front window looking out over the lane towards the bog. Mamma figured that if the divil was coming for us that's where he'd most likely come from. Other mighty saints were posted like Napoleonic generals in flanking positions.

As children, we each had personal protection - spiritual body armour if you like. For this we had the miraculous medal, the brown scapular and the Sacred Heart image. This preoccupation with how personally evil we were created a powerful suffocating sense of guilt. Not a word about the blindingly obvious truth: we were the most virtuous, hardworking controlled, put-upon, guilt-ridden, exploited, God fearing people on earth!

The most unforgivable aspect of our blind denial and dishonesty was brutality to our children. Our catechism commanded

"Children are to be reared in the love and fear of God".

Can love and fear co-exist? In reality, love was an unspeakable four letter word. Fear ruled. Corporal punishment and the sacred mantra: "Spare the rod, spoil the child," were euphemisms for sadism at home and in school. And convent schools, where you'd imagine love might have a place, were worse than national schools in the creative range of punishments and humiliations inflicted. Another aspect of our brutality was the absence of the language or outward displays of affection between parents and children. The language of affection seeps and flows through an entire culture and creates and contributes hugely to its humanity. Apart from the nearby MacAdams family, my entire experience as a child was of a harsh arid emotional desert were people were plagued by fear and guilt. And remember, we committed sin in four different ways: by thought, word, deed or omission. So you didn't have to act to be sinful, just a wayward thought qualified. Likewise, you didn't need to say anything - silence or inaction could equally leave you guilty.

It's painful just thinking how parents' lives were so impoverished by such a perversion of their natural instincts and with it they lost the primary source of happiness in their lives. Instead of homes and schools full of happy, joyful children, we had children who were sullen, resentful and aggressive. As these children grew into adults, is it any wonder that for the rest of their lives, they held a sneering contempt for books, school or education? This was a model proving ground for the truism,

"Childhood is for life".

So this little tale begins with an overview of what life was like on a hilly, boggy farm in the county Monaghan of my childhood, a mere sixty years ago. The rest is about my experiences after leaving home. Here I must enter a plea for your patience. Why would you want to or have any interest in my experiences? I am not a celebrity. I have no claim to fame, but then neither do I have an ego. Still, if you stay with me a little longer I hope you'll find something in this little story that may entertain and reward you.

Chapter 2 - World War Two

Although we were a long way from the action, we were very much in a war. At the time Ireland had so little manufacturing industry; apart from basic food items everything was imported. Kitchenware for instance all but vanished. So we were using tin mugs "porringers" and many wore wooden shoes "clogs". And because there were such heavy losses of ships during the war, it wasn't until 1948/49, two to three years after the war ended, that normal shipping started again. Over this period of ten years, what we missed most was coal. As children, we also missed Santa Claus and for the four youngest members of the Coyle family, Santa Claus existed in name only. Santa Claus never appeared at any time during our childhood. The important point about coal is that we didn't need a fire just to cook and keep warm. Summer and winter we needed a blazing fire to boil mighty back breaking cast iron skillets of potatoes for the pigs we were fattening, a major source of income for us.

So to keep our fires burning, it was a case of to the hills and the valleys to find anything that would burn. In the valley, we had a bog, from which we harvested peat and from the hills furze, "whins" to us, the harvesting of both materials was intensely laborious.

Our patch of bog was so wet, that as we dug out the peat, it just disintegrated, so all we could do was break it up completely with forks, adding water if necessary to produce a great mass of mud. The mud is then loaded onto purpose built wooden containers and drawn out of the bog by our horses and dumped onto waste land. This mass of mud is then smoothed out to a depth of five or six inches and then - the best bit. We went along and formed individual turfs with our hands. Afterwards, given a few days, it was remarkable how they dried out. It looked like a mighty slab of dark chocolate, with sections or squares made by our hands. And it will break precisely along these tracks so that we can now build it into stacks to dry out completely. Often at night as we put turf on the fire we'd be looking to see whose hand print was on them.

Mary and Manus are working the turf together
Old they are the two of them, old and grey
Over the bog the sea-wind sings in the heather
Night clouds lie on the hilltops, far away

They will have comfort now when the nights are colder
They will have turf, aye, plenty of turf to spare
Light she steps with the heavy creel on her shoulder
Load on load for the stack that is building there

Now there is a deeper note than the sea-wind's singing
Soft it comes, on the breath of the dying day
Down in the hollow the bell from the chapel is ringing
And Mary and Manus stand for a minute and pray

Soft and low on the air each long note lingers
Quietly bending their old, grey heads they stand
Making the holy sign with work-worn fingers
Wrapped in the sudden peace that has blessed the land

Is it the light of heaven on the wide sea breaking?
Spreading its glory out like a golden rain
And with the light of the world in their eyes a-waking
Mary and Manus are working the turf again

After getting our turf dry, the prize was to keep it that way and to prevent it reverting to mud, but in pre-plastic times, this was indeed a challenge. Hardly a day passed, winter or summer, that mama didn't call out anxiously, "Will youse get some sticks for the fire?"

This was understandable because a hearth fire of turf and sticks is the very stuff of romantic poetry. Sticks meant any kind of wood, but since there were no trees, it meant either dead whitethorn from the hedges or whins - "Ulex Europaeus" from the hills. That's where they grew in great profusion.

No more for him, the blazing hearth shall burn,
or busy housewife ply her evening care
no children run, to lisp their sire's return or climb his knees
the envied kiss to share.

Furze or whins is one of nature's miracles, growing in the driest, stoniest, poorest soil, far beyond the reach of the plough. Green or seasoned, it is excellent firewood. But while you might laugh around the fire as it burned, harvesting the stuff all but made you cry. And because the turf was always damp, these sticks were vitally important to get a blaze going. For mama it was a case of "no blaze, no fire". Whins are one of the longest flowering plants in Europe, lasting from February through to November and they offer the most delightful scent. At every opportunity I seek it out - and the cascade of memories and emotions it brings. Being such a tough, springy, thorny wood, we found the best way to harvest it was to dig it out with pickaxes. We always talked of this as "stubbing" whins.

In telling this story of childhood it is important to remember that at no time were all nine of us children at home together. As each one left school at fourteen, they sought and found work, work that was menial and low paid. So that by the time I was ten, all my sisters had left home, leaving four brothers. From my parent's point of view, each one leaving meant one less mouth to feed. But a decreasing labour force meant a more arduous and moral sapping struggle to keep life and limb together for the rest.

Chapter 3 – The winter of 1947

One of my most vivid memories of childhood is the winter of 1947, remembered in Ireland as "The Year of the Big Snow". It started one day in early February, a fine salt-like snow driven by a ferocious wind.

In the early afternoon of the first day we realised the snow was getting so deep, we would have to move all our animals indoors. Out in the fields, as we battled to round them up, it truly was a life or death struggle. This fine snow was falling so heavily and the raging wind whipping up what was already on the ground and lashing it in our faces, it was difficult to see. As we moved about, looking for the animals, although only a short distance apart, we would lose sight of each other. Shouting was impossible, not just because of the roaring wind, but reports at the time said oxygen levels in the air had decreased. And I remember so clearly trying to shout but being mystified by the feeling of partial suffocation. It was like a gag being placed around your mouth. One instant you had a breath and the next it was as if there was no air. In a matter of hours, the snow was eighteen inches to two feet deep and each step was a struggle. The temperature had fallen dramatically. Lakes, streams, rivers and wells all froze like concrete. Driven by the icy blast, everywhere the snow hit, it froze instantly. It froze in our hair, on our faces, on our boots, on our legs, on our clothes. When we got indoors we were indeed walking icemen. But even inside we were not entirely free of the snow. Where there was the tiniest chink or opening the ferocious gale blasted snow through it. Under doors, down the chimney, even through keyholes. I remember opening the door of a little cubbyhole to the side of our fire where mama kept flour and salt and seeing tiny flurries of glistening snow falling on the shelf. Somehow it was getting through our 2 foot thick stone wall.

Later that night, sharing the same bed, my brothers and I listened to the raging wind and the snow lashing our windows like a hail of pebbles. We wondered what the next day would bring. Like all children, for my two brothers and me, the snow was enjoyable. But with a storm like this and after my experience in the fields, our anticipation of tomorrow was also tinged with fear. Mama said we had very little paraffin for our lamp, no candles for light - and little or no baking powder, flour and salt for our daily bread making. We simply never had a reserve stock of these things. But there was no concern, much less panic or worry. Stoicism didn't come from Greece - it was invented by mama in the winter of 1947. She said God was punishing us for something. "Didn't the missionary tell us to mend our ways? Look at Godless Russia and China where millions die from famine and floods every year". And that is how it would be until they converted to the one true faith, so we just had to accept what God had sent us and learn to mortify ourselves through prayer and penance. Only in this way would we save our immortal souls and avoid further punishment. And there was another powerful reason from Mama's fatalism. The year before 1946 was Ireland's worst harvest on record. Throughout the months of July and August there was almost incessant rain. For the first and only time ever the Army was ordered out to help farmers take full advantage of the very few dry periods. Townspeople were also encouraged even cajoled to help in the fields and so stave off the very real threat of severe food shortages indeed even famine.

Anyway next morning, we awoke and the first thing we noticed was this icy cold, even, grey light surrounding us and an eerie quietness. It was as if you had lost your hearing. Any sound made, like mama downstairs setting the fire had dullness to it. It seemed Nature had turned the sound down on all things. Everything was quiet and still. We couldn't wait to see out our window upstairs. But there wasn't the smallest chink to see through. It was caked with snow. All the other windows were the same, and because our house had no insulation there was just as much ice on the inside as the outside. We were encased in ice. Downstairs, mama said she couldn't open the door. Frozen snow and ice had welded door and frame as one. When we finally got outside we were simply small, dark objects in this great wondrous, glistening, Arctic snowfield. All familiar features of our outhouses, doorways, gateways, trees, divisions between fields, pathways, the lane over to the bog, all obliterated by a chest high mantle of snow and ice. The truly magical thing about this sight was the myriad ways the ferocious wind had shaped the deep snow as it built up in and around natural features of the landscape. Most common were drifts five to ten feet deep. Then there were many wave-like formations you'd see created by wind driven sand in a desert. In places, the snow was dangerously deep. On one of our hills facing east, there was just a light covering. The wind had blasted the snow into a small ravine, thirty feet deep, just beyond the ridge. So the snow built up until it was level with the top of the hill.

Travelling to school was out of the question. When eventually we did manage this in late March, frozen ink greeted us in the inkwells, while the teacher instructed us to bring fuel from home for our little stove.

Not being able to move more than a few steps outside our door, we started shovelling. The plan was to clear a path to all outhouses. It was freezing hard. So with spades and shovels we able to cut the snow into regular shaped symmetrical blocks and stack them up either side. Now we had a network of narrow paths with walls of sparkling ice linking all the outhouses. But this was the easy part, next we had to cross from the outhouses where all the animals are to where their food is. Hay, potatoes and turnips were stored in our haggard (store of animal foodstuffs), some distance away. As we slowly worked towards the haggard, the snow got steadily deeper. When it was a couple of feet above our heads, we decided to dig a tunnel. After tunnelling about half way, we started from the other side where the snow was at its deepest. After shovelling for some time, we realised that because of the outline on the surface that the wind had sculpted, with a little extra work, we could create an arch. This we did and over the days and weeks that followed we shaped and refined it so in the end we had an arch the Romans would have been proud of.

For the first week of the snow, we couldn't travel far from the house. When we went over the lane to the well, you would drag one leg, then the other out of the snow. After thirty to forty metres, you are up to your waist and panting.

Most of our water in winter came from rainwater of our roof, draining into a large barrel. This kept the house going for a few days. For the animals, we melted snow. But with the amounts we needed, this was slow and tedious. So it was back to the shovels to clear a path over the lane to the nearest water. I recall that morning so well. How we hammered and battered with pickaxe and crowbar to break through. The thickness of the ice was truly astonishing.

For five or six weeks, it froze day and night. On the roads movement of any kind was impossible. The ice storm had also flattened the skeletal overhead power and telephone lines and the Dundalk - Carrick train was derailed. We were utterly and entirely cut off from the outside world. The only news we got was from a neighbour who knew a neighbour who had a radio. In this way we learned that a few local people had lost their lives in deep drifts. Nature's vengeance had in a matter of hours literally paralysed the entire country. The earth was as hard as iron so it was impossible to dig graves. And rationing of essentials such as bread, sugar, tea and butter was worse than during the war. Along with this, great numbers of livestock were lost. The export of live animals was a mainstay of the economy at the time.

While our food supply was meagre we were able to keep reasonably warm. In the Thirties and Forties turf cutting was a major industry in Ireland-our second-biggest employer after agriculture. So turf was plentiful and comparatively cheap. The great difficulty with it was keeping it dry since it was stored mainly in the open. At home our stack had a deep thatch of rushes. Dry, turf makes a bright sparkling smokeless fire, Wet or even damp, a steaming, smoking, smouldering mess. We were fortunate in that we had a little patch of bog from which we got our own very hard-won supply of turf. In large towns and especially Dublin the storm ruined much of the stored reserves of turf . Radio reports said nearly half the population of the city were burning their furniture to keep warm. There was no store of timber for heating and no coal [Britain had banned all exports] what little there was people couldn't afford it anyway. That year death rates in the city doubled due mainly to the cold, but hunger was also a factor. There was a sudden increase in the number of children reporting with rickets, anaemia and other signs of a deficient diet. And of course throughout the 30s 40s and fifties tuberculosis was common. A report in the Irish Independent of 17 March 1947 reads-

"Today the Irish nation faces a national emergency as grave as any in its history. The people face the possibility of famine. Nothing but a superhuman effort can now enable the tillage to be done that will avert starvation. This is a fight for survival."

The sense that a terrible catastrophe was unfolding was powerfully reinforced by the fact that the previous year's harvest [1946] was the worst ever, because that August was the wettest on record. Also and perhaps more ominously 1847 the year of the great famine came more and more into people's consciousness. Remember it wasn't exactly ancient history anyway, my father's father was born in 1830. So connections were being made and conclusions drawn; mainly that the almighty had decided we were now due another full measure of punishment.

In the vernacular of the time people would say- the situation in the country was only a holy divine tarrah. [Terror]

For the first two weeks, all we could do was keep clearing snow so we might feed, water and exercise the animals. I was eleven in 1947, so for me and my younger brother Michael and older brother Peter, this was a magical time. We were creating a snow-scape, shaped to our heart's delight: a network of the neatest pathways, bounded by ice walls as high as our heads, while here and there, a tunnel and our magical arch. Each day, some new refinements were added, using spade and shovel to slice through the frozen snow and to create what shape we wanted. Each night, in bed, we'd talk about what we might do the next day and whether Dada would let us or not. When we started shovelling we knew he approved, because any movement was all but impossible. But as time passed and we were getting ambitious and creative, we were fearful that at just any instant, he would lash out and tell us not to be play acting and wasting time.

While all this shovelling was going on, the cold was intense. We were in short trousers and nobody at home, old or young had winter clothing. What clothing you were wearing was just what clothing you had, with one exception only. Everyone had a change of trousers for Sundays. But we did have our very own private pile of jumble and it was all free! So in the coldest weather, you went to the heap of jumble and found something like an older brother's discarded coat to provide some extra protection but no matter what we wore, we were unable to protect our feet. We just couldn't prevent snow from getting into our boots. We wore long, woollen knitted stockings, so very soon they would be soaking wet. We would keep going so long but then in no time, our feet would be numb so we would go into the fire. Mama would wring out the stockings and hang them over the fire to dry. Remember you only had the one pair. So I suppose you could say we had the unique luxury for the time of having smoke dried knee length woollen stockings.

That year we all got chilblains. Outside our feet and hands would be so cold

- close to frostbite. We'd then rush in to heat them by the fire. The sudden change from extreme cold to heat causes a lot of little blisters to form and our hands and toes to swell. These little blisters get excruciatingly itchy then they'd break leaving us with painful feet and hands for weeks.

One day, we decided to make a snowball. We started on the headland, on the top of our steepest field, by rolling the snowball up and down the headland until it was so massive, we just couldn't move it another inch. We then turned it so that it would run to the bottom of the hill. We wondered how much snow it would pick up on the way down. Weighing at least a couple of tonnes, it started slowly, ponderously. To our amazement, I suppose because of its massive, crushing weight, it was picking up every trace of snow in its path as well as some grass, leaving a vivid, green path behind. It came to a stop at the bottom of the hill, in a dark, little hollow where it got no sun. There it remained, right up to the first week of May.

For the first week, movement was impossible. After that, because it was freezing day and night, you could walk anywhere. All the earth had turned to ice. The deepest snow was as hard as iron. Going into the second week, mama announced

"I have no baking powder or flour, do youse think you'll get to Shercock?"

Without newspapers, radio or phone, our information superhighway was what we heard of adventurous neighbours. But no-one we spoke to had yet reached the road. We had some oatmeal left - our porridge oats - so mama started making bread with it. As she had no baking powder, I remember this bread as rough, thin and hard. Soon, we were out of oatmeal, so our porridge and bread was gone. So now you are thinking that mama's resourcefulness has reached its limit. No, no, no! We still had a big sack of maize meal - an excellent and necessary supplement for our animal feed, especially in winter. Mama switched to making our daily bread with maize meal. This bread was much harder and coarser than the oatmeal but I have pleasant memories of sitting under the kitchen table with my lovable brother Michael. We are dipping our maize bread into tea to soften it. Then we'd see who could make the loudest crack as we bit into it and tried to break off a piece. Even when softened by tea, it was like chewing coarse sawdust. Now we had porridge and bread made from maize. One great benefit of this diet, indeed it is a little known fact, mama had discovered long before anyone else, the benefits of a high fibre diet!

As the days passed, we discovered stoicism had its limits, even for mama. It just didn't cover an on-going shortage of salt, flour and baking powder. And so the inevitable and fateful day came, hastened no doubt by broken teeth and the undesirable side effects of too high a high fibre diet – Dada issued an order. Michael and I were to undertake the perilous and daunting task of crossing overland to the remote outpost at Shercock where we hoped to locate lifesaving stores of oil and flour. And so it came to pass, our intrepid fearless young heroes, ill equipped with just a small, empty basket on arm, without dogs, skis or provisions, bravely and in good heart, sallied forth into the great white, unknown.

On reaching the first road, what we saw would perhaps never be seen again. At the time, hedges along the roadside were seldom cut. In other places, a dry stone wall replaced the hedge or perhaps a piece of bog or marsh ran along the roadside. So as far as we could see, an endless series of mounds and drifts lay before us. In between, the road could be clean and dry. In other places, the road , fields, and bogs merged. Where necessary, we just scrambled up the drift on one side and slid down the other, but most of the time, we were in the fields and this was easy because the snow was frozen solid. Our only difficulty was avoiding being eaten alive by raging, snapping farmer's dogs. But you will remember that our orders were mandatory. We were not to come home without flour and paraffin.

We acquired both successfully, as well as mama's special order: a pot of jam and a white loaf. At that time, there was no packaging or wrapping of any kind. Flour, paraffin in a small leaky container, loaf - everything went into our basket and after climbing gates and hedges and dodging the ever present ravenous dogs, mama said her special treat - the white loaf - had a powerful paraffin flavour. Did anyone object? After two weeks of maize bread, paraffin flavoured loaf with strawberry jam was an exquisite pleasure and indeed opinion around the fire that night was that it was probably very good for us. Didn't many renowned experts in the Celt extol the benefits of paraffin? One was as a cure for dandruff.

"Massage a little into the scalp every night for a week and then wash well with soap and water"

My version of this cure, which I promoted energetically, was much simpler. I assured everyone it was longer lasting and one treatment would be sufficient. Massage in copious amounts of paraffin, leave for a few minutes until well absorbed and then strike a match!

Chapter 4 - Bus journeys to Hell and back

Twice as a child, I needed to make the seventy mile bus journey from Shercock to Dublin. Both trips were to the eye and ear Hospital on Adelaide Road. The first visit was to treat a bad squint in my right eye that needed surgery and some years later I needed to return following an incident with iodine that blinded me. Each time my sister Bridgie came with me. A trip to Dublin on the bus for a child at that time was equivalent to a plane trip to New York today. And for me, it was extra special because I was going with my dear sister Bridgie. But the excitement and expectation bursting inside me would be short lived. For any comparison between yesterday's buses and today's luxury coaches would be in name only. The first thing you noticed about the old buses was the stench and on reading this you'll discover why. Then, depending on the skill of the driver with the old fashioned crash type gearboxes, each gear change was either a sickening lurch forward or a jolt backwards. But the real killer was the vibration. All of the engine's vibration was carried through the entire bus. The floor vibrated. The windows and seats vibrated. Everything you touched was shaking. Everything loose rattled. So many years before it became popular, dear Bridgie and me shook, rattled and rolled for over four hours to get to Dublin. We also for good measure lurched, jolted and vibrated until we got sick, terribly sick.

So now you are thinking, "why exaggerate, four hours to Dublin?" Indeed, but this wasn't your common or garden express service. As our bus criss-crossed parts of Cavan, Meath and North West County Dublin, It was a school bus, a works bus, a shopping bus, an office bus and for Bridgie and me – a hospital bus, in more ways than one, as you will see.

Our ordeal would start half an hour or so after leaving Shercock, Bridgie would turn a very light shade of green, very nice for flower petals but not for lovely Bridgie's face. Then a little later, a frantic scrabble through her things to find the sick bags. Soon, it would be my turn. After about two hours, our stomachs would be empty. Then it would be constant retching for the remainder of the journey. In our weakened state, after the retching, fever took hold. Severely dehydrated, we're both quite ill. There is now a very real danger of fainting and unconsciousness. To prevent this, Bridgie has her head right down in her hands, but in this position she can't brace herself for the fierce lurches with braking and accelerating. If this man drove a cattle truck, he would be imprisoned for extreme cruelty to his animals.

This undignified situation was especially difficult for Bridgie. She was an exceptionally beautiful, young woman, always fastidious about her appearance. Now in the middle of the city, this wretched state isn't one tiny bit enjoyable for her. As a further handicap, she has her raggedy, cross-eyed little brother in tow, wearing his small grey-steel, Heinrich Himmler glasses. But a sanctuary is nearby, my other sister Elsie has a flat at 49, Upper Dorset Street which isn't all that far from Aston Quay where the bus from hell dumped us.

Chapter 5 - Misery

And now some misery. I don't like this part of my story but it's necessary for context and perspective. The misery starts with the relationship between parents and children. At home, this was at the level of "we feed and clothe you as best we can and send you to school" and this my parents carried out heroically. But affection, much less love, did not exist. Or if it did, there was no evidence of it by word or action. This unhappy position is the foundation for a tortured existence for the child. Instinctively, it knows something is very wrong, and in its bewilderment the belief grows that somehow it is at fault, and so unworthy. While they were alive, I had no affection for either of my parents. And for many, many years, I was gripped by a bitter, unforgiving attitude towards them.

In my late middle age, when they were both dead, I came to believe that mama was affectionate and loving but just incapable of showing it. And so now, I don't just love mama, I honour and revere her. She simply gave her life for her family. Her phenomenal energy - seemingly inexhaustible - was superhuman. Not once in her entire life did she take a break from the endless, dispiriting drudgery. A holiday for mama was perhaps half a day each summer in Blackrock, County Louth. A bus collected people after mass, one Sunday in July or August and took them to what we referred to locally as the "Rawks". That was it.

So I had a relationship of a kind with mama because there was never any fear. - how different with my father. Every interaction between us was through the medium of fear and sometimes terror. So an overwhelming sense of rejection was established at an early age and I learned that for a child there is only one pain – rejection. Because with rejection comes a nightmarish, sleep-haunting fear of abandonment and death.

Any child living in a reasonably secure home will accept hunger, disease, ill health, the direst threat imaginable – all as trivial and temporary in the happy and secure knowledge that even if the sky should fall mama and dada will see it safe.

Because of this fear I unknowingly rejected my father and this would have been so obvious to him whether in the fields or indoors as I always kept the maximum distance between us. When he spoke, I froze. When he shouted, I jumped. At the time, an expression I heard so often from adults was that "childer should be seen and not heard". I translated this as "never seen or heard". I would cringe and cower or practically hide so that there was no possibility of eye contact between us. I would prolong the school homework and re-read old copies of the Anglo Celt and then sit under the table with my brother Michael until mama started the rosary.

As I mentioned, in my early years, I suffered with a bad squint in my left eye. Once after a visit to the optician, mama was given drops. She was told "two drops in each eye, twice a day". One particular Sunday afternoon, my sister Bridgie was at home and decided to administer my drops. With the first drops in one eye, there was a stinging, burning pain. I screamed. Dada warned me to

"Stop squealing or else!"

Bridgie applied the drops to the other eye. I was banished upstairs to bed. Some hours later, mama came upstairs and I told her I couldn't see. Only then, did she notice the very distinctive smell.

"Dear God Almighty in heaven!" she shouted "Bridgie's put iodine in his eyes".

At home, we were never without iodine. It was our cure for ringworm which we got from the livestock. Coincidentally, or otherwise, the iodine and my drops were in identical, small hexagon bottles on the dresser shelf.

The following morning, I was completely blind. Mama reassured me I would be ok in a day or two. Dada didn't utter a word. And over the next five or six days while I stayed in bed there was no gesture, no reaction - no contact of any kind between us.

On about the third or fourth day, my beloved sister Elsie arrived from Dublin. She was very religious and prayerful. From the moment mama informed me she was coming, I knew all would be well. I didn't think, or hope, or believe. My opinion of Elsie was such, I just knew. She knelt by my bed and I said tearfully and angrily

"Why didn't you come sooner, you knew what happened?"

She placed a St Jude medal in my hand and urged me to repeat the prayer over and over until I remembered it. The following morning, as mama had asked me every morning,

"Can you see anything?"

I told her I thought I could see the bottom of the bed. Then and now, I know St Jude healed my eyes.

Meanwhile, Elsie had arranged an appointment for me at the Eye and Ear hospital in Adelaide Road Dublin. I stayed there for about ten days. For all that time, I couldn't see anything because each morning fresh dressings were applied that covered both eyes. Then one morning, a surgeon or doctor removed the dressing and asked me if I could see. I said no, my eyes were tightly closed by some sticky substance they were using. He then made a sudden, loud noise by the foot of my bed. I nearly jumped off it in fright and my eyes burst open. The effect was sensational. It was like my first day of life and seeing for the first time!

Looking out the window was breath taking, a symphony of light, colour, movement and sound. Nothing was ordinary anymore. Everything seemed to have life, even trees and buildings. I was again part of the cosmic dance, and so often since I try to recapture that moment. I have come to realise not just the magic of sight but how it can help us sense something of the underlying mystery of our existence.

The following day, I endured another killer journey home on the bus from hell. But without my dear sister Bridgie, this journey would be even more of a torment than the first one. I stumbled off the bus in Shercock feeling like someone who had survived a life-threatening ordeal, just about able to walk, weak and feverish from dehydration. But nearby, a most welcoming refuge - Bridgie's home. So in a short time, in her excellent care, I revived. Then I set off, keeping to the roads because Bridgie said someone was coming to meet me. "Someone" could only mean Dada in the horse and trap.

Going round these winding roads instead of across the fields is a long, tiring walk, but after all that has happened I feel excited, a bit like the hero returning. And a welcome I was hoping for, from my father. I thought remorse for his lack of concern before I left home would for sure break through his fearsome, hard outer shell and we'd be able to speak to each other. Would Teddy our dog remember? And come running madly to meet me? Or threaten me like a stranger?

And Michael will be there. I'm now in our long lane and home is in sight. It looks deserted and where is Teddy who announces everyone's arrival long before they are seen? From a distance I can see the door is open but no sight or sound of life. I walk in, mama is standing by the fire. She is surprised and flustered. She seems unnerved by my sudden appearance. My father is standing by the window that looks out over the lane. If he spoke or if there was any kind of gesture, I would remember it. After the iodine incident and being away for so long, what I was most looking forward to was some reaction that would banish my fear and I would feel accepted.

Outside, it was a warm, misty day in late August. I'd been admiring the golden, harvest fields along the roadsides. My father would be waiting all ready to start with the scythe when the mist cleared and the grain dried. Maybe he'd already started and was resentful I wasn't there to help? Mama is nervous and anxious. She starts to do something and stops - then starts something else. She is speaking to me in a disconnected sort of way. Afterwards I realised this was because my father's silence hung over everything like a threat. After a few minutes, I went back out the door, feeling hardly worthy of existence and of being barely tolerated. My father's mute, silent indifference is crushing. Inside me there's an emptiness that felt like death, I was in a dark, dark place far beyond tears.

I know an easy way out, what was there to lose? I went over the lane to the first bend, down a whinny bank and through a patch of rushes to the edge of a bog hole. We referred to this bog hole as bottomless. We never jumped it for fun, it was dangerously deep. It didn't seem threatening now, It was inviting. I hesitated at the edge staring into the black peaty depths, wondering how long it would take to oblivion.

I'm startled from my black mood by our lovely dog's barking. He and Michael had gone across the fields to meet me thinking I was coming the short way home. Teddy is racing madly towards me. He jumps up on me again and again, crying and yelping. Then he starts running crazily in tight circles around me and jumping with little howls and cries. I know he wants to play his favourite game. I lie down in the grass, he's on my chest. I hold him by the top of his front legs. Then we wrestle back and forth as he struggles with all his might to lick my face. I didn't think then, nor do I now, that this dog we loved was just acting out the pack instinct. Michael is impatient to hear of all the wonders of the city: high buildings, the traffic, especially traffic lights, the Liffey, the hospital and people's names. He thought people in the city had such strange, exotic names.

In later years, when I left home, I addressed all my letters and remarks just to mama, leaving out my father completely. After some time, she wrote telling me of his annoyance and anger at being ignored. I was puzzled by this. What transformation could have taken place? Always when I returned home on a visit, I'd have a stack of presents for him. Especially the most expensive briar pipe I could find and the very best pipe tobacco. This wasn't kindness or affection. It was entirely about proving to him over and over again, that I wasn't worthless. That he shouldn't reject me and be ashamed of me. That I might just possibly be deserving of one tiny hint of fatherly attention or interest.

Over the years and a hundred nights – a thousand nights, lying awake, I conjured with a multitude of reasons to try to understand why my father was like this. Many times I felt that I'd reached a level understanding, but I was unable to forgive. Like Sisyphus, doomed to forever roll the boulder up the hill, just as I struggle and strain the last few yards to the top and the ultimate triumph, I'm overwhelmed yet again by this massive, crushing, poisonous boulder of un-forgiveness and it thunders back down, down, down to the depths of the echoing valley far below, and I must start all over again.

In his ninetieth year, my father was taken into Monaghan hospital for tests, his first time in hospital in his life. This night all eight of his children (except Betty who was in America) sat around his bed. We were chatting. My father wasn't ill. He wasn't receiving treatment of any kind. One by one, my brothers and sisters left his bedside. I'm standing there alone with Dada. I'd been planning to do or say something to show him that whatever terrible spectres haunted his existence, mine were probably very tame by comparison. I'll do or say something to make a start to try to make up for all that might have been, all that was missing, all that we'd lost, all that we might have shared and experienced in life-enhancing companionship, rather than deadening, paralysing fear. Even now, Dada, it might not be too late. My brothers and sisters are looking back wondering what I'm about and calling me on. I'm looking directly at my father. I could never do this in the past. He's half sitting, a tear is building up. He is now as vulnerable as a child. There's a heartrending sadness in his eyes. I put my arm around his neck and touch my cheek to his head for a few, long seconds. This was the last time and the first there had ever been any human contact between us in our entire lives. Later that night, he died. I didn't see his death certificate. I didn't need to. I know my father died of a broken heart.

Chapter 6 - The Rosary

As night time arrived, mama would sit down after a day of drudgery, but not to rest. She sat down to sew and re-sew, to darn what had already been darned, to patch and re-patch, to knit and even to crochet. All this mending and repairing in the vernacular of the time was referred to as" keeping an arse in our trousers". But it was an unequal struggle and poor mamma wasn't always successful as she battled valiantly against the odds. Then at a certain point, she'd just fling the work to one side as if one more stitch was impossible. She'd fall on her knees for the rosary. She and dada, kneeling on the rough concrete floor, the rest of us on chairs or on the stairs. She'd begin, then we'd all join in "thou oh Lord wilt open my lips and my tongue shall announce thy praise, incline on to my aid oh God oh Lord make haste to help us". There might have been tears, anger and stress during the day but now mama was confronting us with her total belief that there were powers reigning over us, way beyond our understanding, and now on our knees and with heads bowed, we must submit ourselves to them.

The fire has died now the rosary truly signals the end of the day. She calls out the different mysteries and each of us in turn is expected to respond and say a decade. Each one has their own rosary beads. The beads sparkle and glisten in the mellow light of a candle or paraffin lamp as they pass through our fingers. There is a quiet solemnity to it as if mysteriously we have all been transformed.

Now and then from my high chair, I catch sight of mama watching me and I see that look, God that look that would just break your heart. Her face is pale and drawn, work-worn and weary. Her head is inclined slightly to one side, in a pleading, beseeching kind of way. Her voice is sad and mournful, like a lament for something lost. Are you thinking of the joy of your child's arms tight around your neck mama, something you have never experienced? There is a terrible, cold dehumanising barrier holding you back. What can it be, dear mama, what can it be? Remember the morning we were waiting for the bus on the Carrick road, another woman was standing nearby when a friend or neighbour joined her. There was a brief embrace. You caught hold of me and said

"Will you just look at them two? And then "No-no, Don't look, don't look".

Where did you learn this? What was wrong or objectionable about this? You know the young of all our animals from the chickens to the foal have this life giving need of close physical contact with their mother, but we can't? What terrible distortion of reality are we living through mama? Is all our praying any comfort or substitute for the pain of what we are all missing mama? Can't we pray to your favourite St Chrisostum, the anointed one of Constantinoble, protector of the pure and the holy, blessed advocate of the meek, the poor, the lonely, the downtrodden and the oppressed? You have all the angles covered there mama. Can we ask him to get us over this wall of ice, and you can reach out open, inviting arms to your own child, just once mama, just once?

The five decades finish but mama has barely started. Now begins one Our Father and three Hail Marys for everyone and everything including the conversion of Godless Russia, followed by the litany of the Blessed Virgin Mary, forty invocations to which we answer "Pray for us" to each one.

V. Lord, have mercy on us.

R. Christ, have mercy on us.

V. Lord, have mercy on us. Christ hear us.

R. Christ, graciously hear us.

God, the Father of Heaven: -- Have mercy on us. (repeat at end of each phrase.)
God, the Son, Redeemer of the world:
God, the Holy Spirit,
Holy Trinity, One God,

Holy Mary, -- Pray for us. (repeat at end of each phrase.)
Holy Mother of God,
Holy Virgin of virgins,
Mother of Christ,
Mother of divine grace,
Mother most pure,

Mother most chaste,
Mother inviolate,
Mother undefiled,
Mother most amiable,
Mother most admirable,
Mother of good counsel,
Mother of our Creator,
Mother of our Saviour,
Virgin most prudent,
Virgin most venerable,
Virgin most renowned,
Virgin most powerful,
Virgin most merciful,
Virgin most faithful,
Mirror of justice,
Seat of wisdom,
Cause of our joy,
Spiritual vessel,
Vessel of honour,
Singular vessel of devotion,
Mystical rose,
Tower of David,
Tower of ivory,
House of gold,
Ark of the covenant,
Gate of Heaven,
Morning star,
Health of the sick,
Refuge of sinners,
Comforter of the afflicted,
Help of Christians,
Queen of Angels,
Queen of Patriarchs,

Queen of Prophets,
Queen of Apostles,
Queen of Martyrs,
Queen of Confessors,
Queen of Virgins,
Queen of all Saints,
Queen conceived without Original Sin,
Queen assumed into Heaven,
Queen of the most holy rosary,
Queen of Peace.
    Lamb of God, who takest away the sins of the world,
Spare us, O Lord.
Lamb of God, who takest away the sins of the world,
Graciously hear us O Lord.
Lamb of God, who takest away the sins of the world,
Have mercy on us.
    v. Pray for us, O holy Mother of God.
    r. That we may be made worthy of the promises of Christ.

Let us pray: Grant, we beseech Thee, O Lord God, unto us Thy servants, that we may rejoice in continual health of mind and body; and, by the glorious intercession of blessed Mary ever Virgin, may be delivered from present sadness, and enter into the joy of Thine eternal gladness. Through Christ our Lord. Amen.

Finishing off mama had a few of what seemed like her own creations who we are called on to pray for us as well.

She finishes with the "Hail, Holy Queen". This prayer told us this earth was a valley of tears and while we were on it our lot would be one of mourning and weeping. We rise and climb up the stairs, feeling relieved that she's eventually got to the end, my imagination conjuring with a host of images of these extraordinary powers she has summoned to our aid: House of Gold, Ark of the Covenant, Tower of Ivory. Mama is leaving nothing to chance but what could possibly be the nature of these deeply puzzling entities? And how or in what way might they help us?

We're all in bed now but my father is still on his knees in the kitchen. He's leaning forward, his elbows resting on the seat of his chair, his head is right down, his face buried in his hands. I feel a surge of anxiety and fear, he looks beaten, cowed, subdued. If there was a trace of affection between us, I'd have my arms around his neck, screaming for him to stand up. "You're not beaten dada. You're strong, powerful and fearless. No power on earth can beat you. Lift your head, dada, stand up, stand up. I can't bear to look at you like this."

As I lie in bed at the top of the stairs, because there is no landing or door I can hear his urgent prayers and the fervour even the desperation in his voice, praying separately for so many things, then finishing each with a Gloria, which I can hear clearly. Then I hear his nailed boots on the concrete floor as he stammers to his feet. All your praying, dada, the fervent sincerity of it, but where was it yesterday when you might have shown a little humanity, where will it be tomorrow? Have you fears and worries that are too terrible to share? Secret frustrations and disappointments locked away deep in your heart, only God and you know about?

At this time of night there isn't a sound anywhere. The countryside is utterly silent, except perhaps for the distant barking of a dog. I'm listening intently. If a mouse stirred I'd hear it. I'm sure dada is wondering if God is listening. How long has he to wait for an answer to his pleas? Then I hear each heavy nailed boot fall to the concrete floor, the timber stairs creak as he climbs up in his bare feet. He passes right by my bed. I'm on the outside. Michael is next to the wall. Will he reach down, just a touch, a word, a goodnight?

Chapter 7 – A typical day at home
between March and October

Almost all the action on a small farm in the 30s and 40s takes place between these months. It's the period when all the crops are planted and harvested. The young of all the animals are born and reared. And insofar as it was humanly possible, we sweated and strained to extract mud from our wet, marshy bog to make turf to fuel a fire that was needed just as much in summer as winter, since we had to boil mighty backbreaking cast iron skillets of potatoes for our pigs. The day started with mama first down the stairs. Our fire just went low overnight, so in no time she would have it blazing again by adding dry sticks, usually whitethorn or whins. Breakfast was easy. Mama would have made a skillet of porridge the night before so everyone had porridge with fresh milk most of the time. From time to time it could be buttermilk or skimmed milk which we hated. The menu might also include bacon or a boiled duck or hen egg.

Before school there was an urgent all-important job to be done. The cows needed to be milked and mama would take what she needed for our daily use along with some to churn for our butter. The remainder we transported on a wheelbarrow to the end of our rocky lane in time for the creamery man. And just like buses or trains these days, he didn't wait. Then, at the end of each month we collected a cheque for our milk. This cheque, I can tell you, was looked forward to with an eagerness and expectation unsurpassed in the history of financial transactions.

We churned what milk mamma had put by every 2 to 3 weeks. The milk is allowed to go sour, then as it begins to Curdle -very like natural yoghurt mama would announce the opportune moment for churning to begin.

The churn is a small wooden barrel with a close-fitting lid. This lid has a 2 1/2 inch diameter hole right in the middle. Now a wooden staff 4 feet long has a 10 inch diameter wooden disc fitted on the end. So churning is the action of moving this disc via the staff up and down through the milk. And the more energetic and turbulent the action the faster the butter is produced. As very young children we learned to churn. If you are too small to reach the staff you could stand on a stool. After 20 minutes or so of vigorous churning the great excitement of seeing tiny globules of butter forming on the surface. Mama would then collect all these globules up add some salt and then beat it into some shape with a wooden spoon.

Unfortunately, cows don't give milk all the year round so in the months November to March our milk supply dropped to zero. When this happened, mama would send me to a neighbour's house with a small half-point bottle to ask if they could spare a drop. And drop is the word because our neighbours supply was as meagre as our own. I'd arrive back home with not much more than a few tablespoonful's in my little bottle.

After milking, it was off to school across two of our neighbours' fields to reach the road and then a further three miles to the school itself. It consisted of a small building with two classrooms and two lady teachers looking after between thirty-five and forty-five pupils. When school finished, the cows and goats would be brought indoors again to be milked. In summer they were never brought in. They grazed all day in the fields then as darkness fell they assembled in a favourite, dry sheltered spot, lay down and chewed the cud for the night. A cow has four stomachs. As it grazes it swallows the grass only partially masticated. It is then stored in the Dewlap. At night it is regurgitated in small lumps, this is known as "chewing the cud". No other scene in nature that I know of evokes such a wonderful sense of peace and plenty. Through the night cows have been lying quite close together chewing contentedly in the quiet stillness of the countryside. All around them the air is rich with the comforting smell of fresh warm milk. So each morning in summer we went to where the cows had spent the night. As we approached they'd stand-up and enjoy a great stretch. This stretching it seems often produces a slightly undesirable side effect –toilet function no.2 is performed with great urgency and considerable energy. Most of it will reach the ground but the cows long hairy tail will intercept some. The spot where they've lain is remarkably warm and dry, elsewhere the grass is wet. Then kneeling in this warm spot with the bucket fixed between our legs and our head resting against the cows flank we'd milk them. You were well advised to keep your head in this position because cows like to swish their tails a lot, now if you were leaning back you got the full force of that long wirey hair which was like a whip lash laden with a goodly measure of its dung. Then you'd have the job of cleaning yourself with wet grass.

It was believed at the time that cows loved music, and were easier to milk and gave more if we sang to them while we worked. But I think there was a bit of reverse psychology at work here because milking twice a day could be a chore no one was too keen on. But of course if you were singing while you worked you couldn't possibly sing and be unhappy at the same time. Then there were times while we were milking and giving our best possible renditions of "moonlight in Mayo" or "Il take you home again Kathleen" or perhaps my version of "Kevin Barry" or "the Minstrel boy" a cow would lash out with a vicious kick sending milker and milk flying. This not only reflected very badly on the singer but now with clothes saturated with Milk you had to get off sharpish to school. Nothing wrong with a bit of fresh milk on your trousers. But then about the fourth day your classmates and others got a bit sniffy as the smell of stale milk filled the classroom.

The final job of the day was our school homework: sums, poetry, Irish, English, history and Christian doctrine entirely in Irish. We all sat around the kitchen table and worked by the light of an oil lamp or flickering candle. My most pleasant memory of long winter nights at home was when a neighbour called "on a ceilidh". Remember no one knocked. But there would be a stamping of feet outside the door then lifting and dropping of the latch and straight in someone would come. There was always a salutation. God save all here or God bless this house. Our favourite neighbour, Mickey Hearty, always posed riddles for us which we never solved to his satisfaction. It was always

"Well no yiz jist haven't got it right yit" or "yiz will jist have to think some more about it".

Here are some of Mickey's riddles:

Brothers and sisters I have none but that man's father was my father's son. What's the relationship between the speaker and the man?

There were these twins who were born in March but their birthday fell in September. One was twenty and the other was twenty-two. One lived as a bachelor and the other married his mother. Now riddle me that, Mickey would say.

This man coming from the market arrives at a river. He has with him a fox, a goose and a sack of corn. He can only take one of these in the boat with him crossing the river. If he takes the fox the goose will eat the corn, if he takes the corn the fox will eat the goose. How does he get all three safely across the river?

At weekends, mama would ask us to go out and catch some rabbits or go to the lake for fish. Rabbit is a seriously underrated dish and mama's rabbit soup remains unsurpassed.

We fished from an old leaking boat that was parked at a lake nearby. We were in mortal danger with this boat because none of us could swim so someone had to bail out constantly. This was coarse fishing, perch, roach or pike. Sometimes we didn't land a single fish. Other times we had so many we didn't know what to do with them. They would be swimming round our bare feet and legs in the water at the bottom of the boat until it was time to go home. Mama's favourite fish was the eel. Most of the time these were very hard to catch, but at certain times of the year we could pick them up in fistfuls in tiny streams and ditches near the lake. Around home the eel was a mysterious even mythical creature. People said it was all but impossible to kill them. Some said the only way you could do this was to run them over with the iron wheel of a cart. I remember someone telling a story of how he was looking forward to his dinner of eel and bacon. He said they were both sizzling away nicely on the pan,

"Bejaysus", he says "I'd only turned me back to make the tae and the cursed eel had downed the bacon."

Home supported a menagerie of animals, each one very important in their own way, but standing supreme above all was our horses. Without horses to plough and till the fields, we simply did not survive. On a small hilly farm their work is endless and cruel beyond words.

Dada would plough all winter. The plough is a very heavy iron implement. Two horses are yoked to it and the plough is then drawn through the hard, stony earth to a depth of nine or ten inches. The ploughing went on almost continuously from November to March and this dammed ploughing involved me doing the most detestable job. Towards the end of each day, the horses would be utterly spent. Every last trace of their phenomenal strength exhausted, their noble spirit broken after months of this work, and my father would be in a similar state. And I don't know of a more physically demanding job on this earth than ploughing Monaghan's rocky, hilly fields with horses. But at times Dada wanted more than the horses could give. So, he'd make me follow close behind them with a rough stick to keep them going. At times when I was less than enthusiastic about this, I suffered along with the horses. Many times since, I've prayed to the horse God for forgiveness.

Along with my younger brother Michael, we would avail of every opportunity to spoil them. Whether it was with the foal in the fields or the work horses in the stable, we'd be patting, brushing, keeping the mane and tail looking well, or cleaning out their stalls each day, but they're remarkably clean animals so this was easy. We'd be sure to leave a deep bed of straw for them at night. Turnip, apple or any kind of grain, they would eat out of our hands. They would scoop up the offered food with their large, flexible lips, keeping their huge bone-crushing teeth well clear of our tiny, fragile fingers. And we had names on them so we talked to our horses continuously.

With the ploughing finally done, the worst is over for the horses. The lighter work of breaking the soil and preparing for planting and sowing begins. We had fields of hay, oats and flax. But the most labour intensive job was the potato crop. It started with Dada making drills in the fields to be planted. To consider the labour involved here, give this a moment's thought. After the field has been ploughed, then harrowed and re-harrowed to break the soil down, Dada will start one end of the field with what we called a drill plough to create furrows into which we plant the potatoes. He will have opened hundreds of these furrows before we can go to the next stage. This involved getting all the manure produced by all the animals through the winter out and spread in these furrows. It was a time consuming, heavy, dirty, mauling job.

Thinking of the next stage, I'm feeling my eyes go moist as Mama is involved. She is on her knees in a little dark outhouse where we have our seed potatoes stored. There is a curiously attractive smell in this little shed. The life cycle of the potato is at its turning point, so there is a hint of decay, mixed with something fresh from the mass of new dark green shoots and all mama's slicing. Her job is to prepare the seed potatoes that we will plant to maximise the potential of each individual potato that she picks up. Given that two healthy buds will grow into a vigorous new plant, Mama will cut each potato two, three or maybe four times. There will be no wastage, every single potato is precious, not even a piece of skin will be overlooked. Every year, without exception, Mama did this job and did it alone, and as she cut and sliced endlessly, my brothers and me carted the seeds to the fields and placed them one foot apart in the manure in the furrows. Dada would be following with the horses and the plough - covering them.

Compared to the potatoes, sewing the hay, oats and flax seed was easy enough. Dada would have a large sheet tied around him, forming a large pouch in front and then holding it closed with his left hand, he went along shaking the seed over the ground with his right. All the crops were in the ground by April - then we prayed for rain.

By the middle of April, chicks and ducklings will have hatched and calves are born. With the arrival of May, a climactic moment is at hand - the imminent birth of our foal.

By May/June the fields are a sight to behold. After all the heroic work - our reward. The lush, healthy, verdant green of each field is indeed joyful and inspirational - promising an abundant harvest. But of all our crops, flax deserves a special mention. Three foot high, dark green stems topped by a rosette of vivid, blue petals and it sways, waves and dances in the wind. As a crop, it is a sight unsurpassed. However, this beautiful sight belies what this savage crop has in store for us.

Because it is made of such tough, fibrous stems, it cannot be cut. It must be pulled by hand out of the ground. And it is a dead weight. A small sheaf is four times the weight of oats. Because of this, we tie each sheaf very securely with bands made from rushes. My brothers and I would spend weeks beforehand making thousands of these rush bands. The entire crop must now be submerged in water for two weeks. This process starts the rotting of the useless part of the stem so that the fibrous part (ultimately linen] can be harvested. If you remember, think how heavy it was before we put it into the water. Now, an able bodied individual can just about lift one sheaf out of the water to spread it on the land to dry.

When it dries we collect it up again and tie it. It's so light now that a gentle breeze would blow it into the next town land. Before that happens, we load it onto the horse's cart, so high you wouldn't believe it because it is so light. The final step is to transport it to the flax mill.

Compared to the flax, the reaping of our hay and oats was easy, but still laborious. Both these crops were cut by a combination of scythe and horse-drawn mowing machine. Me and my brothers followed the mowing machine , gathered the crop and tied it in sheaves. We then put these sheaves into small stacks, later as it dried out into bigger stacks, and finally into two very big stacks while we waited for the steam driven thrashing machine to arrive. Crucially, both the hay and oats needed to be kept dry otherwise the seed would rot. his machine separates the grain from the stems of the plant. The thrashing usually took place in October and was indeed the climax of the farming year. While I say the thrashing was a climax, it was only in the sense it was completed in one day.

The final act of the farmer's year, however, was the harvesting of the potato crop. This job could go on for several weeks into November. The machine used was drawn by two horses and consisted of a specially designed wheel turning at the back which broke up and scattered the potato drill. We didn't own one of these machines, so my father arranged with the same farmer each year for me and my brothers to hand pick his crop and when we'd finished, he'd come and dig ours.

This man, whose name was Packie Brennan, was a jolly, talkative man and it was so enjoyable working with him compared to the tension at home. He knew us really well since we were there every year picking his crop with his children who were about our ages but attended a different school. At one o'clock, his wife would appear in the field with our dinner. This was always the way unless it was very cold or wet. The fields then had high, thick hedges so there was always a sheltered spot to sit down. There was something curiously attractive and deeply satisfying about finding this sheltered spot, finding a flat stone or just a bundle of sacks to rest on while we enjoyed this excellent meal in the open air.

Mrs Brennan's speciality was rice, lots of it - beautiful, sweet, hot, creamy rice with a hint of cinnamon or nutmeg and then our second course - mugs of hot tae, with as much curreny bread and jam as you could eat.

All this was lovely. Nevertheless, twice each day for me, a sensitive, awkward and embarrassing situation arose. There were three Brennan children: Kathleen,

Peter and John. Father Brennan for his own good reasons paired one of the Coyles with one of the Brennans, with each pair sharing a big, wicker-type creel to collect the potatoes. Somehow, I always found myself paired with Kathleen.

Along comes Packie, whistling, humming a song, shouting friendly and encouraging remarks to his happy band of pickers. The machine splits the drill, scattering the potatoes, clay, stones and everything else. At the bottom of the field, the horses wheel away and plod their way back up for the next drill.

Kathleen and me and the others go along, each pair in their own section of the drill. All is well until about midday. I get the urge to go, but where? At home in our own fields and just men present, you still looked for some privacy. Never, ever with any female within a mile.

At first I ignored the insistent signals. As I look around in panic for somewhere to escape to, I can see Packie looking down at us from the headland. I know I will have to leave the field, but there is just no bush, tree or anything to go behind. Kathleen can't lift the heavy, wicker creel herself so she will be just standing there looking at me or waiting for me on her own. Another drill is dug and picked. Now I am in pain and starting to wet myself. Suddenly like a thing possessed, I start running frantically, stumbling and falling over the drills towards a gap into the next field. With all the others watching and thinking I have gone completely mad, I feel as if I am crossing no-man's land under heavy fire! And if I was, I couldn't run any faster. Business done, I return to Kathleen, wet and feeling as if some great, unnatural event has happened. And for the rest of the day, I'm wondering what will Kathleen do? As the only female in the field, her predicament is even more acute than mine.

This was a very busy time of year for us because when we'd finished harvesting our own crop, as well as Brennan's, we'd help our other neighbours. In between, we'd collect blackberries from the roadside and the neighbours fields. Each year mama warned us

"If we didn't collect enough blackberries we'd have no new boots for the winter".

When we'd finished picking these berries, we loaded them in buckets before carrying them into Shercock where they were weighed and priced. We were quite well paid for them.

Chapter 8 - Bulls and Boars

Hardly a week passed in summer without moments of high tension and drama,. Mainly to do with our animals giving birth. We would all be standing by anxiously and helping in any way we could until the new-born gulped its first breath. Almost all births take place during the day. But uncannily the mamma pig always waited until after dark I can't recall it ever happened once during the day. It is uncanny. It was always a night-time job. So someone had to stay up and keep watch because the mother will so easily lie on her own piglets and in certain situations, she will eat them. Sheep lambing and goats in labour were no bother at all.

For us children being present at the birth of our animals and then caring for them day-to-day was a deeply appealing and a wonderful bonding process. But each year our care if not love for them suffered an emotional painful indeed savage blow. Not all male pigs in the litter will be allowed to grow into hogs. And not all male calves will be allowed to grow up as bulls. So all our male pigs and all our male calves will have to be castrated. This is because they will then fatten much more quickly and the entire point of the exercise is to produce meat for human consumption. My father will carry out the surgical process when the animals are about 6 to 8 weeks old. For this to happen they will have to be completely immobilised. Naturally the animal squeals and roars and struggles with every last tiny grain of its strength to break free and save its life. But me and my brothers hating and detesting in equal measure what we are doing have to get the animal on the ground, tie its legs together and then mainly by lying on top of it keep it still while my father performs the surgery.

If experiences like this didn't dispel our childish ideas of care and love for animals the next event in our farming calendar certainly did. This was a day of the greatest tension and high drama-The day we killed our fattest pig. This is a harsh, cruel procedure so just a basic outline of the gory details. The animal is dragged manually from the pigsty as its roars and protestations rent the countryside. Outside in a selected spot it is hit from behind by an able bodied man with a sledgehammer. In the instant it falls over unconscious someone else knowing precisely where its heart is delivers the fatal coup de grace. Mamma then rushes in to collect its blood for our black pudding. Now begins the laborious task of cleaning all the hair of its body butchering it and storing it in layers of salt in a wooden barrel. We kept this barrel in the coolest darkest place we had-the upper storey of our barn. Then from time to time as needed we'd bring in sections and hang it on a hook over our hearth fire. As these procedures take place year after year as children we soon learn that in our battle for survival there was little room for sentimentality especially with regard to our animals.

After the foal the kid was our favourite animal and the cleanest. goat's droppings are completely odourless, hard, black, dry pellets like a bunch of black peas. And kids are even more appealing than lambs. The goat is surely one of nature's supreme designs: tough, hardy and so tame, they are just pets. The other animals on the farm get dosed for one thing or another. Goats are never sick so never get dosed. They have the most extraordinary and varied diet. They eat so many plants other animals don't touch, including some that are regarded as poisonous.

Milking in wintertime took place in complete darkness apart from a blinking lantern. After we had milked the goats, Michael and I would frequently sit on some straw with them and sometimes between them to keep warm. They were always warm. We'd just sit there stroking their heads and ears and occasionally there would be a soft, timid bleat. I'm sure they thought that we were goats.

Now, for all these animals to give birth they must be impregnated first. Remember these are pre-artificial insemination days. Dada being expert in these matters knew when it was time to take a cow to the bull. To do this, we would fix a rope to the animal's head, then with one or two of us in front and one behind with the rope, we'd set off for the farm where the bull was kept. Getting our cows impregnated was easy enough; the same procedure for our sow was distinctly more of a challenge.

We always kept a sow at home and each year she gave birth to between ten and fourteen piglets. We then fattened them up and sold them. So each year, our sow had to be brought to the farm where the licensed boar was kept. This farm was a mile further along the road where the bull resided.

Getting our sow there was the single, most challenging task for us as children. With two or three of us, it wasn't too bad. But once, for some reason, Dada said I was taking the animal on my own, probably as a special punishment for something. A rope is tied around one of its hind legs. As you can imagine, the pig is heavy, fat with very short legs, so is slow and ungainly. Its sole aim in life is to eat. You fill its trough - slurp, slurp, it empties. You fill it again, it empties again. You then let it loose into a field where it shoves its snout into the clay and the animal happily stays there in the clay, all day, eating anything that moves: worms, grubs, larvae and even some clay.

It is completely and utterly heedless to any kind of urging, coaxing, shouting and beating. The task of one person getting a sow from one point to another five miles distant, and back again, would surely qualify as one of the labours of Hercules. So, with the rope around its leg and duly equipped with a big stick, I set off over our lane. The lane is completely open to fields on one side and wasteland on the other. Since pigs have no interest in the stones that make up the lane the battle between pig and me is well and truly joined.

After one hundred and fifty metres, we reach the first of four gates. I go in front now to open the gate, the pig thinks "oh, great" and bolts backwards into the field. This performance is repeated through the other gates. Eventually we reach the glen road. Frequently referred to as the stony road because all repair work was carried out with loose rough stone. This isn't too bad because of dense hedges to either side, although the animal will fight to get into any gap, any gate or laneway, just to get off the road.

The most infuriating hazard for the remainder of the journey is dogs. There were so many dogs. And they seemed to sense that both human and pig were handicapped and this makes them attack with enhanced enthusiasm. The dog has all the trumps and there is nothing more attractive to it than sinking its teeth into the pig's soft, fat, hind legs. But just as this tormenting dog swings in, presents my opportunity to deliver a sharp, venomous, temper-easing crack of my stick that sends him on his way, yelping. This particular day, I had been on the road about an hour and it started to rain. Three and a half hours later, when I get home, Dada asked me what took me so long and Mama if I was wet. I was soaked right through like the proverbial, drowned rat.

"Get those things off you," Mama said "before you catch your death, and get up to bed".

This was the only option when we were wet with no other clothes to change into. Mama would then hang the clothes over the fire and when they were dry you could get back up.

Chapter 9 - Keeping the school fire burning

In my last two years in school, aged thirteen and fourteen, our teacher seemed to think that I should do some jobs for her - I suppose the modern equivalent of work experience. One of these jobs was to collect coal for our heating system. This was a small pot-bellied stove behind her desk. Any coal we had was dumped in a corner outside and was always soaking wet. So most of the time, the only thing generated from our heating system was smoke. The principle being if there's smoke, there must be fire! And if you have a fire, you must be warm, so everybody's happy, ok? One or two mornings each year, our teacher would announce

"Pat, go up the road, get Ned Mckittrick's ass and go to Shercock for coal."

Ned lived in a low, rusting tin-roofed house just up the road. Two small windows and a half door distinguished it from a hen or duck house. The bottom half of the door kept animals out in summertime and let in air and daylight. It also kept people out.

When a stranger knocked, Ned would come out and chat over the half door but if the entire door is opened, then the stranger will just walk in. Ned thought it an honour to be asked for his ass to transport coal for our school.

I knocked and Ned came to the door.

"Sure you can have the ass to get your coal. Yiz must be perishin down there without a bit a coal. I'll come and help you get him harnessed and yoked to the cart."

This was my first experience with an ass. I thought he might respond much like a horse. This ass didn't. He just didn't respond to anything I said or did. His clip clop, clip pity clop pace was equivalent to a small, child's walk. I tried leading him, no change. I climbed up onto the cart and gave him a good lash of the reins on the backside. All he did was flick his ridiculously, big ears as if a fly was irritating him. I was now thinking I wouldn't make it back from Shercock before the school closed.

As you get near this village, there is a long, steep hill leading up to the shops. Half way up the ass decides he will have a rest and despite my pushing, pulling, dragging, beating and lashing, he won't budge. Around me, some local boys have stopped to laugh at the performance. They call their friends. Soon there is a crowd of them. Not only does the ass refuse to move, but I have this chanting, jeering mob, laughing with great hilarity at the antics of this red neck and his ass. It seems as if the animal's brain is switched off and no signals are reaching his legs. I was so exasperated I could have shot him.

He is just standing there as he would in a field, his head hanging right down. huge, sad, saucer eyes, with eyelashes like chimney brushes, ignoring all my efforts to get him moving. He looks like he has some terrible, secret sorrow and the anguish of it all is more than he can bear!

At this point, I thought I would nip into a nearby entry out of sight, hoping my tormentors would disappear. When I came back out, I was just standing there wondering what to do, then slowly he lifts his head, he swivels his mighty jaws a few times as if trying to eat an outsized piece of turnip. Then the jaws open to their widest and a sound comes out, which for a small animal is just absurd. It's the loudest, harshest sound - grating, grinding, teeth tingling. If you didn't see the animal, you'd think you were near a great steel mill as mighty sections of rusting steel were being drawn back and forth across each other. He is screaming his anger at this cruel world and the harshness of his existence.

When the raucous, tearing and screeching stopped, he seemed to come alive again. A lash of the reins and to my great relief, it was clip, clop, clippety, clop to the top of the hill and McEntee's for two bags of coal. The journey back to school went well and without a stop. He even seemed to quicken a bit. Everyone in the country who works with horses and asses say the animal speeds up knowing they are travelling home.

Chapter 10 - My Pantheon

Whereas home was cold, our childless neighbours spoiled us. And since they always needed help, we never hesitated to cross the fields to spend some time in their company and in their houses. From this time in my life, I created a pantheon of three very special people: one man and two women. This man whose land was next to ours was about fifty and lived with his mother and very aged father. I saw very little of the father. He suffered with a very bad back and was bent almost double. He may have been deformed. He just hobbled about with the aid of a stick. I felt so good about his home that I visited at every opportunity - up over a dry stone wall, between his land and ours and then up a little hill. Now you didn't approach Packie's house or walk up to it. You came upon it, or even stumbled on it, in a hollow just beyond this little hill. There it is, all but invisible, small and thatched, it is nestling there. It seems to lean into the hill as if for comfort and shelter. This is the environmentalist's dream house. It does not obtrude on the landscape, it is part of it.

There is no half door, or little porch. I would just walk in and always to such a welcome! At the time, no one knocked, knocking implied you may not be welcome. Inside with the door closed, it was almost dark, like a cave. The walls and roof beams blackened by a smoky, hearth fire. Right in one corner facing west, a tiny window. I can't remember ever visiting Packie's house when his mother, Biddie, wasn't there.

"Oh, come in child, come in, you're welcome, pull up a sate, come and sit here by the fire. I'll have the tae made in a minute".

There were no chairs with backs, just three-legged stools and forms (long wooden benches). Then she rushes to tend the fire which was the surest sign of a welcome anywhere. "No fire, no tae, no welcome". Using great, long tongs she piles up the turf around the kettle followed by an urgent blast of the bellows to create a blaze. She is always dressed in great, wide skirts right down to the floor. She moved so quietly and gracefully and spoke gently and softly. She seems to have a reserve and dignity that belied the grimness of her day to day existence. From time to time, she asked me to read letters she had received. I remember one from a sister who was a nurse in Wigan. She would ask me to write replies. I remember needing to stand up and just being able to reach the little window for light, when I am reading or writing for her.

"Tell me now, child. What book are you in at school? Aren't you just great with all that larnin? And helping poor Packie with the preddies."

Packie didn't have a lot of preddies (potatoes) and couldn't afford to pay anyone with a digger to harvest them, especially with only one horse, so his method was similar to many in the same circumstance. His one horse pulling the iron plough would split the potato drills one by one, while he and I and sometimes his mother, would go along on our knees and with our hands, scatter the clay and dig into it with our hands to find all the potatoes. This was referred to as potato hoking. You dear reader may feel this was primitive and arduous work. It wasn't. The unique and special smell of the freshly disturbed earth and reaping the bounty of so many potatoes that the earth seems to have produced from nothing and even the digging for them with your hands and with a companion you can chat to, makes it pleasurable and therapeutic.

Chapter 11 – An Irish Wake

Packie had the face of someone who is completely happy with his lot, chubby and rounded, with a permanent little smile in his eyes. This face has never known frustration or anger. Everything we do just seems to happen – no effort, no strain. He chews a straw or a match stick all the time. I can read his mood from the chewing. As we chat, he'll stop momentarily switch the straw from one side of his mouth to the other. When this happens, he will be silent for a minute. This signals he is coming up with some new aspect of what we have been chatting about.

Everything with him was

"Azy, azy, azy".

And then every few hours we would go in for something to 'ate'. This couple churned and made their own butter as we did and frequently with Packie, lunch consisted of chomp (mashed potatoes with salty home-made butter and a mug of butter milk). He was either very smart or an insightful natural leader, always leaving me in no doubt of his complete conviction that I could achieve anything. One day in the field after lunch, I had a bad fit of the hiccups. Packie said

"Hauld on there a minute now, Pat"

He popped into the house and returned with some salt.

"Throw that over your left shoulder", he says "and bless yourself"

The hiccups stopped instantly and I have had none since.

Taking it "azy" meant sitting on the grassy headland, with the sun shining down on us. One day as we chatted, he told me that if I'd help him when I could, he would leave me the place in his will. One day when I arrived, he tells me his father has died during the night.

"Now you'd do the wake with me, won't you?"

There was a pause, and he says directly to me.

"Now, what would you need for the wake?"

I remembered the talk around the fire at home many times about wakes. I did know what was required, but this delegation of responsibility was a bit overwhelming to a thirteen year old.

I compiled a list: Guinness, clay pipes, tobacco and cigarettes for the 'min', sherry, cake and 'curreny' bread and jam for the 'wimen'. And an endless supply of hot, hot tae.

"Will you harness the horse, Pat, and go to Shercock for me?"

From the ass and cart to the horse and cart is one extreme to the other. The cart has five feet high iron-shod wheels so the body of the cart is correspondingly high. When sitting up on it, I am just a bit higher than the horse's back. Packie's cart has seen better days. The timber sides are caked in years of dried farmyard manure and here and there, great jagged chunks are exposed where bits have rotted away. As the cart moves forward over the rough, rutted roads, the wheels slip back and forth on the heavy iron axle so there is a continuous grinding and rattling. Packie's horse would be referred to as an "auld stager" in his final years, dirty, no brushing or grooming, mane and tail, just a great matted tangle, but probably no split ends!

When I arrive back, I can see Packie is chewing faster than usual – he is a bit anxious. When he sees I have everything on the list, the chewing eases.

"Now, we'll go and have some tae and curreny bread and jam for ourselves".

After the tae he says,

"Do you think we might have a sup a'sherry?"

I wasn't sure.

"Do you think we should?"

"Bejasus Pat, I think we shid". He replied. "We've only got an ojus (odious) night ahead of us".

As I sipped this sherry, my face started to get warm. In minutes, my face was flushed and hot, like a really bad blush. We're both quiet while we sip the sherry. Finally, he says.

"You know Pat, we'll need buckets of tae and I only have that small kettle there, wouldn't it be only a holy dread to run out of tae?"

Remember no electricity then. I said

"I'll run home and ask Mama for our big iron kettle."

"Grand, grand, I knew you'd know what to do".

When I got home , Mama says

"What on God's holy earth are you doing, your face is on fire."

I told her I was running because Packie needs our kettle. We would need buckets of tae at the wake. As our plans develop, he leaves me in no doubt that I am the senior staff officer and he trusts me to plan the order of battle. There are no drapes or curtains on Pakies Windows if there where they would be drawn closed, mirrors would be covered and clocks turned face down.

As the mourners arrive they head straight to the bedroom where the corpse was laid out. They kneel by the bedside for a little while and join in the rosary, which would be repeated continuously for the entire night. When one woman finished, another would start again. The men didn't stay long praying. Back in the kitchen, they'd sit around on benches with their backs to the walls, with the women around the table and the fire. The talk would be almost entirely about the deceased man's life each one recalling particular incidents. Some would exaggerate certain incidents a lot so that by the end of the night the deceased man would be a hero beyond compare. I know all the neighbours well, especially the men. So as they come out of the bedroom and sit down, I hand each one a new, white clay pipe, along with an ounce of cut plug tobacco, while the cigarette smokers receive a twenty packet of "Sweet Afton" - the best cigarettes of the time. On the front of this packet is an illustration of the river Afton in Scotland. Underneath are two lines:

"Flow gently, sweet Afton, among thy green braes, flow gently. I'll sing thee a song in thy praise".

I'm prepared. Lots of bottles of bottles Guinness are open and ready. I'd hand each man a bottle of Guinness and then, most importantly, place another open bottle on the floor at their feet. And as the one on the floor was picked up, I'd take the empty and place another full one in its place. For a man to be left sitting with an empty bottle was equivalent to a mortal sin. For the women, we'd organised big plates of sliced cake and currney bread layered with jam ,and of course the sherry.

From what went on in pubs, I knew there was a very close connection between the amount of Guinness and sherry consumed and the liveliness of the party. This was especially true of myself. Normally, with a crowd about, I'd be hiding somewhere in the background. But after my sup of sherry with Packie, I was hyperactive. I flitted about in the shadows and around the adults' legs with the Guinness and the sherry. But in truth It felt like I was floating about somewhere just below the roof beams.

Now and again, Packie would stop chewing, give me a nudge and tell me in a low, anxious voice to slip so and so a little extra. Maybe something left over, like tobacco, cigarettes or pipes, for someone whose horse he needed to borrow, or perhaps to help repay for a mowing machine loaned to him.

The custom at the time was to refuse anything offered however small and to refuse again, and maybe even a third time. While all the time, everyone knew that the more strenuously the favour was refused, the keener the other person was to receive it.

"Another little drop of sherry, Mrs McConnon?

Oh, no, no, you and Packie are far too guid. I've had plenty already!

Ah, go on, go on, you will, just a little."

"No, no, you are going too far too much trouble.

Well, just this time, Mrs McConnon, just to give Ned a good send off. He'd want to know you were enjoying yourself at his wake.

Ah well then, just a wee drop, if you have enough to go round."

For the good name of the deceased's family, it was vitally important for all attending to enjoy themselves and with the food, drink and tobacco, we were off to a good start. But at some point soon, we would have to organise music. We are prayerful and mourning the deceased passing but we must also celebrate his life with music. These are the two essential elements of the wake. Packie is genuinely concerned and now he is hyperactive because he is shyer and more uncomfortable with the crowd than I am. Another nudge and he says,

"Who'll sing Pat? Who'll sing? Who'll start them off? Jaysus, it will only be a holy dread if we have no singing."

Knowing him so well, and because he confides in me, and with the false courage inside me from my sup of sherry, I enjoy a sense of power. I can get the music going. I can't speak directly to the crowd, but I can go to someone quietly in a dark corner.

At wakes, someone singing was the usual start to a music session. Then someone playing a melodeon, a tin whistle, a flute or any musical instrument and the crowning glory if at all possible was dancing.

The solution to starting the singing was right under my nose. This man's name was Pete Marron, in his fifties, small, neat, clean shaven with a glowing red face. I remember asking him innocently, how even in the coldest weather, he could be so warm. The lane to his house branched off ours, then took a dive into a little valley and a thatched cottage at the end where he lived with two sisters, Maggie and Katie and their mother. He was our most frequent visitor at home, arriving on a "ceili" (chat) at least once a week. And I think he liked coming because we always asked him to sing. When mama saw him in the lane, she'd warn us

"Make sure you ask him to sing, he loves to be asked to sing".

Knowing him so well, I was completely at ease speaking to him. I was begging Pete to sing. He would protest again and again.

"No, no, no, not at all. There's much better singers than me here."

At a certain point, I knew he was primed and ready to go. I tell Packie. Packie calls out.

"Whisht, whisht, everybody. Will yiz whisht Pete's going to sing. Shush now, shush."

A voice calls out, "Good man, Pete!"

Except for the low murmur of the rosary through the bedroom door, the place is now quiet. Then with the earnestness and passion of a prima donna, Pete launches forth,

"Shur, it's just a couple of weeks ago
I left the Cobh a Cork
And I wasn't very long sailing
Til I landed in New York
There wasn't a soul to greet me there
A stranger on the shore
But when I go back to Eireann's isle
Tis I'll be welcome there....
Friends will meet me on the shore
They'll greet me with a smile
So many there, I've never known
I've been so long away
But my mother will introduce them to me

And this to me she'll say
Shake hands with your Uncle Mick, me boy
And here's your sister Kate
And there's the girl you used to swing
Down by the garden gate
Shake hands with all the neighbours
And kiss the colleens all
You're as welcome as the flowers in May
In dear ol' Donegal

When Pete finished, there was a loud roar of applause and great shouts of,

"Guid man Pete," and "that's the boy can sing".

Hearing this, others are just aching to be asked. Someone calls out,

"Who's next now? Who's next?"

"What about May McElroy there, that one would only charm you with her singing. And she knows lovely Irish songs."

And someone else chimes in,

"And one of the nicest voices you have ever heard."

A little more encouragement and May sings "An Spailpin Fanach" (the wandering labourer).

Go deo deo aris ni rachad go Caiseal

Ag diol na reic mo shlainte

No ar mhargadh na saoire i mo shui cois balla

I mo scaoinse are leataobh sraide

Bodair na tre ag teach tar a gcapaill

Ag fiafraigh an bhuilim hrelta….

Time passes and the singing stops, but there's still the low murmuring lament of the rosary from the little room at the back. The mood grows sombre and melancholy, flickering fire and candlelight play with unearthly figures reflected on the walls and between the roof beams. In the gloom some faces only appear when matches are struck to light pipes and cigarettes. I'm squatting in a dark corner at the end of the table just level with Pete Marron's knees. But looking back I realise I wasn't the only one in the dark. Remember this is the time of pishogues, fairy forts, stray sods and lone bushes, but tonight especially with a death everyone will be thinking of ghosts and banshees. Prayer, singing and drinking has woven a spell.

Some say the dead man's spirit and indeed the spirits of others are present. Others say they see them. It is late now, but no one wants to be the first to move and there will be a degree of fear crossing the fields on the way home. In the melancholy atmosphere at wakes, there was always talk around the fire of banshees, ghosts and stray sods. As children our greatest fear at night time was of seeing a ghost . It was always talked of as a malign threatening spirit. The banshee was a female spirit that roamed the countryside at night screaming a lament for the one who died. If you walked on a stray sod on the way home your only hope was to put your coat on inside out. Otherwise you would go round and round in circles in a field all night and not find your way out until daylight.

"Let not ambition mock their useful toil,
Their homely joys nor destiny obscure
Nor grandeur hear with a disdainful smile,
The short and simple annals of the poor."

Chapter 12 - The second person in my Pantheon

Joining Packie, this honour belongs to a Protestant lady named Mrs Rose Violet McAdam. She lived nearby with her husband, Thornton, and two children: Thomas and Mary, who were both in their early thirties. By the standards of the time, they were prosperous. At planting and harvesting time each year, my two brothers and I waited for their call for help, like children eager for Christmas, hoping and praying they hadn't asked someone else, or somehow manage without us.

When the call came - and indeed it always did - we would make our happy, gleeful way through the hedges and ditches across the fields to their farm. Their rough-haired collie, Tiny, barked out our arrival as soon as we set foot on their land. A beautiful dog, we loved him even when he was angry and protective. Still, we were fearful of going any further until one of the family called him up.

Whoever called him would invite us into the kitchen where the rest of the family would greet us, with smiling, even admiring looks. It was as if they had prepared a little reception for us. This left us a little uncomfortable, not being used to such attention.

"Now do you remember which is which?" Rose Violet asks her husband.

"Of course, I do, there's Peter the eldest, then Pat and Michael. What would we do without them, they are such good workers.

"Yes, Thornton, aren't they just wonderful."

This beautiful lady used this expression frequently about something we said, about our work in the fields, at home or at school.

Ever since, I have thought of this word as sacred. It's locked away deep in my subconscious, to be used only in the most exceptional circumstances. Every time I hear it, I think of her. Time and space are irrelevant. I'm back with this lovely lady and rejoicing that I have known someone so special. I can open the floodgates on a torrent of thoughts, thoughts that could not have been expressed at the time. Thoughts that for so long, hammered on my conscience to be set free, but weren't - and so have left me with a sense of guilt. Thoughts and memories that have grown more real and more vivid with passing time, and so I revisit her constantly in my dreams, revisit the almost unreal happy atmosphere in the company of this family, and how clearly they enjoyed us as well. I revisit dear Mrs Macadam's womb-like kitchen - an all too brief heaven of warmth, security and love.

When we finished in the fields at evening time, we went into the kitchen where a banquet was prepared for us. Mrs McAdams fusses around us, spoiling us like we were her own long, lost prodigals.

The kitchen is of modest size, dominated by a mighty Aga cooker. On the opposite wall, stands a Welsh dresser with shelves of willow-patterned china. In a corner, a grandfather clock chimes out in soft, soothing tones. High on a wall, sits a radio and I can hear the deep, resonant tones of Alvar Lidell telling of so many dead in fighting between Jews and Arabs in Palestine (1947).

It's always warm and always filled with the comforting smells of baking, tarts, jams and pastries. An oak table in the middle of the floor scrubbed almost white has a Tilly lamp on it (best model at the time). It gives excellent light with just a hint of blue. There is a happy, easy banter going on between the parents, their children and us. Between the parents themselves there is a childlike playfulness, like one evening the father playing the tearful child, saying he didn't have his fair share of gooseberry pie. He should have more, he protests, because he is bigger than the rest of us. Rose Violet says he has eaten too much already, that's why he's so big. And it ends with the mother running around the table with this huge dish of pie and the chasing father pleading for more.

So often since, I've wondered about the appeal of three ragged urchins to these lovely people and I've realised the probable reasons. We were of an age where we could possibly be their grandchildren. We were so overwhelmed by their kindness and praise we would be looking up at them with permanent, adoring smiles. We were always there very early and this counted hugely with these very industrious people. When they spoke to us, any response they got would be painfully shy, slow and hesitant. Our manner was most respectful. Also, we were hardy and wiry and well used to the work in the fields. So we responded to their approval with extra energy and enthusiasm, scooting back and forth over the fields and up and down the drills.

Chapter 13 - Mrs Culleton and wee Hughie

The third and final person in my private Pantheon is a Mrs Culleton. She lived in a low rusting tin roofed house along the road to school. She was on her own with a young family – husband supposed to be away working in Dublin or England. She'd be out on the road chatting to us going and coming from school. Now and then she'd ask us in for tae and bread, with homemade damson jam

.She had a very old gramophone with the original HMV horn-type amplifier, playing John McCormick, Richard Tauber and Kirsten Flagstad records. One morning she appears on the road with her eldest. She says

"Will you take Mickie to school?"

I was eleven, maybe twelve. I remember being surprised, even slightly shocked at this. Although I knew Mickie, I didn't think he was ready for school. I am looking down at this little thing with thin yellowish hair. He just looks pitiable, pale and sickly looking and with a squint worse than mine. Mounted on his nose are the cheapest glasses. With both hands, he is clutching a small, brown paper bag – his lunch. He doesn't look up when I speak to him. His voice is low and shaky as if tears are about to burst. I thought he should be tucked up in bed and given drinks of warm goats' milk to strengthen him a bit.

I ask him for his little paper bag and take his hand. My brother Michael takes the other. Along the way, I talk non-stop to reassure him, telling him the great time we'll have at school. I am fearful that at any minute, he'll bolt and dash back home, home to mama whom he loved, no doubt. Mickie wouldn't have known it but I loved her too. This little waif makes me feel I am a commanding presence, a giant, big and strong, with the ground shaking under my feet. If ever there was a child to which my first poem learned at school applied, it was to him.

"He has gone to school, wee Hughie
And him not four

I wish you saw the fright was in him
As he left the door
But he took a hand of Dinnie
And he took a hand of Dan
And with Joe's old coat upon him
Ock, the poor wee man
I watched him turn the corner
Of the old turf stack
And the more his feet went forward
So the more his head turned back
I followed to the turnin',
When they passed it by
God help him! He was cryin'
And maybe, so was I.

Many, many times I have thought of him since and prayed – whatever road you have travelled Mickie Culleton, I hope it hasn't been too hard.

Chapter 14 - Ducklings and Foals

Those of you literary types who I fantasise might be reading this will know of complete books written about a single incident or a day in someone's life. Now consider what could be written about one day in the life of a small farmer in 1940s or 1950s Monaghan.

On our twelve acres of stone, rock and bog we grew a range of crops and maintained a menagerie of animals: hens, ducks, turkeys, pigs, sheep, goats, cows and horses, cats and dogs and a ferret. And whilst the winter's day would be marked mainly by the milking of cows, the feeding and cleaning of all the animals and keeping the fire blazing, in summer, say between the months of April and September, so much of what happened each day was from the domain of the magical. For us children, it was mainly to do with the young of all the animals. The incubation, birth and care of chickens and ducks, to the birth and care of lambs, calves, kids, piglets and a foal each year.

Now most children will be familiar with excellent Walt Disney films on animals, such as Donald Duck. At best, these films are a case of art imitating life, but of course life is the real thing and holds all the magic. Each infant animal has its own very particular features, but all in common involve both male and female. Therefore, children reared on a small farm soon learn not just about birds and bees but in this case ducks and drakes as well. And now with due respect to Walt, I'd like to tell you about the incubation and birth of ducklings.

The mother duck will lay her clutch of eggs in a safe and secure place around the farmyard. She then must sit on them for twenty eight days, keeping them warm. When she leaves her eggs to eat or drink, she must return quickly before they get cold. A drop in temperature below a certain level would bring incubation to a fatal stop. After twenty eight days, the ducklings will have developed inside the eggs and now start battering on their shells to enter the world. Over the course of two days, all will have hatched. Mama duck will now move a short distance from the nest, usually just outside the door of the duck house. Then, with head bobbing up and down, she starts an incessant quacking.

One by one, the ducklings struggle and stumble (their large webbed feet aren't meant for walking) and with tiny butterfly wings flapping uselessly, they more or less fall out of the nest as they respond to mama duck's call. When all twelve to fifteen of them are outside (she must be able to count) and still quacking non-stop, she heads for the nearest water. In a perfect line behind her, follow her ducklings. Their feathers a faint yellow colour, large reddish beaks and webbed feet, way out of proportion to their bodies. Without beaks and feet, a tiny ball of yellow feathers, the size of a small egg, and only a few ounces in weight. This bewitching parade sets off over the lane. As they progress, they all sway from side to side, left foot forward, a swing to the right, right foot forward, a swing to the left. And they have tiny voices, so as mama goes "quack, quack" in front, she is serenaded from behind by her swaying, swinging, tiny brood with a barely audible "peep, peep". A sight to charm anyone lucky enough to see it.

When they reach the water, the mother still quacking takes up a position in the middle of the pond or bog hole, head still bobbing and waving from side to side. As before, the ducklings cannot resist her call and again, fall, somersault or just tumble into the water. With 95% of their bodies now above the water, they are truly in their element. But evening draws in and now mama duck wants them safe back in their nest. This time there is a difficulty as the ducklings can't fall up or out of the water. Their big webbed feet are now a handicap so we would be on watch for this and lift them out of the water. If they remained in the water after dusk, they would be the easiest of prey for any wild creature bigger than a mouse.

Many times during the day, danger will threaten: a cat nearby, a dog or most frightening for mama duck, a rat. At the remotest sign of danger, mama sounds a frantic emergency screeching quack, quack. In seconds, the ducklings respond. And in such a short time, simply disappear under her wings and feathers. Looking closely you might see the tip of a beak, or webbed foot, just peeping out.

Chapter 15 - Birth of a Foal

In terms of size ducklings lie at the bottom end of the appealing scale. Above them are kids (young goats) and at the top – the foal. The mare carries her foal for eleven months on average; it can vary by as much as three weeks. Then one day in late April, early May, the ideal time, dada would tell us of the imminent arrival of our foal - a time of great excitement and high drama, and for good reason. The successful birth, rearing and training of the animal to the various harnesses, otherwise known as 'breaking in', and finally the eventual sale was by far our biggest single source of income.

The birth always took place out in the field. It happens remarkably quickly but with a few minutes of great tension between cutting the umbilical cord and getting the foal to breathe. Now breathing, the animal struggles to get to its feet, with me and my brothers helping it, as the mother licks and nuzzles her new-born. The mother knows us so well, probably by our voices or our smell, but any stranger or another animal near her foal turns her into a lethal, kicking, stomping, biting fury. In less than half an hour, although shaking and trembling on incredibly spindly legs, the young foal will be on its feet.

It is now of the utmost importance to get it to suckle for the first time. One of us puts a finger in its mouth and leads, whilst the others coax and push it to its mother's teats. Once it has started suckling, the foal is inseparable from its mother for months. It simply never leaves its mother's side. No other mother and baby on the farm stay so close for so long.

At about six months, the foal starts to eat grass. At this point, we separate it from its mother. Then for a few weeks, we would draw milk by hand from the mother, reducing the amount each day to encourage her to stop producing altogether. We discarded this milk not realising that their horses' milk was a major part of Genghis Khan's Mongol troops' diet. Regrettably, we never tried it.

Chapter 16 – Irish culture in the 1940s

The year is 2013 and you turn on the evening news. You see great throngs of men parading on the streets of Iran or Pakistan. They are carrying small whips, the whips have several tails and the men are lashing themselves so that their backs are raw and bloody.

I'm sure most people watching would feel good they were not part of that brutal, sadistic culture. But in Ireland in the 1940s, members of at least one religious order practised this kind of masochism. Though it is true it was done in private as a penance for their own or society's perceived sinfulness. Any such type of penance was referred to as "mortifying yourself". At the time, any kind of pain or misfortune was looked upon as positively redemptive. This was a valley of tears - to live was to suffer. One particular individual named Matt Talbot was held up as an exemplar of what it was to be a good Christian. This reformed alcoholic put himself through all kinds of self-inflicted pain and privation, during which he was said to have mystical, transcendental religious experiences.

At home, whenever any of us complained about something mama would say:

"Remember, the more you suffer in this life, the better it will be for you in the next. Look at Matt Talbot; we must learn to mortify ourselves like him."

This was the age of "spare the rod and spoil the child" – the age of corporal punishment. At no time ever did any child that I knew, or any child across the extended family, speak of anything other than brutality at school. And our school with women teachers was regarded as far less punishing than most. To many parents, sparing the rod translated as spare the fist, the boot, the belt, the pulling of ears and hair and a great variety of everyday humiliations at home and at school. A little rhyme often heard at the time summed up children's attitude to school.

Friday night is my delight and so is Saturday morning, but Sunday night I get a fright thinking of Monday morning.

How could it be otherwise, when the state gave this brutality its blessing? How could it be otherwise, when the church taught that children were inherently sinful - born with an inherited, sinful nature: original sin? An un-baptised child could not be buried in consecrated ground and the church's teaching on the rearing of children was replete with expressions of the child's unworthiness. Children with Down's syndrome (Mongolism to us then) were shut away and never seen in public. Children deformed in any way or with defects of any kind were thought of as ill omens, bringers of evil. You were given this cross for some reason - somehow the children were to blame for their own misfortune. It seemed we had taken on the Buddhist notion of Karma - whatever happens to us, good or ill, was entirely due to our own good or evil actions in this or some previous existence.

At mass every Sunday, the priest scolded us and warned us. Once a year, sometimes twice, we had fortnightly long missions. The urgent work in the fields came to a "swearing under the breath" stop in order to get to the church. And though the work was vital, everyone stopped. They didn't stop entirely out of religious zeal. They stopped because their neighbours did. For James Coyle to continue when his neighbours had stopped was equivalent to stealing a march on the enemy. It wasn't playing the game and if the others met at the mission and he wasn't there, his name would be mud. He really would be damned.

You may think that for a stressed farming community, one service a day would save us. But no, we were urged most persuasively to attend in the early morning as well. Only by making the effort to attend morning and evening would we prove our worthiness of the many special blessings reserved just for us. Unlike the infidels and hardchaws who would only get the leftovers for attending only at night. These were big churches for such small communities. They would be packed right to the doors.

Before the main event, there would be prayers and invocations for the success of the mission. Then the missionary himself, a man of saintly appearance, would appear. He is wearing a long, brown habit - a flowing gown right down to the floor, along with a long, rope-like chord around his waist with huge tassels on the end. He moved slowly to the pulpit and ascends the steps. He briefly surveys the massed throng of poverty-stricken peasant farming families below him. The church is silent. There is a growing, rising sense of some great event about to unfold. Now with arms reaching outwards and upwards and in a tone urgent and emotional as if he is about to announce the second coming, he calls out

"Brothers and sisters in Jesus Christ, prepare, for you know not the day nor the hour."

For the next thirty to forty minutes, this man, who was an excellent orator and no doubt sincere, quoted St Paul, St Thomas, St Augustine and others that only mama would know about. From time to time, leaning over the pulpit, reaching down and out to us, he implored and beseeched

"Mend you ways before it is too late. Remember what St Paul says about the sinner who repents?"

And then as happens every evening, a most solemn and moving conclusion with incense burning and bells ringing: Benediction.

We all emerge from the dark church blinking in the bright evening light with mama looking bewildered. I'm sure she is perplexed about how she is going to mend her ways. My father with stalks of hay stuck in his bootlaces loosens and adjusts his sweat-soaked collar. He puts his cap on hurriedly, then takes it off again and wipes his face and forehead with his hand. His gaze is fixed straight ahead. Not a word is said to anyone. He takes off for the stables. We all hurry to keep up. I'm in the lead because I'm the most fearful. He needs help to harness and get the horse yoked to the trap. He will not want to be kept waiting. There is still time to get a bit done in the fields before darkness falls.

What were we guilty of? Crime was remarkably low, the prison population for the entire country was only a few hundred. On the other hand asylums were grossly overcrowded. We crammed our fellow citizens into what were frequently referred to as the madhouses. And I have always thought of this as a true measure of our natural self hatred at the time. What were the criteria for committing such great numbers of people to these vile places? With no cinema, no theatre, no newspapers or magazines, no TV, no radio and with all the so called evils of today's society unheard of. Where or what was the source of the supposed evil in our lives? It would indeed be a safe bet to say that out of that packed congregation there wasn't an individual with a real sin.

Such an exaggerated emphasis on the spiritual left people feeling guilty and inadequate and created a culture of self-hatred. Young people were emigrating in alarming numbers. And with the marriage rate so low outside experts were forecasting the death of the Irish race. When the poet wrote "the savage loves his native shore," he wasn't thinking of Ireland. Hundreds of thousands of those who departed would never return. Very many indeed disappeared never to be heard of again. I knew some. When you speak about this, others admit to knowing someone who sailed away, never to be heard of again.

Any major UK city has great numbers of elderly single Irish men living alone. Sad, lonely and desolate they've cut off all ties with home, if they ever had any. They have rejected their birthplace, the very source of their existence, the very wellspring of all that might be dear to them and indeed sustain them through bad times. What experience of their birthplace could cause such a deep-seated trauma? No other emigrant group presents this kind of deplorable scene. It's uniquely Irish. It's a depressingly sad but enlightening testament to a lifeless, loveless culture in their homeland.

Chapter 17 – First romance

These days, do school children notice or take any interest in their fellow pupil's social status? How well turned out they are, the quality of their clothes, their shoes, maybe the kind of house or car their parents possess? I'm fairly certain this doesn't happen. But in the Monaghan of my youth, it was very much part of the social scene.

Maybe you live in a two storey house, a thatched cottage or a rusting, tin roofed shack with a hole in the roof for a chimney? Do you own horses, a mule or an ass? How much land do your parents own and how many cows?

At school, you would be very aware of who arrives with new clothes, especially shoes. Who is still barefoot when the rest have put their shoes back on? Who has nice lunches, others dry bread, others nothing. Who has a bought satchel, or a rough home made one? But most conspicuously, who just looks well cared for, clean and happy?

If you stood at the gate to our school, you wouldn't need extra sensory perception to categorise each family as they entered. So plain to see and scoring on all counts – the Burns family: Mary the eldest, Kitty, Pete and Betty. Mary was a year younger and a class behind me. Now picture the classroom scene. As our teacher faces her pupils, on her left are the desks for third class, then fourth, fifth, sixth with seventh on her extreme right. Two pupils at each desk, boys and girls all together. But boys and girls at this age don't mix voluntarily. They are contemptuous of each other. A boy would never sit at a desk with a girl. If a boy got something badly wrong, the girls would have a great laugh and vice versa, with one exception.

Each day, as I looked across to the row of desks on my right, I can see Mary Burns. At first I was just looking in an envious way. Later I'd be looking in an envious and admiring way and later still in a longing way. I was eleven and a half or twelve years of age and however unlikely or improbable it seems, I was intensely interested in Mary Burns.

On the one hand, I am comparing my lowly status with her privileged world, but there was something else. In looking at all the children in the school, boys and girls, she would attract anybody's attention. She had presence, charisma, that certain something which is usually a combination of personality traits.

For me, it was just a case of look - there's lovely Mary: lovely, lively confident Mary, healthy, happy, glowing and always smiling - a smile that spread out all around her like bursts of radiation. A smile that said "I'm loved, the whole world loves me. I only know love and so I love everything and everybody. If you are in the same room or if you can see me, even at a distance, or just hear my joyous, girlish laughter, then you also will become part of this dreamlike world of mine, a world completely carefree and happy."

My fondest wish each day was to find some reason or excuse to speak to her. I'd speak to the other girls in the class but not to Mary - except maybe to say a very shy, very self-conscious, embarrassed hello. I was devoid of confidence and it would certainly not be a case of false modesty to say I was lacking in social charm. On top of this, I was small for my age and dressed in handed down clothes that had been victim to a lot of mama's repeated stitching and patching. My right eye had a bad squint and I was wearing steel rimmed glasses with very small lenses. I thought of myself as a miniature Heinrich Himmler, the Nazi SS Chief. (At the time I was reading a lot about the Nazis and particularly the Nuremberg Trials of 1945 and 1946). But picturing Himmler in miniature with a bad squint would be stretching the imagination beyond its elastic limit.

Then it happened. The fates took a hand. It is two o'clock in the afternoon, poetry time, not Mary's best subject. The poem we were given for homework was one of my party pieces so I knew it really well. We called it a poem, but it is really a ballad, the ballad of Michael Dwyer.

Mary is asked to recite the first verse, she begins:
At length brave Michael Dwyer, you and your trusty men
She stumbles, and then stops.
"So, you have learned one line." Our teacher shouts.
"Did you bother to do any homework at all?" Her face has turned red, she is angry. "Now try the second verse."
And the teacher snaps out the first line of the second verse:

"The soldiers searched the valley and towards the dawn of day."

Mary repeats it and then continues:

"Discovered where the outlaws"

Silence.

"I asked you to do two verses," she roars,

"you hardly did two lines, you just ignored what I asked you to do. You made no effort at all."

With this, she grabs Mary's hand. The cane lashes down four times on soft yielding flesh, then the same on the other hand. Our teacher then tells her that because she didn't learn the first two verses, she now demands she learns the entire poem for tomorrow.

"Now go and stand in that corner and face the wall until school finishes".

This was the most hurtful humiliation at our school. The atmosphere in the classroom is now threatening and fearful. You don't have to get lashed yourself for the violence to affect you. Everyone who sees the shame and pain has their humanity undermined. Our teacher's anger leaves us all fearful. Anything could happen. Anyone could get it before this anger is spent. All our noses are in our books, studying as if our lives depended on it.

Mary is standing there with her back to us all, her head is hanging and her shoulders hunched. Her beautiful long, lustrous hair is almost completely covering her face as if hiding her humiliation and shame. Her body shakes as she sobs. She is holding her book with one hand while the other hand is tucked tightly under her arm to help ease the burning, stinging pain in her swollen fingers. After a bit, she switches to the other hand. The pain in her hands will pass, the emotional pain, perhaps never. She is like a delicate flower, broken, crushed, trampled on.

I did manage some little confidence in the classroom setting, whereas in the social sense it was zero. But as always happens in human relations, the emotions swamp everything – my lack of confidence, my self-consciousness and my fear of rejection counted for nothing. I know I am going to speak to Mary. But it can only happen in the pushing and barging on the way out, before we get to the gate when school finishes. That way, no-one will notice.

In normal circumstances speaking to another boy, much less a girl, after they got a lashing would be just silly. It was very much a case of, you got it today

- it will be my turn tomorrow. It's not a rare event. Every day, one or two will be in tears.

When school finishes, Mary turns to collect her satchel, head still bowed and eyes downcast, the humiliation and shame is keener for her than anyone else in the school. She is a model image of the obscenity of violence to children. I can't take my eyes off her. I can see she is unable to lift her head to speak to anyone. As we all jostle at the door I hang back so that Mary is just ahead of me.

When I am beside her, I just stammer out the words,

"Mary, don't try to learn the entire poem. She knows that's impossible."

She turns slightly towards me, pushing back some hair that is stuck to her face.

"She never carries out her threats Mary, you'll see, she won't ask you to recite at all tomorrow, you'll see, you'll see."

And this was one of the reasons I was so fond of our teacher. She would give someone a terrible time one day and tomorrow, after promising them hell, she would either ignore them or do something to make up.

Together, we go out the school gate onto the road. Mary will be turning left down the hill, I will be turning right. She hasn't spoken but I am watching, watching, hoping for signs of that silent language children have. A certain look, a glance that can be so eloquent. I start to walk backwards up the hill, still watching for some sign. Mary continues downhill, hunched and downcast. She doesn't turn - no glance back. Now I am hunched and downcast. I can only hope and pray that my advice for tomorrow is correct.

Next day at school, Mary's warm and engaging smile is still missing and there is an undercurrent of gloom from the previous day. Mary is no doubt dreading the afternoon's poetry and English class. And I'm quaking with the fear and nervousness that I could be wrong. If Mary is called by our teacher to recite again, then she is just an unfeeling brute. If I am wrong, what a fool I'll be in Mary's eyes. I'm watching, looking and listening to everything our teacher does and says - trying to judge her mood.

Lunchtime comes and the classroom has been quiet all morning. Our teacher hasn't raised her voice once, not one reproving word has been said to anyone about homework or class work. After lunch, she called third and fourth classes for mental arithmetic. Because of how classes were arranged in the afternoons, this meant there would be no poetry for Mary's class that day. Mary will know this and in an instant her mood and mine will lift from fear and despondency to elation.

Yesterday, school was a harsh, bitter place and our teacher sadistic and cruel. Today there is peace and our poor teacher can be forgiven. At times, some of her pupils drive her to distraction. I think she hates herself when she is cruel and she has inspectors to satisfy about teaching standards.

Third and fourth classes are standing in a semi-circle around our teacher so that she can't see the rest of us sitting at our desks. I look across to my right, towards the front to where Mary sits. I just want this delightful creature to acknowledge my existence. "Please Mary, just turn your head." I am sure she knows I am watching. Yesterday the lashing cane brought you pain and humiliation Mary. Now with each second that passes and if you don't turn I'll suffer more than you. After an eternity her left hand comes up slowly to her face and pushes all that beautiful, wavy hair back. Her head turns slowly, gently, shyly, with her left hand still holding her hair . I see her face. As our eyes meet, that gentle bewitching smile forms around her mouth and spreads slowly to her plump, freckled cheeks. The gaze lingers. This smile signals she has cast her spell, a spell that would last, and I am the most willing of victims. She takes her hand away and her hair folds slowly back to hide her face again.

The drama of the poetry incident and my prediction about its outcome was a life-giving boost to my confidence. School was now a happy and inviting place for me. Each day marked by a number of small, but emotionally satisfying moments.

Each morning, Mickie would be waiting at the end of his lane with his mother and seeing this kind, affectionate lady, third in my pantheon of the most worthy, was the perfect start to the day. She would repeat stories her son had told her of what happened the previous day at school and lately how nice one big girl in particular was to him.

About the second week he had his own a satchel - a converted shoe box. Inside, were his sandwiches, a small bottle of tea, a pencil, a picture book and tiny plasticene animals we made together the previous day.

I thought of this delicate little figure with his squint and weak eyes as a three year old version of me. He was so small - I couldn't believe he was four. Taking his hand in mine made me feel mighty and strong and not as weak and powerless as I thought I was. So paradoxically, this and later events will show this was a mutually beneficially relationship. I was getting at least as much out of it as him. Then onwards we went to school, with my head swimming with delightful thoughts of seeing Mary.

Chapter 18 - A Row at School

At school, our teacher beat us with three foot long bamboo canes. They broke frequently, so quite often she didn't have a cane available. Once she sent me out with a knife to cut an ash cane from the hedge and the irony here is, I got lashed with it. It was the only time in my ten years at school that I got slapped.

It is the first week in September, the start of the autumn term. It's a warm, sunny afternoon and teacher announces sixth and seventh class will have our Irish lesson outside in the sun. We are standing in a semicircle and the lesson begins. After a few minutes, she asks a question of the first pupil in the line. The child cannot answer.

"Hold your hand out."

As usual she grabs the wrist, whack, whack, whack, whack. The same question to the second pupil, no reply, and on to the next child. Now, it's my turn and I've had so much time to think, but I have no answer. Still, I'm standing there feeling so smug. I've never been slapped. I just know she'll find some excuse, she won't slap me. She'll go on to something else. I'm wrong. She takes my wrist, whack, whack, whack, and whack. My world collapses. How could she do it?

She knows how I support her, work for her and never let her down. My pain and disappointment soon vanish with what happens next. My brother Peter is next to me.

"Hold your hand out," She demands.

"No, I won't." He says in such a determined voice. Consternation. It was simply unknown for a pupil to challenge the teacher. She's spitting venom at this defiance, she grabs his wrist. He breaks free and with both hands grabs fist-fulls of her big head of wavy hair. Now, he being half her size is dragging her head down. She is struggling desperately to break free. After a few minutes, doing the dance of the dervishes, wrestling each other, round and round with gravel flying in all directions. He then releases the grip on her hair, but then pulls the branch from her hands, breaks it into little pieces, runs into the classroom and crams the bits into our little pot-bellied stove, comes back out and takes his place by me as if nothing had happened.

Our teacher, who is clearly proud of her appearance and always so well turned out, is now in shock. Her hair and clothes look like she has been dragged through a hedge backwards. She calls out to a Finnegan lad to run for the Guards. With that, Peter Finnegan and his brother Pat take off out the gate. Almost in the same instant, she has the presence of mind to send someone else haring after them to call them back. Our teacher then dismissed all her pupils.

But Peter Coyle is angry and the episode for him has to have a final, climactic scene. He calls me to attention. "The Finnegan's were going for the Guards. We are not letting them get away with that". He was aggressive, but not violent. He seemed to enjoy fighting and couldn't understand me hating his fights. When he had a fight with another lad, he manufactured some reason and arranged for me to attack his younger brother. (He was my fight promoter). Peter and Pat Finnegan were the same ages as us and in the same classes. We'd had earlier fights, mine always promoted by Peter. He tells me threateningly what I have to do.

Just outside the school gate, my brother Peter attacks Peter Finnegan. I had a one minute satchel fight with Pat. In the satchel fight I held a distinct advantage. Mama had made my satchel from an old flax bag. It was a really tough, rough material with an extra-long strap attached. On the back in 6inch letters were the words "Ulster Monarch". This was the variety of flax seed we used. With this extra-long strap it was a lethal weapon as I swung it at my opponent. Satchels were then put aside for the main event: punching, kicking, pulling of hair and a bit of a roll about on the road. The Finnegan's abandon the field of battle and we all go home. Next day, Pat Finnegan and I will be back at our desks together and friends again. On the way home, Peter and I talk about how we can hide this from our parents. For we are in mortal dread of what our father will do to us if he finds out.

Remember these were the days when the teacher was second only to the priest and the priest was God. No adult, no parent and certainly no child ever challenged the teacher. Indiscipline in school was unheard of. It did not exist. This was because of the iron-clad alliance between teacher and parent. If you were punished at school, woe betide you when your parents found out. Being punished at school meant it was richly deserved so when you got home you're entitled to a further full measure at least.

Sixty years later, I still marvel and wonder at the enormity of what Peter did. But from that point on, our teacher took very little interest in Peter's education, so in the end, he was the one who lost. Each evening when we arrived home, we were fearful, dreading mama's initial greeting, wondering if she or dada had heard of the incident. A week or so had passed and this one evening as we trudged in the door, mama tells us anxiously,

"He wants yiz out as soon as yiz have a bit. He's started on the back field." (Mowing the corn).

This was ominous because we always went out anyway. Dada was harvesting oats with the scythe in our back field. All our fields had names. I can relive each moment as it happened. He is standing at the bottom left corner of the field. He has the scythe standing on its seven foot long shaft, blade upwards, as if about to sharpen it. He's a fit, athletic man - just under six feet tall.

Peter is standing nearest him, about three paces away. I'm beside Peter and Michael (RIP) who is just behind me. He's nine, I'm eleven, Peter is thirteen.

"Which of yiz took the cane from Molloy?"

Peter, without hesitation "I did."

Dada turns to me, his face isn't flushed and his eyes aren't blazing with primeval fury - signals I expect. Nodding towards me he says

"You tell me what happened".

With a shaking, trembling voice, I begin to tell him. Sometimes I hesitate, he demands:

"And then what did Peter do?"

As I'm telling him, he puts his hand up to his face as if to stifle a yawn or a sneeze. When I finish, his hand comes away and he starts to laugh uncontrollably. Between bouts of hysterical laughter, he repeats what I have just told him.

"He won't let Molloy slap him." More laughter.

"Then he fleeces the head off her, wrassles the cane off her," More laughter. "Breaks it in bits and puts it in the fire!" He then turns away from us, wiping tears from his face. He's now bent double laughing. Then barely able to control himself, he stutters out.

"Then they bate the Finnegan's".

He starts cutting the oats again, but from time to time, crumples up with laughter as he repeats to himself what I have told him. Peter and I are gathering the oats after him as he cuts. We're tying it in sheaves. We look at each other in silent disbelief. Instead of terror, we have never heard him laugh like this. And for these few moments I'm at ease in my father's company - a unique experience.

Chapter 19 – My Last Year In School

At school, good timekeeping was just as important then as now. At nine in the morning, our teacher would arrive on her bike and open the doors. Not later than ten past nine, she would lock them again. Anyone coming after this time had no option but to return home. Before she opened the doors, we would all be milling about comparing homework. These ten minutes or so for so many of the class would be a frenetic, anxious time. Those who didn't complete their homework, or lacked confidence in their work, would be scribbling madly as they copied from someone else. Being a year ahead of Mary Burns was in my favour, having covered all her work the previous year.

From the moment Mickie and I went in the school gate, holding hands, I would be looking out for her. I'd mope about near where she was. Will she look towards me? Will I attract her attention for a few seconds? Will she turn away from her friends? I was using Mickie as a decoy, a lure to attract her. This worked every time. Mary bending down would take Mickie's hands - I suppose to get him to lift his head. I am listening to her gentle, comforting talk and I'm thinking how jealous I am. This isn't supposed to be all about Mickie. I was sure it wasn't. And by now I knew that the little lad was in a way, my proxy. At least I could dream some of Mary's lovely endearments were meant for my ears as well. She is fulfilling all my dreamlike images of her. She is so sure of herself and had such emotional stability. I, on the other hand, was an emotional shell. To her friends, or lads in my class, it looked like she was feeling sorry for this little lost soul and had nothing at all to do with me. But in truth, there were two lost souls.

As the weeks passed, these little encounters became more frequent and perhaps I began to sparkle a bit as well because about this time my squint was corrected. Indeed as happened, over corrected! My little friend Mickie is also thriving. Before, looking so lost and forlorn, his eyes fixed on his feet. Now, he was gazing up at me, confident and trusting. I'm caring for Mickie, but he is also helping me, and Mary's beguiling, heart-warming words are life giving for both of us. It was only on poetry days that Mary's charm gave way to anxiety and unease. It is so clearly etched on her face and by now I share her anxiety. I want everything at school to be perfect for her. I can't bear to think of anything banishing that smile. I think she knew this from my reaction when we talked but most especially from the magic and the eloquence of the many silent moments when our eyes met and it was like "now let's see who looks away first".

This particular afternoon we are called out for poetry. Leaving our desks, if I step into the aisle on my left, I will be four to five places away from Mary as we stand in a semicircle around our teacher. If I step into the aisle on my right, I am likely to be right next to her. This day I step right. Mary is called to recite. She is shaky and nervous. I am more so. "Please, Mary, don't get stuck. Please, please sweetheart get through this cursed poetry somehow." I am saying the lines with her under my breath. She's going well - then stops. In the very instant she stops, instinctively I come out with the next few words. It was as if someone else spoke them. With this, Mary picks up again and sails on to the end. I am looking at my teacher with my mouth open in astonishment. I thought I was in trouble. She's looking back at me as if I had uttered a gross obscenity. She then looks to Mary and back to me. She says nothing but the expression on her face has changed. She's happy and amused. I'm sure she senses that something is going on between Mary and me.

My emotional state at this time is now entirely dependent on what happens at school. Relationships at home count for nothing. I know that tomorrow, I will see Mary and the world is a beautiful and magical place.

The tide has indeed turned. A major event in both our lives takes place. In secret, without fanfare or trumpets and with the minimum of witnesses (just parents), my sister Bridgie marries Mary's uncle - Frank Burns. Given the dire economic conditions of the time, this Burns family were indeed remarkable. Of six brothers, four set up business in Shercock, a small village. A fifth brother, Mary's father, runs a business out in the country. The sixth stayed on at home on the family farm. Now there is plenty for Mary and me to talk about, especially after she meets my dear sister Bridgie, the loveliest girl in the land. And as we are related, we can talk and not be bothered about what our classmates think.

Autumn of that year comes, my last year at school. Any pupil promoted to a higher class moves to desks for that class. I'm in seventh and take a desk on the extreme right. Mary's moving into sixth, so can select a desk in any of the last two rows. On the day of the changeover, I remember sitting at my desk wondering who's going where. I am all but praying Mary will get into a desk near me. On the desk right in front of me there's a quality leather satchel and some books. Imagine my delight and astonishment when I realise they are Mary's but she's nowhere to be seen. She's done the equivalent of the German's by claiming the best poolside seats by placing their towels on them the night before.

My last year at school was like a happy dream. Mary is right in front of me. Since the entire class of pupils is between us and our teacher, it is perfect for the passing of little coded slips - we were texting! And the focus of each and every day for me is entirely about whether or not Mary will ask for my help. I am just longing for her to pass back a little note, something like: how do you do number six?

"A farmer applies for a loan of £1500 from his bank to buy a farm. The bank agrees to lend him the money at a rate of 3% per annum with repayments of £15 monthly.

Question 1: how much interest is due the first year?

Question 2: how much interest is due over the entire period of the loan?

Question 3: How much compound interest will be due if the farmer fails to make any payments the first year? "

Now while everything seems perfect on the surface, underneath is a growing unease. I'll be fourteen on the 17th March 1950 so I can legally leave school. My father may want me too, leaving is my secret dread. But children had no rights, so what I wanted wouldn't be given a thought.

Also, at home mama was genuinely disturbed that not one of her sons was a priest. She regarded this as a shame on her personally. At the time, a priest in the family not only bestowed great blessings in a religious sense, it also gave the family greatly enhanced social status. I don't even have an altar boy, she used to say. None of us were altar boys because the two churches we attended had schools attached. These schools produced all the altar boys for the two churches. Our school, Sreenty, was four miles from the churches. Mama was determined. She arranged private lessons for me on the Latin mass, so two evenings a week I travelled to the priest's house for one to one tuition.

Chapter 20 - Holy Smoke

Now Mama has her altar boy. The weeks pass and from time to time, I'd see her and my sister Bridgie sitting in the corner at home in secret conclave, now and then, with sideways glances at me. One Sunday afternoon, there is white smoke. They announce I am to become a priest. They told me I had a vocation. Mama said the parish priest who taught me Latin told her I should be sent to the Millhill Fathers in Kilkenny as a seminarian, where I would be on the fast track to the priest hood. As a seminarian, there would be no fees and all my needs would be provided for. This is an exciting, even exhilarating time for mama - her happiest, dearest dream, her fondest wish will at last come true. My sister Bridgie's place of work is only a short distance away. Now coming home a lot, she and mama sitting in a corner, talking in low hushed tones, with just an occasional remark to me, how privileged I am to be called and how God will shower blessings on all of us. And mama is treating me differently. She is watching me all the time and when she looks at me, it's in a most respectful, almost reverential way.

My schooling is nearing its end. One Sunday at mass, the priest announces from the altar that two scholarships are on offer to the parish from St Patrick's agricultural college in Monaghan. Boys between the ages of fourteen and seventeen are invited to do the exams.

This was of less than passing interest to me, I enjoyed a higher calling. I am one of God's chosen ones, I had a vocation and would soon be leaving the clay behind me. In the all-embracing religious culture of the time, to be told at age fourteen that you had a vocation was sensational. I was someone apart, special, and because my religious faith was almost total, I believed it.

However, from time to time, a small but lively energetic thought rose up through the heavy, deadening religious overlay – Mary Burns. I was in a dilemma and bothered about how I would see her when I left school, that I might not see her was unthinkable.

Time for another secret conclave. In no time, mama and Bridgie emerge from clouds of white smoke again, the decision is an easy one. Either way, it's win-win. I'll do the test for the scholarship and fail or succeed, I still have the option of the Millhill Fathers in Kilkenny. As with everything mama said, whatever happened was in God's hands and as things turned out, it was the agricultural college for me. And ever since, I've been inflicted with the disturbing thought of just how much God has to answer for.

The scholarship's test was held in the college but I only have tiny images and flashes of memory of it. No memory at all of how I journeyed there or how I arrived home. At the time, getting there and back would have been a logistical challenge. From home to Carrick, then to Blayney, then to Monaghan and the college is a couple of miles outside Monaghan town. I remember the test was in the study hall. All I recall was the very last paper, a page of English text that I can best describe as heavy and dense, like something you read and then think "what the hell is that all about?" The question was "describe in so many words your understanding of the above". Anyway, as it came to pass in due course - I was informed I was awarded a scholarship. It was for one year's duration and would cover everything bar personal requirements. The college sent a list of these. Mama didn't take much interest in the list - she said the holy priests would look after my needs. I must have believed her because even as these words form on the page, I still can't believe how I left home with so little. In my innocence and naivety, I must have been so trusting in what mama said, or just been completely taken by the great feeling I had – leaving home.

Chapter 21 – A Scholarship to St. Patrick's Agricultural College

Dear reader, if heroically you have stayed with me so far, I genuinely hope the next chapter doesn't stress your endurance to breaking point. You have no doubt experienced in your life a bad day, a week, or perhaps a year. A number of unfortunate events hit you, one after the other. You battle valiantly to deal with one, then another strikes. There's no recovery time. You begin to believe the fates haven't just conspired against you, they are vindictive as well. You have been singled out for harsh treatment and it simply couldn't be coincidence. You'll see it was a bit like this for me as the next morsel of our little story unfolds.

I arrived in St Pat's Agricultural College in Sept. 1950 and from the first day, I knew I shouldn't be here. Apart from another lad who was the same age, I was the youngest of the group of students and the smallest. And if I take size as an indicator, I was the only pre-pubescent, the only one with glasses and the only one still wearing short trousers.

Many years later, still wondering why I seemed so out of place, size wise, I enquired of Monaghan County Council about the class of 1950/51. They sent me details of every student's name, age, address and school's attended, I discovered that this was a right motley crew. Most had left other colleges, others expelled. They came from so many different counties as far away as Sligo and Waterford, with only three from Monaghan.

There was a fully functioning farm attached to the college, a large herd of cows, a lot of pigs and big acreage of potatoes and sugar beet. The students were fully involved in all the farm work, spending each morning milking cows by hand, looking after the pig herd and working in the fields. During the afternoons and evenings, we studied agriculture, horticulture, botany, zoology and soil Science. For recreation, there was table tennis and football. Everyone else was in shorts and football boots. I played in my short trousers and ultralight slippers which was regular footwear for altar boys.

Feeling very conspicuous in my short trousers, I wrote in urgent desperation to mama. Some weeks later a parcel arrived. I felt a warm, surging glow of excitement, my first long trousers. And now I needn't feel so conspicuous.

That morning in the dormitory with five other boys present, I ripped open my eagerly awaited parcel. The other boys were reading their mail and opening parcels. I quickly read mama's note.

"The trousers might be a bit big but I know you'll grow into them."

I pulled them on, confident that what she meant would be insignificant. But these weren't long trousers – these were long, long trousers. I was a smallish fourteen year old - these would have fitted a grown man. For the first time, perhaps the only time ever, I felt so angry with mama. A rage of resentment and disappointment welled inside me. In other circumstances, this would be a hilarious practical joke. This is no joke, mama. With my tight jacket and the legs of my long trousers rolled up – everyone laughed. I suppose I would have looked a somewhat curious, even comical figure –small tight jacket rolled up trousers, chaplinesque you could say, so to the other students I was indeed a great source of fun.

Wednesday afternoons were free. Everyone put on their best and walked in to Monaghan town. The main attraction was a matinee in the Magnet cinema where the boys gorged on chocolate, ice-cream and soft drinks. I tagged along the first week, but saw no film and I didn't do any gorging.

The following few Wednesdays found me in the library. It boasted a substantial number of books for such a small place. Then one afternoon, the lad who got the other scholarship from our parish found me. He asked me why I didn't join the merry throng going into town. I didn't expect him to believe my lie, he asked me to go with him.

The heart of Monaghan town is called the Diamond and it's a very attractive layout. All the best shops sit in a cluster here. Before the matinee in the Magnet Cinema the boys head for the Diamond, in small groups, from their respective dormitories. My friend, Pat Larkin and I are together, isolated, and in my case, shunned. At the time, one big store called Wellworths dominated the Diamond, it was modelled on Woolworths. Inside, one counter with mighty glass jars of the cheapest sweets, so many for a penny. Another counter, with two penny offerings, and so on.

Soon it was clear, my friend Pat had a seriously deficient cash flow problem, not quite, but almost as bad as mine. The penny counter took all his business.

On the way home, he is sharing his sweets with me. This one bag, he says, was unbelievable value. He got so many for a penny. But he didn't like them. He offered me the lot. Pat was enjoying a bag of Camphor Balls. Unfortunately, Camphor Balls didn't figure high on my list of priorities. Any moths in my wardrobe were most welcome to what they found, that is if they found anything.

Our study hall consisted of a long narrow building with rows of desks along either wall and another two set of desks in the middle, at the top end. A lad from Donegal and me sit at these desks right in front of the lecturer's table. Five nights a week, there was a two hour study period. This was the only time discipline was strictly enforced. No talking, no play acting, heads down - it's study time.

At some point most nights, the Dean of Studies, Father McDermott would arrive in. He'd glide up and down the middle aisle, reading. He was so quiet, he seemed to hover. The only sound in the place was the flicking of pages being turned. Sometimes, he would sit at his desk, looking out at us. Being so near, I found this unnerving. When he did speak, we knew it would be something about behaviour in general - a reproving telling off, talking-down-to kind of talk. He was fond of pithy, moralising aphorisms like

"Coyle, what is the meaning of the expression: 'There is a marshal's baton in every knapsack'?"

Or

"Procrastination is the thief of time".

He would then pronounce on the wisdom and power in these expressions. Four to five weeks after my arrival, it's study time and I am sitting at my desk when something hits the back of my head. I turn around and see a small ball of paper on the floor. I thought someone is having a bit of fun, maybe it is my friend Pat Larkin who threw it, then I am hit by another and another. Each time I look around, everyone's nose is in their books. Not the tiniest clue to who is throwing them. After this first incident, the paper throwers took a break for a while, but it would start again when some particular piece of work needed to be completed or a test or exam was to take place the following day. This night the Dean of Studies comes in, sits down at the top desk and it's clear he is in a black mood. Perhaps the cleaners have complained. Before he came in, the paper bombers had been active and there are a lot of small paper balls and airplanes made from paper at my feet and under my desk.

"Coyle," he says, "how do you account for all the rubbish at your feet and under your desk?"

"It's not mine, Father."

Now the tone becomes harsher.

"Not yours," he says. "There's all that litter right under your own desk and now you have the effrontery to deny it's yours. Look around you, why can't you be tidy, like everyone else? Coyle, you are a squalid mess. Clean it all up, this instant and I don't ever want to see such a mess again."

This incident was a model for an on-going series that lasted my entire stay. My tormentors were a core group of four to five, with others joining in from time to time, for the fun. The method and the outcome was always the same, crucially, the victim would be found guilty and so suffer the consequences. And apart from the Study Hall, the great variety of work around the farm and the fields provided an infinite variety of opportunities for the pack to set up their target.

Being innocent, but always getting blamed, I was in constant fights as I feebly attempted to assert a tiny degree of self-respect, but it was an unequal struggle. Eventually, I gave up and endured. So each night, when the paper bombers had been active, I made frantic efforts to clean up before the Dean of Studies comes in. But I can leave this until the last minute because I know he will come precisely on time.

One night, sitting there waiting for the next missile, unable to do any work, paralysed by anger and frustration, I accuse another lad of throwing. He says

"I didn't throw anything at you, Coyle, but even if I did, what are you going to do about it, four eyes?"

I'm back at my desk, having come a poor second. The Dean of Studies strolls in. My Heinrich Himmler, grey-steeled glasses, bent and twisted, cling to my cut nose. He does his usual routine. He's been sitting at his desk for some time. I can't believe he still hasn't noticed, with the previous incidence still fresh and all his talk of good order and discipline, I am waiting for the sword to fall. He has already threatened me with expulsion, I have no defence. If I try to, I'll get the same retribution as before or worse. Maybe this time, he'll accuse me of self-harm. The brooding presence speaks.

"Coyle, a little while ago, we discussed the meaning of the expression 'discretion is the better part of valour.' Did....you.....learn....anything?"

Lesson number one: In this situation, discretion as a choice is no choice. All the encouragement the aggressive bully needs is to see his victim taking the easy way out.

Lesson number two: When it comes to moral courage, many adults can be more childish than children.

Lesson number three: Hold a healthy scepticism of people with grand titles.

The one bright spot in all this was I enjoyed an excellent relationship with all the instructors, except for this Dean of Studies and the Agriculture instructor, who were both pathetic and wilfully blind to what was going on. So obviously looking the other way and ignoring the source of the trouble. It's so feeble minded to come down hard on the easiest target and give the impression of imposing discipline.

The Botany teacher was the opposite and pointedly so. He was exceptional. So I developed a real interest, if not a love of the subject. Come hell or high water, I would not let my Botany teacher down. So when we sat for a test, or at exam time, I really did know my Angiosperms from my Gymnosperms.

On my last day there, the College Principal Father Hackett, a small, kind gentleman offered me a lift to Monaghan town. From there, I would catch a bus to Castleblayney or Carrickmacross. He wished me well, saying I should keep in touch and come back to visit when I felt like it. Father Hackett wouldn't have known, but the thoughts of keeping in touch or going back on a visit was hysterically funny. I felt I could only reclaim my life at the most remote distance from the place. I couldn't even bear to think or imagine what could ever drag me back.

I watched his car move away through the streets. I wait until it has vanished out of sight. While it was in sight, I still felt some connection with that detestable place. Now it is gone, standing there for a minute or so, I had the feeling of emerging from a nightmare, then the joyful realisation, it was all over.

It was a warm, sunny morning. I wanted to run, roaring and shouting through the streets:

"I'm free, I'm free, I've survived. I can live again!"

Sitting on the bus to Castleblayney, I thought of how I would banish this experience, utterly and totally from my consciousness. I knew this would be easy, because I was already delighting in thoughts of seeing my sweetheart again. I would never tell anyone, or talk about it. No-one would ever, ever know. It was a place of shame and humiliation, so I would bury it forever as if it never happened.

How wrong I was. Forty-six years later, on my last day in Eircom, I picked up a Northern Ireland telephone directory. I was looking for one entry, one Sean Grant of Moneyscalp, Castlewellan, Co Down. There it was, just one entry under this name. Without doubt, this was my man. He, I believed, though I couldn't be sure, was the ringleader and most to blame for my difficulties. Down all the years, justice was still screaming to be done and honour and self-respect restored.

Chapter 22 - First Job

I'm on my way home, but home is not where I want to be, all I am thinking about is how, where, or what kind of job I can get. And above all, I must see my sweetheart. She'll be finishing school, what will she do? Will she be leaving home? It's not like I can phone her, or get on a bike, or horse and trot over to her home. The only possibility is to meet her at mass or when she'd be in Shercock shopping or seeing her new cousin Helen (Bridgie's first child). Although I hadn't seen Mary for some time, I was in no doubt it would happen soon.

Meanwhile, it was as if your loveable sister is absent, your thoughts and memories of her have an added vividness with the small but all important difference, my sister didn't look at me with warm, bright eyes for so long, I had to turn away in bashful, blushing silence.

Sitting under the table at home, I started answering every "situation vacant" ad in the Anglo Celt and Irish Press that offered hope of any kind of job. In the forties and fifties, the main source of male employment was agriculture. Young girls leaving school entered domestic service, but the word here really is servitude. Living in the homes of their masters doing the most arduous work seven days a week for a miserly pittance, they were little more than indentured slaves.

Along with agricultural work where the boys slept in the barns and outhouses of their employers their main source of work was what was known as "serving their time". Each and every type of business took boys on at age fourteen in what we may call in the form of apprenticeship. The point is the limits of anyone's ambition at the time was food in your belly and a roof over your head.

Boys and girls finishing school was a plentiful source of cheap labour. These adverts would be phrased as,

"Strong youth urgently required ..." **or** "Young female to help ..."

However they were phrased – these expressions were simply metaphors for child slaves. There is no other word for it because remember children had no rights or status and were predisposed to evil. No history has ever been written of the extent to which the Irish economy of the time, such as it was, was based on child slave labour. Every business, without exception, depended on its child slaves working very long hours, six days a week in most businesses (including pubs), or sometimes seven days - all for the reward of subsistence wages.

In the case of the "strong youth" ad, what it really meant was the young lad would be paid a pittance to do a man's job - but without the overhead of paying the reasonable income a grown man would expect. Young fellas of my age voiced their own particular version of the strong youth's ad:

"Horse dead from overwork, strong youth urgently required."

In September of 1951, aged fifteen, I received a reply to one of my many job applications. It was for a young assistant to the Head Gardener at a gentlemen's residence near Rush, County Dublin. I was asked to present for interview at an office in Dame Street. My dear sister Elsie met me. After the bus journey, I was in my usual fragile state. I recall so well, she gave me a right talking to at the state of my boots. We went in great haste to where my cousin, Anne McEnroe, worked - as it happened, also in Dame Street. There I had a chance to recover and polish my boots before setting off for this gentleman's office.

This gentleman went by the name of Douglas Figgis. He was Chairman of the Board of Dublin Port. On the thin side, tall, grey hair sleeked back, sixty plus and very smartly dressed. He exuded that certain, serious, imperious kind of look. You sensed he wasn't someone you could have an in depth discussion of the weather with, or offer the latest pub joke. His office is very impressive and happily, he didn't check my boots. He told me about the job, what was expected of me and that I would be paid £1 per week. Naturally, I agreed to everything and was given a starting date.

On my first morning, in my first job, the lady of the house gave me very firm instructions on how I would address herself and other members of her family. When I had reason to speak to her, I would address her as Lady Mogret (Margaret); her husband as The Mossteh (the Master); her daughter as Miss Pomelah (Pamela) and finally her son as Mossteh Crisstafoh (Christopher). I didn't like this. And so throughout my entire stay, I never - not once - uttered any of these titles.

She referred to me and other staff there as the sawvents (servants). Out in front, she led me to this little room, the shoe room and declared my first job each day was to polish every shoe. My next job was to look after three beautiful hunter-type horses whose names were Carna, Flicker and the nicest and the biggest - Silver. Each day, it was shoes and horses first, before I started my gardening.

Lady Mogret herself was the most attractive lady I have ever met. Aged fifty or so, greying hair, always so well turned out. Every time we met, or whenever I saw her, early or late, she looked as if she was about to step into the spotlight. Apart from her figure, clothes, hair and make-up, she was gifted with a most appealing and attractive manner of speech (except when she was in her condescending mood). She practiced inflection a lot. When saying a word such as *immediately,* the tone wasn't so much a straight line, more of a sine wave.

The most extreme example was when her husband Douglas was some distance away and she needed to call out to him. The first syllable quite low, but the second, long drawn out and soaring into the heavens so that it would be heard over most of North East County Dublin! "DoooGLOSSSSS!" I have often thought since because of her voice and her way with language, she was most probably an operatic diva-even a real prima donna.

I lived in the servants' accommodation along with three other much older men who managed the farm. The head gardener inhabited the gate lodge with his wife and two sons. His name was Michael Sherry, about fifty, very pleasant manner, hardworking and wonderfully humorous. Horseracing was an obsession with him, along with an endless repertoire of accompanying humorous stories, which he had a way of telling. At times, I thought he had kept them all for me, as if he was telling them for the first time. Frequently, we would both be convulsed with laughter as he told a different story. I think Lady Margaret knew about this, because I remember times when our uncontrollable laughter turned to petrified silence as Lady Margaret, using her full alto-soprano range, called out "SherreeeEEEE".

While there was time for fun, there was major work to undertake. Each day, we prepared an order of fruit, vegetables and flowers for the Gresham Hotel in Dublin. Meeting this order on an on-going basis meant planting and growing in phases, through spring and summer, so that the different batches matured at different times. While most of my time was spent in the walled garden and inside the extensive glass houses, I was also responsible for the maintenance of a croquet lawn and grass tennis court.

Both children were in boarding schools. Christopher was in the UK and Michael Sherry reckoned he was at Eton. When he was home, at weekends and on holidays Christopher would come and talk to me. He was a grand chap, probably three to four years older than me and of course, I was flattered by his company. Each time when he came to the servants' quarters he carried a rifle and a rugby ball. He seemed keen to put in some passing practice and to demonstrate to me how it should be done. Afterwards, we would wander off and take pot shots at crows in the trees. Frequently, he would don the full riding gear and canter off on one of the horses. I wasn't invited to join in this. He probably knew Lady Margaret would consider this a step too far for her junior servant.

One weekend, when all the family were away, the other servants dressed me up in the full riding regalia including tall black hat. I saddled up Silver, the biggest of the three horses. This is my first time in a saddle. What followed was one of the most frightening experiences of my entire life. I rode the horse out of the yard, where the loose boxes were, intending to go for a gentle canter to get used to the saddle. I have this feeling, this great feeling of acting out the character of what we referred to then as the *landed gentry*.

But as I leave the yard, this horse suddenly took off on a mad, runaway gallop - up along the long winding gravel path to the nearest paddock. Whatever I was doing, was driving the horse crazy. Into the paddock, on a mad, flat out gallop. He heads for a grove of trees with so many low hanging branches. I feared we won't get through this alive. Nothing I do has any effect. I am hanging onto his neck and mane for dear life. Not easing in the slightest, he heads for the paddock boundary. He is galloping so crazily, he seems blind to obstacles. Just as I thought he was charging straight into the high boundary paling, he wheels away back to the entrance of the paddock. Back along the gravel path to his loose box, I have to stop him. He is big and the door to his box isn't that high, but there is no stopping him. I just cling on in desperation. My right foot is out of the stirrup, so I am half on, half off, stretching out along his neck like an American Indian attacking Custer cavalry. There is no other way to get through the door alive. Somehow, we made it. After this life threatening ride, I had a lot less affection for Silver.

The entire business of the farm and the garden seemed to be Lady Margaret's show with Douglas hardly ever appearing, so there were times when it was clear she was under some stress. She was assisted by two live-in housekeepers but they never stayed long. I would see new faces every seven to eight weeks. It was the same with the farm workers. She would come to see me frequently in the morning when I was doing my daily grooming of the horses. I can't recall her ever complaining to me about any of my work, probably because this was the best part of the work scene for me, being completely at ease spoiling the horses.

This one morning she astonished me, saying she had sent one of her housekeepers packing. There was a deep sigh. She says:

"Coyle, you can't possibly begin to imagine the difficolty one has, trying to find sawvants one can trost" (sic).

Maybe the trouble was rooted in the wages. When I told the gardener what my income was, he said I just had to ask for more. But don't ask her, he cautioned, ask him.

"But I never see him" I said.

"He'll be in," he said, "I'll let you know when".

Even with Michael's help and advice, I was genuinely bothered about whether or not I could manage meeting the Master and asking for a rise. And I could not call him Master. When the day came, my friend Michael said,

"Tell him you want an extra half crown. (Half-crown is two shillings and sixpence - remember we were using sterling then.) If you don't say how much he will just give you one shilling."

For me, speaking to the man, much less asking for a rise, was a major act of courage. But Michael coached me well. At the opportune moment, I spoke up,

"Mr Figgis, for the extra work I am doing, I think I deserve a rise of half a crown."

I was much relieved when he agreed. However, he said, he would consult with Sherry from time to time and if my work wasn't satisfactory I could expect a severe reprimand. In another time and place, he might have added, "and be reduced to the ranks."

You could always tell when the master and lady were arguing because instead of her calling out Dooglas in the usual way, she'd come to me and say,

"Coyle, summon the mosstah, I wish to speak with him immediately."

Standing beside her, I had an almost irresistible urge to call out Dooglas just like her. I was so impressionable I thought she wanted me to do this. Michael had me practising while they were away, so eventually I could imitate her with pitch perfect precision.

He'd often ask me to call out "Dooglas" while the other men were getting an extra half hour in bed, or playing cards after an extended lunch break. This sound ringing out unexpectedly was not good for their nervous stability. But the vernacular of the time was my natural speech, so my inclination would be to say,

"Dougie, me auld brancher, herself is chewing the rag up at the house, will you gup and spake to her?"

My sweetheart has now finished school and I was hoping she would get a job away from home so I could write to her. I hadn't been at my new job in Rush long when mama wrote asking me why I wasn't coming home at weekends. Travelling home was just what I wanted to do, not for mama's sake, but to see Mary. But the very thought of the journey, on what I labelled the hospital bus, sickened me.

Into the breach steps my sister Bridgie once more. She knows van and lorry drivers who pass through Rush at weekends. At the time, the general area around Rush and Lusk produced a major part of the country's vegetables, tomatoes and strawberries. The van and lorry drivers were on the road, either very early or very late. So at weekends it was ideal for me to catch a lift home, return and still keep good time.

Home at weekends meant mass on Sundays. Mass on Sundays meant parents and children together - Mary would be there with her parents and we would probably snatch the briefest conversation, but this was sufficient reassurance because I knew we were moving to a time very soon when we could write.

I was reasonably happy in this place. At the time, having any kind of job was a source of pride, and for me, having some money was sensational. However, after my living expenses each week, very little remained.

Chapter 23 - Blackrock College

A year passes at Rush, and I knew I didn't have the courage to ask Dougie for another pay rise, so it's back to the "Sits Vac" in the Irish Press. It was the national daily at the time and sadly no longer in print. I can't recall how many applications I posted but I got a response to the one I most wanted.

'Young man to assist in the gardens at Blackrock College.'

If I can use a surfing metaphor, I really am on the crest of a wave. Being called for interview was mighty. Nowadays, Blackrock College has competition. Back then, it was synonymous with Ireland's elite in politics, religion and business. Being a rugby college only added to my interest as Ireland had recently won the Triple Crown.

I jumped off the bus and looked across the road at this great wrought iron arch that frames the main entrance. For a youngster from Monaghan, with fragile self-confidence, it was intimidating. I thought I'd be overwhelmed intellectually by anyone I met in these hallowed domains.

If my application is successful, I'll feel privileged. With gloating satisfaction, if anyone asks me where I am, or what I am doing, I'll simply say I am in Blackrock College and leave it at that.

Some distance up the avenue the college buildings come into sight. Small groups of happy, laughing students are passing to and fro. I was thinking of Pat Larkin and me at the penny counter buying sweets. These boys in their suits looking so well cared for inhabit a different world. Here and there, I spot a Professor or Lecturer in flowing colourful gowns. Carrying bundles of books and folders close to their chests, they cradle them in a protective, almost comforting way, as they stride about earnestly. I am wide eyed, impressed and wondering if any of them should acknowledge my presence, should I bow, bless myself or genuflect? Ever since, I've thought of this as the perfect image of dedicated scholarship. Little did I realise that just a few years later, I would imitate this exactly with my City and Guilds notes, but I had no colourful gown and I don't think I strutted as confidently.

I continued on to Reception where I was to meet Brother Luke, the gardener. The reception area was a showcase of the college alumni such as President De Valera and Archbishop John Charles McQuaid.

I was studying the scholarship achievements of these demi-Gods when Brother Luke introduced himself. He's in full clerical habit, all black, with short black hair and frequently he flattens a fringe across his forehead with his hand, a bit Hitler-like. He didn't look like a gardener. He's in his mid-forties, with a pale, clean look – as if he quickly freshened up to greet his new understudy.

There is a lot of activity in the reception area, so we start to walk down this great, long corridor, lined with busts on either side. His walk was a real giveaway, a countryman's walk. Country people doing so much walking over hills and dales and long winding, endless country roads, have this habit of bobbing back and forth with each stride. It's like they're trying to get a bit more distance with each step. At the end of this corridor, we go into a pokey, little, not so much office as den, and unlike my previous employer, Lukie's office, fails to impress. And as examples of the infinite range of human personalities, Lukie and Dougie would be wonderful models. Dougie stern and regimental, Lukie solemn and cold, utterly humourless and in all the time I worked there, not once did we share the tiniest morsel of humour.

Just like my first interview, this one was entirely a one-sided affair. It was a case of,

"Yes, brother, no brother, I'll jump through hoops, brother, somersaults and cartwheels brother".

I was anything but a hard-nosed negotiator and my answers were as brief as possible.

Anyway, I was offered a job. I would live in the college with full board and my wages would be almost three times what Dougie paid. I'm no longer a servant. I go by the grand title of member of staff. And as Brother Luke said, I could avail of the college library. So who is to say, when I am in the library, I can't also act the young scholar.

Returning back down the avenue, my face held a permanent little smile. Although I could not see Brother Luke convulsed with laughter too often, I did see the other compensations. And I know I'll feel so good being amongst all these educated people. I didn't just admire them, I all but paid homage.

Now back to Dougie and her ladyship. How am I going to tell them I am leaving? In the interview, I just sat there and listened or answered questions. This will be much more difficult. What personality I had could best be described as passive - even meek. Just below the surface tugged a deep reservoir of self-hatred and the poison of low self-worth. I had been well conditioned this way psychologically and emotionally. If her ladyship announces I am just another disloyal and untrustworthy servant and she won't let me go, I am fearful I will accept this and stay. And I'll need to ask for a reference. At that time, you could not get a job or move from job to job without a reference from your prior employer. I was concerned about what kind of reference she would give me.

What will I say to Michael Sherry, friend, teacher - and indeed father? I must work a week's notice, so each day with Michael will be difficult. Am I letting him down? Will he think how much he has done for me, all the life-giving humour, all the laughs we've shared - and now I am walking out.

When I eventually built up the courage to tell Michael, he made it all easy.

"You have to go where you will have a reasonable income, here no-one will stay because they won't pay - what they really want is bonded slaves."

When I told her ladyship, I can't recall any reaction.

The work scene in Blackrock was a lot like Rush, we were planting and growing entirely to supply the kitchen and plant flowerbeds but there all similarity ends dramatically. Wages, meals and accommodation were all substantially better and the library - I remember just looking in wonder and astonishment at so many books - where would I start?

Also, my first sight of a shower. Staff could use the students' showers within a very limited period in the evening. I'm glowing with satisfaction mingling with the educated classes.

And in a matter of minutes, I can be in the city at weekends to catch a lift home to Shercock and the joy of a few stolen minutes with my sweetheart. With so much extra money, I began to buy clothes and any surplus I gave to mama when I was home. I remember seeing or perhaps just noticing polo neck jumpers for the first time and thinking - "this I must have." In the shop in Blackrock, I went to the counter and told the girl I wanted to buy a polo-necked cardigan.

The garden at the college was the perfect example of every gardener's dream: two acres of the best soil, facing south, surrounded by a twelve foot high, thick, red-bricked wall. This magnificent wall provided shelter and absorbed warmth from the sun. The result was a micro-climate and ideal growing conditions for a great range of plants.

The only entrance to the garden was through a couple of three foot wide doors in the wall, so the biggest piece of equipment in the garden was a wheelbarrow. Inside this magnificent space, there is one huge glasshouse and a smaller conservatory. Inside, you'd fine various sized growing plots, Lukie (Brother Luke) and me duly equipped with spades, forks, a shovel, a hoe and a wheelbarrow.

Each morning, I would be in the garden at half eight. Lukie would show at nine thirty. How could I be so lucky? He trusts me. He feels no need to check I am on time. I thought it couldn't get any better, but it did, in a very limited sense. At midday, he departs again, eventually reappearing in the afternoon. He leaves well before my finishing time. At first, I thought this was a temporary thing, but later realised it was a fixed, even rigid, routine. I never really discovered but he must have had other duties elsewhere.

Now dear reader, you are thinking, such freedom, he is letting you get on with it, this is ideal. Well yes, but mostly no. About the third or fourth week, each time he would depart, he started outlining how much we were behind with this job or that. If we didn't get this finished, we would be late with something else and then there was another job that should have been completed weeks ago.

This genuinely worried me because the "we" he's referring to really means me. As a result, I worked with every ounce of energy I had, in fear, that if I didn't catch up on all these jobs that were 'behind' I might not have a job. Also, in keeping with the mood of the time, I was most deferential towards priests, nuns or other religious people. And he had this uncanny, infuriating knack of having me always answering no, implying failure. Ignoring all I completed, he'd ask about a job when the answer was so obvious.

"Did you get started on the pruning of the apple trees?"

"No brother."

"Or the black currants?"

"No brother"

"You didn't?"

"No, brother."

I recall at times being so exasperated, baffled by how he could so consistently turn his back on all the excellent work completed and only point out the next job to be done.

This attitude and behaviour would be regarded by today's norms as thoughtless, negative and even cruel. But the good Brother Luke was not abnormal - he was a product of his time. To him, acknowledging much less praising a young person was to encourage laziness or what was referred to then as 'getting above themselves' and tantamount to encouraging the very serious sin of pride.

None of this bothered me all that much because overall I had a great time. The college was a very lively place, with frequent gatherings of the great and good - for the many sporting and social events.

It is now the winter of 1953. I am seventeen and thinking of the ultimate glamour job - a chauffeur gardener. I imagined this perfect, idealised image of myself in uniform driving the most expensive car. When not driving, I would clip some hedges, cut grass and plant flowers. Then at any odd moment, himself or her ladyship would call out to me, in a Lady Margaret-type tone, to drive them to some grand event such as the opera or a classical concert. In pursuing the "Sits Vac" columns, a number of jobs for Chauffeur Gardeners always stuck out. If I am to achieve the ultimate, this sublime pinnacle of achievement, I must learn to drive and yes, there was a school of motoring in Dublin, the only one in Ireland. At the time, if you owned a car, you could simply drive it away. At least another ten years would pass before a driving test became compulsory.

Over that winter, I went into the O'Connell School of Motoring on Aston Quay and took driving lessons, always at night-time. My instructor and I spent a lot of time driving around the Phoenix Park, but later through the city streets. I also completed what they called the owner-driver maintenance course. After the test, I was presented with a diploma which I still have. (Now, don't you sneer, it's all I have.)

The diploma reads: "This is to certify that Patrick Coyle has this day been found proficient as a driver and has also passed a car maintenance course."

Can there be any stopping me now? As a "Sits Vac" junkie, it's back to the columns of the Irish Press. I started sending in my applications for every Chauffeur Gardener position advertised. I was so confident my gardening experience combined with my brand new driving diploma were my passports to greatness. If there were three positions advertised, I'd apply for all three. You see I had a fiendish, ulterior motive, it was the best possible way of seeing the inside of the grandest houses in and around Ballsbridge.

After a couple of interviews, I discovered my dream job was a mirage - a cruel illusion. All my perspective employers were Duggie Figgis clones. What they called my income would be more accurately described as a small contribution towards an income. My illusion shattered, I re-focussed my great gardening talents, not to mention my driving diploma, elsewhere.

You will recall that this is 1953, Coronation Year in the UK, the Second World War ended just eight years previously. German and Japanese manufacturing industry wiped out in the war, hasn't yet begun to recover. So the Brits and the Americans have the markets of the world all to themselves. There was huge demand for labour in the UK and adverts started appearing in Irish papers for all types of jobs.

Chapter 24 - England and Arundel Castle

This day in the Spring of 1954, as I go through my daily ritual perusing the "Sits Vacs" columns, my eyes suddenly light up and my ears go back.
"Applications are invited for the position of Trainee in the gardens of the Duke of Norfolk's estate at Arundel in Sussex. Transport and other expenses will be paid for all those called to interview."

I applied. Sometime later, I was asked to attend for interview. This truly set my mind racing. Blackrock College and chauffeur gardeners is one thing, Arundel Castle and the premier Duke of the English realm is surely the big league. It was also not insignificant that he was Catholic. I mentioned to another lad in the college, Matt McKiernan, that I was thinking of going to England. I didn't mention the interview. He said that he had already made up his mind to go. He seemed keen we'd go together. As the time was coming fast for my interview, I was in a bit of a quandary - I would have to ask Brother Luke for three or four days off to go to England. It must have been that I had no holiday time remaining. I remember thinking I couldn't ask this man for a favour. He might ask for an explanation and in my innocence I would tell the truth. I decided I'd leave. If I didn't get a job with His Grace, I would join Matt wherever he decided to go.

Chapter 25 – A Date in Howth

As the time nears when we are due to sail, this interview was on my mind, but I have a more immediate and pressing need, I must see Mary Burns before I go. Once in England, I have no possible way of making contact with her, so I hatched not just a Plan A, but B and C as well. The Duke was the Duke, but darling Mary was my life. I'll visit home the weekend before I go. If I don't get an opportunity to speak to her at mass, I'll ask my sister Bridgie to find out where she is - when she eventually gets a job. If I can't bring myself to ask Bridgie, I'll make up some story and call round to Mary's home. On the Sunday morning, she isn't at mass with her family - I thought the Gods were against me. She always attends. This Sunday above all, she is missing. I speak to Pete, her younger brother.

"Mary is in Dublin, she has just got a job", he says.

Pete's few words had such an impact on me that it took a while for them to register. I stood there watching after him as he ran to catch up with his parents. Mary working was something I'd waited two years for. I hadn't the presence to ask him where she was working. No matter, she's in Dublin. I'll sit on the side of O'Connell Street, all day, every day - she's bound to pass sometime. If there was a scale for happy joyful excitement, I am stuck at max. After a few minutes, walking on air, I recover some balance. I realise that just as Mary arrives in Dublin, I am set to leave. As the whirlpool of thoughts settle a little, I realize I need to go to Shercock to see if Bridgie knows Mary's address.

Bridgie will be startled to see me because none of us ever went to Shercock on Sunday. Nevertheless, going to England was a major event, so I was armed with a good excuse. I just hope, even pray, she'll know Mary's address and I don't have to ask her to get it. I pretend to ask in a "by the way..." fashion, otherwise she'll ridicule me for being so silly.

Bridgie is surprised to see me and is genuinely concerned about my upcoming departure to England.

"Have you any idea what that place is like? Money isn't everything, you know? You don't know a soul there . You won't have a single friend to turn to."

Anyone she knows who went there, all went astray.

"There's Willy Brown, he was there a while, now I see him at mass on Sundays and he has neither prayer book nor beads in his hand!"

She made me promise to write every week and try to phone as well. *Try* being the operative word as so many calls failed. I am fidgety, anxious and unable to bring myself to ask the all-important question. Up pops a wonderful, unconscious prompt.

"Any news of my old school friends?" I ask.

"What would I know about your old school friends, they wouldn't be in here? (the pub)"

Then as she shuffles some scraps of paper across her mantelpiece,

"Mary Burns was in to see Helen and Peter (Bridgie's children, now age four and two, Marys niece and nephew). She left the address where she's started work, I don't know why; I don't have time to write to nieces and nephews."

I copy the address and skip all the way home, smiling at the cows and hobbled goats in the fields. Clutched in my hand is Mary's address and contact telephone number and I'm soon to be working in a castle. I've achieved Nirvana! There's no-one on earth I envy, no-one else could possibly possess an existence so perfect.

Next evening in Blackrock village, I eventually find a telephone kiosk that works. I'm as fearful and nervous as if I am about to set in motion a world-shaking event. Well, indeed it is. I'm arranging to see Mary for the first time, apart from school or mass. She says she finishes at six so we can meet at seven.

At seventeen, I am taking a real interest in my appearance. I am all growed up, if you will, and I remember enjoying great vitality. Dispensing with my Heinrich Himmler glasses, now I own glamorous horn-rims. My head boasts an excellent head of jet black hair. I was, after all, modelling myself on the "Brylcream Boy" ads – "not a hair out of place"

Mary is waiting at the legendary Howth Tram terminus. When I first see her, I stand still, in shock. She is transformed. Never have I seen her wear lipstick before. Never have I seen her dress like this. The bodice of her summer frock modestly enhances her developing womanhood. She looks bright and glowing, like a beautiful flower opening to the sun after a summer shower. And then getting a little nearer, to greet her, the delightful freshness of Eau de Cologne. Her entire appearance declares quietly but elegantly "I'm a proud, beautiful, young woman". She was. And I wanted to say so. The thought was there with so many others, like a pent up dam. And my heart is aching with the pain of being unable to say what I feel.

"Darling sweetheart, you are a delightful picture of female loveliness."

But in my shyness and paralysing lack of confidence, the words were stillborn. We start to walk, blindly. I feel so overwhelmed and proud to be with her, it feels like I'm under a powerful spotlight. And the village has come to a standstill. Everyone watching me with the most jealous and envious looks.

We come to a point where a well-known climb to the highest point in Howth Head starts. It is a warm, sunny May evening. We start the climb, neither of us said anything about where we were going, just strolling aimlessly. At first, we were some yards apart, now we are a bit closer. I feel I should take her hand, but I am so charged with emotion, I think that as soon as our fingers touch, I'll disappear in a little puff of vapour. After a while, there is a gentle, childlike touch and clasp of hands. For so long I had been dreaming of this, now I am sure we will be inseparable forever. I adored Mary. I was obsessed with her. I was possessed by her.

My head and my heart are bursting with so much I wish to say. Will I manage to overcome this insurmountable emotional barrier and express a little of it? As we move upwards, sometimes I go in front and I pull Mary up. At some point, I want us to sit down. Then with a supreme effort of will, I'm hoping I'll manage to say something to ease the boiling cauldron in my head. I see a rocky outcrop - it all but invites us to rest.

At home in Monaghan, there was a spot just like this on the top of one of our hills. The top of the hill forms a plateau. A short distance on the other side, the land falls away steeply. Just on the edge at the top, a mighty flat stone projects over the edge. In the enchanted landscape around home, this was my favourite place. Many times, I sat on this rock, my legs dangling in space. Down below is a little valley. This is a secret, hidden place - a place of fairies, banshees, stray sods And ghosts, no-one went there after dark. At times, I thought I was the only one who knew about it. It runs east to west and the only way in is through a cleft between two massive rocks on the east end.

In the late evening, it fills with a golden liquid light. On the plateau behind me, just yards away, the cows would assemble and select their place to lie down. They will chew their cud through the night. There is a homely, comforting smell of milk and something spiritual about how these gentle, placid animals all coming close together for companionship and company through the night. Looking across to the hill on the other side, nature is coming out to play and feed. A dense thicket of bush, whin and briar provides excellent cover. As the sun sets, the fox and her cubs will emerge and a bit later, the badgers.

But this evening on Howth Hill, my thoughts are far from badgers and foxes. The point where we sat down is quite high up. I remember looking out over the sea and it felt like we were floating in space. My head certainly was. As we chat, Mary is unhappy that just as she arrives in Dublin, I'm on my way out. God, if only I had known a few days earlier. England and Arundel Castle wouldn't hold the tiniest interest for me. I have already handed in my notice. I can't go back on that, not with Brother Luke. There is little hope of finding another job. But Mary is fascinated by this idea of a job in Arundel Castle. She talks and laughs about it as if it had a fairy tale dimension to it and I reassured her that when I get to know the ropes over there, she'd be able to join me.

Now and then as we chat, there are long pauses. And I see that happy spellbinding look, so open, childlike and trusting, devoid of fear or doubt. She has a soft soothing radiance as if she has no knowledge of hurt or pain, much less experience of them. I feel she is looking into my soul and reading my mind. I'm sure she expects we should kiss. Kissing, I'm sure, would be commonplace for her at home, but this is different. I desperately want to, and I am living a beautiful dream even thinking about it, but here and now, I am completely overwhelmed by the prospect of such intimate contact with this creature that inhabits all my dreams.

Above us, the sun is setting, but I have no thought of returning to Blackrock. Maybe time will stop and the beauty and innocence of this moment, sitting hand in hand in the glorious evening sun, will be fixed for eternity. But as darkness descends and we have to go, I realise I won't see her again before leaving for England. Suddenly, I feel the cold pang of fear. A little while ago, I was preoccupied with seeing her and this interview in England. Now, it feels as if I am running away.

As we stand up, I'm holding both her hands so tightly. Does she sense my anxiety? The real impact of going to England strikes me. Oh God, when will I see my darling sweetheart again? But my fear is eased, knowing that I will be able to express in letters what is impossible for me, face to face. I hint awkwardly about this to her and she teases me playfully about what I might say. Her happy, soothing eyes brighten as they search my face for answers. At moments like this she has this teasing, playful, confident way. I think she has some secret knowledge - that she inhabits a world of dreams, a world I cannot even imagine but only glimpse when I am with her. It is a world of beauty, magic and love, the love that shines in those enchanting eyes, charms all around her and unfreezes my cold heart.

How dearly I want to know that world of hers - to learn it's secrets. Would I ever know? The thought that I might not terrifies me. The thought that there was even the possibility she would smile like this for someone else - that another boy would delight in her loveliness, her company, and the joy of her uninhibited, girlish laughter, was more than I could bear. But this was just the tiniest, passing flicker of anxiety. By every moment with her, every touch, every word, a multitude of brief, shared experiences, from those early, tiny but joyful encounters, I knew heaven had sent her to me and I would love her and care for her for the rest of my life.

Darkness falls as we happily, hand in hand, make our way down to the village. Nothing much was said. It was if spoken language was unnecessary. There was this excited, euphoric state where words would intrude, unless they were few and special. But as we approach Mary's lodging, I'm torn by anxiety – how will I say goodbye? If there is no kiss, I will be sick with guilt, thinking Mary will feel unworthy or unattractive. Worse still, I'll be revealing the cold, unemotional desert I have come from.

And there was no kiss, just a hurried but happy goodbye as I ran to get back to the city and the last bus to Blackrock. I hated myself for this and that I had the opportunity but expressed so little of all that she meant to me. I was living a beautiful dream, being with her. Compared to this, everything else in my life held so little value or meaning. Without doubt, in the not too distant future, I'd be asking Mary to marry me. This is what I was thinking as I rushed to get the tram. This last tram from Howth that night - destination disappointment and despair.

Thoughts of the interview dwelled inside my mind, day and night. I thought a generation of young fellas would envy me such an opportunity, yet I became anxious and nervous. Lying awake at night, full of doubt about whether I could cope. I envisaged meeting someone cold and domineering who would just chew me up and spit me out. I was so overly respectful of all people in positions of authority, like Brother Luke, or the high and mighty around Ballsbridge.

And how about finding my way? In my time in Blackrock College, one of my favourite walks was along Dun Laoghaire pier, right to the point where the mail boat passes into the open sea. One evening after I had been invited for interview, I went into the office on the pier and enquired about the cost of crossing to Holyhead.

The attendant asked me where I was going in the UK because the same ticket covered boat and train. I told him my destination. He seemed to know what he was talking about. He said it would be train from holyhead to Euston in London, from Euston across the city to Charing Cross by tube, and then from Charing Cross going south to the nearest station to the castle. This meant travelling through the night and into the next day.

The train from Holyhead to London was notorious for very long delays and there were questions in the Dail at the time about British Rail's treatment of its Irish passengers on this route.

Chapter 26 - The Black Country

So this bright, promising afternoon in May 1954, Matt and me, suitcases in hand, stood together on Dun Laoghaire pier. Two others who Matt knew, also seeking their fortunes, joined us. Believe it or not, we were, or rather they were, deciding our destination. The boat dropped us at Holyhead, but then where would we go? It came down to Birmingham, Coventry or Wolverhampton. One of Matt's friends called Ward, much older than the rest of us, loud and talkative, brimming with enthusiasm at being to Wolverhampton before, knew exactly where we would get work and digs. As well as all the talk, he smokes a lot. Most of the time, he talks with the cigarette in his mouth. If it isn't, it is just poised an inch or so from his mouth. It's like the smoking restricts the flow of talk, or maybe it is vice versa. I didn't contribute to the conversation much. The prospect of the interview dominated my mind. I needed a few days to sort out the confusion in my head.

Arriving in Holyhead, the train was true to form. It lumbered slowly through the night and eventually reached Crewe. In a few minutes we are moving again, but slowly, very slowly. Then there is a squealing of brakes, a hissing of steam, some shunting, lurching and we stop. After waiting for two hours, with no movement or announcement or information of any description, serious anger is building up in our crowded carriage, so I thought I would get off and look for someone to speak to.

In the darkness, I opened the carriage door and almost fell out not realising there was no platform. We were some distance outside the station, rail lines and rolling stock, spread out into the distance. Crewe is the biggest junction in the UK. I would have great difficulty finding someone to speak to. I think it was around six in the morning when we finally reached Wolverhampton.

The four of us are standing at Victoria Square, just up from the station. I thought what a grimy, dreary town. A trolley bus is coming down a street towards us. As it turns into the square, a young woman in trousers with a piece of toast in her mouth, jumps off the back, races forward while the bus is still moving quite fast, and grabs a lever-type device on a pole beside me. As she holds it down, there is a clanging and a few great electrical flashes and sparks overhead. She then races after the bus, toast still gripped in her teeth, and jumps back on again. Women never worked on the buses at home and this was the first time I ever saw a woman in trousers.

Where to? What to do now? Ward, our guide and would be mentor, speaks first. "Up through the town centre and St Peter's Gardens, we will find seats there and we can relax a while."

Forgetting how early it was, I was thinking what a half dead town this is. On an elevated site overlooking the towns' main square, the gardens are a dazzling delightful oasis of colour - from the mass planting of tulips, under planted with primroses - the perfect combination. A few seats nestle along the network of paths. Not a soul is in sight. We sit down, with our suitcases strewn around us. I'm on a seat on my own and soon fall asleep. It didn't seem very long, but maybe four or five hours later, I awoke. I recall vividly as if it was yesterday, I can hardly believe my senses, my bewilderment at the mass of humanity flowing all around us.

This is Wolverhampton, the heart of what is known as the Black Country - birthplace and cradle of the Industrial Revolution. Four miles east "Cradley" – home of the first blast furnace in the world. A bit further on is Ironbridge – where the first iron bridge ever built is still in use. And some distance further north is Sheffield Forge Masters, location of the world's first steel mill - built in the late eighteenth century.

Around us, the Main Square and streets off it are jammed with people, trolley buses and cars. The gardens are crowded. My suitcase is at my feet but half blocking the narrow pathway. People skirt around it as they pass, looking for a vacant seat. A man sits on the bench beside me feeding the pigeons.

As I try to collect my thoughts I glance towards him. There is no acknowledgement, he continues feeding. I look towards the other three. Ward is stretched out full length on his own. The other two are draped over the ends of another seat, all fast asleep. I'm now wide awake in the middle of a warm, pleasant May morning. I'm embarrassed. The four of us are occupying the three best seats in town. If I were a local looking for a seat, I'd be thinking that these drunken Irish layabouts sleeping rough are a damn nuisance. The embarrassment lasts a little longer. All the other suitcases are providing an obstacle course leading to steps down to the main square. There is a stir. The great leader lights up and speaks.

"Fall in line, full steam ahead, suitcases in hand, destination: Waterloo Road, an Irish ghetto."

He knew where he was going alright. This is a long tiresome road what one hundred years earlier would have boasted the finest townhouses of the gentry. Near the bottom, Mr Ward knocks on a door. It's hard to imagine but we are all taken in. Where would this Mr Evans, the landlord, put us all?

Soon, all is revealed. I'm assigned a single bed in an upstairs room with five other beds. All beds are in use and it's a tight squeeze between them. Every room upstairs and downstairs, except the dining room, is crammed full of beds. The house is simply packed with Irish building workers.

A smallish window at the gable end looks out over an endless vista of red-bricked houses and a dense forest of chimneys. It created a powerful impression of the density of population in this town. All of us in the house are on full board: breakfast, dinner and a help yourself supper. I'm thinking mealtimes will be interesting, how will they cope?

I'm up early the next day to squeeze inside the one small bathroom, just toilet and hand basin. Afterwards, down to the dining room which is big, yet almost filled by a very substantial table. The breakfasts come flying in, plates loaded with sausage, bacon, egg, black pudding, mushroom and tomatoes. All the meals were exceptionally good and astonishingly prompt. The twenty or so men in the house are nearly all in their early twenties, good company, full of chat and especially keen to help and advise us newcomers. The railway metaphors are memorable.

"So, you have just pulled in, have you?"

"Have you just pulled in from another town or have you just arrived from over the pond?"

"Any idea where you'll get the start? You'll have no trouble getting the start. Balfour Beatty, McAlpine, Murphy, Wimpey are all mad looking for men."

"You'll be alright in this kip for a while, next week I'm pulling out."

"I think it's cat here".

"I'm pulling out next week. I'm going to Coventry where my friends are on a lot more money than me".

Almost everything they refer to is either, cat, pigeon or melodeon.

With breakfast finished, the great leader, with the three Musketeers in tow, head for the nearest building site. He speaks to someone who informs us the site manager will see us shortly. I don't want to be anywhere near this place but I am tormented, indeed paralysed by indecision. Next day, I'm supposed be on my way to Arundel. I never mentioned this to the others. If I did, they would probably think my head was gone. If I don't pass the interview or if they tell me they will let me know the outcome in a week or so, what then? I can't go home. Will I supply a Wolverhampton address? Meanwhile, I will arrive back in Wolverhampton and try to explain to the others. Any of these choices holds very little appeal. My trouble is that I've joined up with these three and I just cannot muster the courage to say

"I'm off fellas, I'm trying my luck elsewhere. Maybe I'll be seeing you, maybe not."

We'd been waiting a long time without any sign of the site manager. This suited me fine. Quite how it happened, I don't know, but I upped and left the building site on my own. I'm just moping along, confused, trying to sort my thoughts out.

A short distance along the road, I find myself standing at the entrance to the Goodyear tyre and rubber plant. It's enormous, with several thousand employees. The sights and sounds of so much concentrated human activity in one place astonish me. Giant chimneys pouring out smoke. And a multitude of smaller ones hissing and spewing steam. A constant level of sound reverberates through the air. The whole area seems to pulse and throb like it was a living, giant organism. In the background, a constant clattering and clanging of rail wagons and everywhere, the stench of rubber. It's black and smoky, but mostly smelly.

Outside, a huge hoarding lists "Sits Vac", there is a sign indicating "New Job Applicants". With my thoughts in such disarray, I'm like a sleepwalker. I didn't so much go in as find myself inside. I'm handed a job application form. Several other men and women are filling in theirs. I'm stupefied by indecision. I write a little bit, stop, then another line, most of the time I'm looking out through the half open door hoping against hope someone will come and call me away. Between stops and starts I read the terms and conditions of employment on a notice board on the wall opposite. I'm unnerved by the impersonal, cold, business-like atmosphere. Not a word about how good the weather is for the hay, or getting the turf out of the bog.

Frequently, I look towards the exit, asking myself 'what the hell am I doing here?' But just can't bring myself to walk out. In the terms and conditions, I stop at a line that shocks me to my senses. There is a great list of jobs, but anyone below a certain age would have to take an extended period of training at a greatly reduced rate of pay.

Others, who have come in after me, hand up their forms. New applications must be submitted before midday. The girl taking the forms is hovering just behind me. She's sees my slow, hesitant progress and asks if she can help. No doubt she could if only I told her my real difficulty. Speaking to anyone I had confidence in would show clearly what the right decision was. In a way, I am trapped, unsettled, and a little desperate. I hurriedly complete the form. It's like sitting an important exam where you are stuck on this one question. Initially you know precisely how to work it out then , in an instant all the key elements you were so confident of become lost in a cloud of confusion. I am now so conscious of the office Assistant watching me I hurriedly complete my form.

And I made a fateful decision that would create difficulties for me in the years ahead. In order to avail of the maximum rate of pay, I lied about my age. I gave 17th March 1930 as my date of birth, making me six years older than I actually was.

In that instant, the die was cast. The Duke of Norfolk and Arundel Castle slipped away, out of reach, and beyond recall. Fear and indecision had robbed me of the ability to see clearly what I was in England for, in the first place.

It feels like all the promise, glamour and excitement of just a few days ago has been lost, stolen, and of all the many twists and turns my future held, the changing of jobs, the driving inner need to prove myself, and so many years of daydreaming, mind wandering, and imagining, no decision, not one ever prompts the thought - 'what if?' Yet this one does. Uncalled for, unbidden, it bobs up persistently, from the depths of sixty years of numberless changes and a multitude of life-changing choices, it tunnels its way to the surface of my mind as if calling for an answer. Just what might have been if I'd taken the position at Arundel Castle? We'll just have to blame Karma again, dear reader. But is it good or bad?

I hand the girl my completed form. My lie doesn't help my sense of well-being. Will they query it? I don't have long to wait.

"Personnel will see you now, Mr Coyle". The man on the other side of the desk doesn't look up.

"Sit down, please". Everyone I have met so far has a disturbing seriousness about them. He reads my form aloud,

"No skill, training, no educational record. You have some gardening experience and you're good with horses. We have no pressing need for gardeners or horse handlers here."

He's looking at me now and the stress in my belly has eased a lot - not a word about my age. He says,

"All I can put on your record is unskilled labourer. You can have one of these open positions if you pass the medical."

I knew what medical meant, but not the detail and if I had known, I might have ran screaming from the place and not stopped until I got to Sussex. But it turned out to be ok, only partial exposure, just the top half. I think they just wanted to confirm I had a heart.

The medical officer was Irish, Dr Byrne-Quinn, later to be Mayor of Wolverhampton. He looked at my form and I promise, dear reader, these are very close to his precise words. Shaking his head, he says,

"I'm baffled, I'll never understand it. Over the years, I've sat here and seen so many like you and they just get younger and younger. Here it says you are twenty-four, but you're just a lad, you don't look a day over sixteen".

Perhaps the good doctor hadn't read the company's terms and conditions.

In the early fifties, emigrating to England was thought of as a serious move. For many, it meant they wouldn't be seen or heard from for years. Sadly, some never again. This was often due to a lack of capacity whether travelling by sea or air. If you wanted to journey home from the UK in the summer months, you'd need to book in February or March at the latest. So many failed to travel because they forgot to book early enough, me included.

To attempt to speak to someone on the phone was a matter of some hilarity.

When I called my sister Bridgie in Shercock for the first time, I passed through so many different manual exchanges, eventually reaching Shercock 17, the Post Office.

"Hello this is Shercock 17, who do you want?"

"I'm Pat Coyle; can I speak to my sister please?"

"Hold on, now, I'll run down the street and get Bridgie for you".

"Hello, hello can you hear me?" Says Bridgie.

"Yes, I can hear you, can you hear me?"

"Yes, I can hear you." A long pause follows in disbelief that we are speaking to each other.

Bridgie says, "It's good to hear your voice, I can't believe it's you, are you still there?"

I answer yes. "When are you coming home? "she asks

I answer, "I only got here a month ago."

"I know, but you have to book"

"I won't forget."

"Did you speak to Eddie McElroy?"

"No, where is he?"

Bridgie, a little irritated. "He's there in England."

"Well, there's only about fifty-five million others so I suppose I will eventually."

Operator cuts in. "You're out of time caller.

I say, "Bye bye for now Bridgie, I'm out of" … beep, beep, beep.

The girl at the desk informed me that if I waited a while they'd let me know whether or not I could start. In a remarkably short time, I get the news - report for work the following morning, to a particular departmental manager. The hourly rate of pay was hardly believable. What would I do with so much money?

However, there were three shifts, including nights and I didn't know what I'd actually be doing.

Meandering my slow, lazy way, back to our digs. I'm suffering one of my bouts of self-hatred. I will take this job. The pay is irresistible. Yet all my instincts tell me to get on the train for London and Arundel. Somehow, I feel tied to this trio I've travelled with and I don't possess the moral courage to break free. But foremost in my mind is a letter to my sweetheart. No doubt, she will be disappointed with my decision. I know how intrigued she was and looking forward to my news about this castle.

I have hours to pass. The digs will not be a welcoming place at midday. Looking for a shop where I can buy writing paper and envelopes, my eyes and ears take in the sights and sounds of this strange place. The contrast with home is bewildering - so much industry and business. It felt, sounded, and indeed smelt like the entire area was one giant blacksmith's forge. At the time, Britain claimed to be the workshop of the world, it was and this is its pulsing heart. This area of the West Midlands was known then and is still referred to, as the Black Country. Sitting as it is in the middle of inexhaustible seams of coal and iron ore. Bringing these two together over the last one hundred and fifty years has drawn a black grimy veil over everything.

In the early afternoon, I head back to our digs. I thought I'd lie on my bed upstairs out of sight until the others started coming in. I was surprised to find I wasn't the first back. In the dining room, Mr Ward is holding an audience. The easy, relaxed air of merriment so early in the day tells its own story. Matthew McKiernan has a permanent grin. Now and then the grin grows into a little bursts of subdued laughter Te he he he he he he he. He is either very consciously aware of the effects of the alcohol, or perhaps he thinks unrestrained laughter might be a sin.

Ward is on one side of the table on his own. He wears cheap reading glasses, similar to my old school ones. He has a thin red face. Some greying hair clings to an almost bald head. He wears a long grey grimy rain coat. Both elbows rest on the table, with one hand supporting the other holding a cigarette. The cigarette is always poised in reddish brown nicotine fingers just an inch or so from his mouth. It appears to be an indispensable prop to the non-stop chatter. He talks continuously. He's worked in England before. He's graduated so feels he must dispense his superior knowledge to these innocents before him. Tell us how this strange and alien place works. Telling us how many he knew, such as us, who fell innocently into various traps. And the fun he had at their expense, because all the time he knew so much better. I think he was an original practitioner of schadenfreude. His sneering, mocking, attitude sets a blazing red light flashing in my head. Not so long ago, I was the butt of his kind of humour.

Already I'm ignoring him and there is a simmering hostility between us.

After some time listening and paying homage he says,

"So where did you skive off to, Paddy?"

"I had a look at Goodyears."

"Oh," he says, "right kip that place. They stream in one door and out the next."

"I'm starting work in the morning."

"Oh, you won't last there Paddy. You'll be doing shifts you know. You'll be doing nights. Did you know you'll have to do nights?"

He then tells me they didn't get the start, but they found a great pub with the best pint in the entire universe. And we're going back there later on.

After dinner, in order to prevent a complete breakdown between us, I went with them to this pub with the elixir of life. But I can't partake of any of it because I'm on probation. And I have a pin in my lapel to prove it. I can't recall the exact circumstances, but at some point in Blackrock College I took a pledge to abstain from alcohol for two years, by which time I would I would have earned the right to join the honourable ranks of the pioneers. So each time the others sunk their beer I ordered an orange juice.

The night passes peacefully and the next day, well-fortified with vitamin C, I arrive in my new place of work. I was shown how to use my clocking in card. Afterwards, this departmental manager introduced me to my machine. It consists of a sloping bench, four feet high, three feet wide and six feet long. At either end sits a spindle, while nearby there are trolley loads of fabric about three feet wide and fifty feet long. On these rolls, the fabric is very untidy and loose. My job is to place one of these rolls on the spindle and attach the fabric to the other spindle. Next, I put my foot on a pedal which drives an electric motor which turns this spindle while I guide the fabric onto it. The result is a neat tight roll. When I've done twenty or so, I take them to the tyre building shop, where I duly collect another trolley load of untidy rolls. This performance is repeated again and again, each shift, each week, each month. A process you could say conceived by an alien mind to deaden the spirit and rob victims of their humanity.

After the first few hundred rolls, I was doing this job unconsciously. I spent each and every shift daydreaming. Most the time, I was with Mary planning our dream life together. I would own a white E-type Jaguar sports car, in the showrooms at the time. A design which I think remains unsurpassed. If not a Jaguar, a red Aston Martin would do. We spent a lot of time in this car, showing off to friends. Or we might be on a boat in a Mediterranean harbour.

Later on, to enjoy the cool of the evening, I would drive Mary up dangerous steep winding mountain roads to my villa in the hills which I knew she would find enchanting, with great cascades of delightfully coloured and scented jasmine, wisteria and Bougainville flowing over every door, balcony and window. Naturally, in front there was a view out over the ocean and at the back in the distance snow-covered mountains. A big plot of land means I can manage a herd of goats, care for hives of bees, grow a great range of the goats' favourite herbs and tend enough fruit and vegetables to live on.

When I had rushes of self-pity about the job, I only had to think of the money or look at the people around me, or at the departmental manager, and in an instant I was a happy labourer, indeed you could say a happy high roller.

The manager had long since succumbed to the death inducing boredom. His demeanour was grim and threatening. He looked like he'd been condemned for some evil deed of which he was entirely innocent. He just patrolled up and down this vast workshop left hand held high on his chest clasping some clock cards and a pencil, not like a scholar with notes and folders, more superior army officer type, with swagger stick. Now and again, he'd step up onto a little makeshift stand and sit down. And from there he'd look down with lifeless eyes at the serried ranks of the un-dead working like denizens at their spitting, whining machines. Frequently he comes towards me and stops three or four paces away, head held unnaturally high, like a guards officer on parade. He's looking down his nose at me, no name, no greeting, not once did he use my name. Then in his rank Black Country accent says. "Want to wake oova"

And this look never changed. all hope had long since been abandoned, there wasn't one tiny instance of engagement between us .My few attempts at humour were soon drowned by that cold dour countenance.

I never wanted to work overtime, but thought if I refused he'd sack me. His name was Marriot, but because I resented his attitude so much, in my daydreams I invented all kinds of names for him which I thought reflected his personality. I thought of many names, but the one I preferred was Ebenezer

Troglodyte Hogwash. There were times when he asked me to do overtime but I was so engrossed in my daydreams I almost said "yes I will Mr Hogwash, when I'm finished milking the goats".

Since I always worked fast, whenever I took my trolley load down to the tyre building shop I'd speak a few words to the men working the machines there - that is to anyone who had a few seconds to spare. I remember at the time feeling the need of this, I suppose for reassurance that we were all still human. And whereas my job is mind numbing, I think they're probably worse off. The tyre building shop is over two hundred metres long. On one side of the central corridor lie hundreds of small machines driven by compressed air. As valves open and close, they spit and blast as the operator goes through his tiny part of the operation, before passing his work on to the next stage. On the other side of this corridor sit hundreds more, this time electrically operated machines, which hum and wine as revs build up and slowdown. All these men are paid by the unit, so each one works frenetically to keep up and not let the side down

It's similar to a scene from the Charlie Chaplin film "Modern Times". Charlie is standing by the conveyor belt with an outsize spanner. The conveyor belt starts. Charlie makes a couple of small very quick jerky movements with his spanner as he tries to tighten a nut. Lines of people to either side are each assigned slightly different roles. Charlie hesitates for an instant - great sad eyes rolling in his head as he looks heavenwards. He scratches his head and another part of his anatomy. In that instant, he falls behind. He makes the most frantic efforts to catch up. He is working like a demon but just can't make up the few seconds he's lost. In a state of panic, he climbs onto the conveyor. The scene fades with Charlie disappearing into the bowels of the great machinery, striving desperately to tighten the ones he's missed.

I finish my shift in early in the afternoon and stay on the bus as it rides into town. I'm looking for writing material that I failed to get the previous day. I'm late with a letter to my sweetheart. The digs, my machine, the factory, the whole Black Country scene holds a stark grimness, but just a thought of my darling sweetheart in Howth and I'm enveloped in a beautiful trance like dream. Mama will also be watching the lane for the postman.

On my own in the bedroom, I get the letters off. Soon all the young fellows return and there's a stampede for the bathroom. All washed and changed, they're keen to know what I was up to, but especially if I'll be coming with them for a few scoops later. Their attitude surprises me. I was so pleased to be invited, even elated, but puzzled. Didn't they know I was a reject? that I didn't have friends? While in Rush, I was too young to drink in the pub. Some evenings I strolled along the beach or visited an amusement arcade, always on my own. Most of the time, I stayed in to read the newspapers from end to end and listened to the radio. My favourite station broadcast a memorable call sign. Each evening I tuned in to the deep grave tones of this announcer

"This is the American relay service relaying the voice of America from Tangiers." Remember reader, at this time the Cold War was at its hottest so most of what I heard was propaganda - but I lapped it all up.

When I moved to Blackrock, I went out frequently to a cinema in the village, or watched the rugby teams practising. Only a few of the staff lived in and the few that did, such as me, stuck together because they worked together. Being on my own in the garden, I didn't have all that much contact with the others. In front of me now, here's this group of young fellows keen to recruit this quiet, serious newcomer to their ranks.

Skipping along Waterloo Road that evening, we are like a bunch of young schoolboys leaving school on the last day before the summer holidays: non-stop banter, humour and laughter. We are so noisy other pedestrians are looking at us. I'm tagged on at the rear. I'm quiet, but inside I'm singing and dancing. I'm truly ecstatic, and for the first time in my life I feel accepted by a group. And this feeling of companionship and belonging is sublime. For the first time ever, I'm just one of the boys and these young fellows confirm I'm probably quite normal. We're on our way to a pub called the Chequer Ball – situated right beside Wolves Football ground.

This was the age of the drink round. The first person in the group buys for everyone else. Then the second buys for everyone, and so on. Seven or eight of us make up the gang. The first lad asks me what I'm having. I say orange juice. It's as if I've sounded the death knell.

The place falls silent. They all look at me. He comes a bit closer and quietly repeats orange juice, as if he was hoping no one else heard . Another lad repeats orange juice and calls out so everyone else can hear

"I thought that was for expectant mothers".

Once they've all got their pints the serious business starts: darts and rings competitions. The dart players give me a crash course in the game and elect me scorekeeper. Everyone is well behaved. Each buys their round and the night passes. The orange juice is a black mark against me but I've got their wholehearted imprimatur to remain scorekeeper. And the orange juice works in my favour. After a certain level of alcohol is consumed, I'm still be sober enough to keep the score both literally and metaphorically.

Everyone smokes, so to further confirm my status, I join in. To try and impress them, I buy the most expensive cigarettes there is. "Passing Clouds" was one brand, but my all-time favourite was "Peter Stuyvesant" because there was a notch in one corner of the packet. When you offered your friends a cigarette, you flicked the packet a certain way and a cigarette popped half way out. I knew this would really impress them all so I practised in the bathroom in the digs and anywhere else I could, where no one could see me, until I mastered it.

That night in the pub, I pulled out my eye catching packet of Peter Stuyvesant with its blue red and gold bands. The others are standing around waiting for their cigarettes. I flicked the packet as I had practised so well and just as the Cowboys did in the movies, but no cigarette popped out. I flicked again, and again, irritated and annoyed that I couldn't show them the man I was, same result, no cigarette. The all had a great laugh telling me this only worked in films.

The following day I'm a happy high roller. I'm in a state of euphoria with my new friends, my status in this group, and looking forward to the next night in the chequer ball. And so a routine is established: home from work, dinner and Chequer Ball.

However, into the third or fourth week, possibly due to vitamin C poisoning, I'm considering mutiny. While I'm a high roller, I can daydream, so the boredom is tolerable. The Chequer Ball brings darts, darts and more darts, hour after hour, right through the night. Keeping the score means I can't daydream. It's a dilemma. This group's acceptance and approval isn't just life enhancing, it is my life. You may think - what's the difficulty? You just don't go.

To understand, here's a thumbnail sketch of my personality at the time. My state of mind was a continuation of the rejection well-established at home and in the college. It's accurate to say I didn't have a personality. I was in a permanent approval seeking mode. At any given moment, it was case of: I am just what or how you want me to be, my sole aim is your approval. If I don't win your approval then the shell of outward appearances shatters and my feelings of rejection and worthlessness are further reinforced.

And yet, there must have been some little self-will. I stopped going to the Chequer Ball and I didn't venture out with my travelling companions either.

Each week, I wrote letters to my sweetheart, mama and my sisters Brigitte and Elsie. I discovered the town's magnificent library, the swimming baths, and the College of Technology - later Wolverhampton University. Often at night time, when I was in the bedroom on my own, the landlord would pop in and chat a few minutes. I was in the house a little over a month at this stage. This night he tells me about other houses him and his wife own. He asks me if I'd like to move to this house his wife runs. He describes a fine big bedroom I could take sharing with just one other person. He asks if there is anyone I'd like to come with me.

This is about perfect. When Matt McKiernan comes in I tell him. He says I'm coming with you. That night we did a moonlit flit. Our new abode was just half a mile away and only one hundred paces from the Wolves football ground. Our new address is 336 New Hampton Road East and as promised, it is a fine big room downstairs with just two beds. And Mrs Evans is a lovely landlady. Matt's good company and we get on fine but he likes the pub, so for his sake we venture out a few times each week just for the hour before the pubs close.

I am now discovering this town and how much it has to offer. When I look at the College of Technology's syllabus, I realise what Goodyear's Personnel officer meant by no skill, no qualification and no education. The courses available and the range of skills needed to drive an industrial community are practically endless. My mind is made up - I will attend this college, join the library and learn to swim.

At first, I went to the swimming pool three or four times each week. Later, I would go every day. I also spent a lot of time in the library. The College of Technology was just half a mile from where I lived, so I went there frequently at night just to avail of the great range of newspapers and magazines.

Back in my new digs, I read and write my letters. I remember so well mama's response when I told her I was working at night in the factory. She said she couldn't believe I had to work at night making tyres. She thought the only people who worked at night were the Russians making rifles.

My new home is a major improvement on Waterloo Road. Still some pressure on the bathroom in the morning - but otherwise very good. All Mrs Evans guests are Irish except for one Englishman with a pokey little room to himself. He was referred to as the cock lodger. Early one morning, passing by his room, eager to be first at the bathroom. I see tiny wisps of smoke coming from under his door. I hesitated at first because it was so early, but when I decided to knock there was no response. I knocked harder - still nothing. I opened the door to be enveloped in a cloud of dense acrid smoke. I called Matt and we dragged the English lodger unconscious from the room. We want to put out the fire but there's no sign of fire. Eventually, we discover a lighted cigarette had ignited the mattress. Great red hot smouldering lumps of mattress were falling onto the linoleum floor under the bed and producing the poisonous smoke. Mamma would say he was horrid lucky. The last thing of note about my stay in these digs was meeting another lad about my own age by the name of John White. We both had nationalistic tendencies and we talked and argued endlessly about the Irish British question. A few years hence as our story unfolds, we'll meet John White again.

The routine in this house is very much like that in Waterloo Road. In the evenings the men return from the construction sites, clean up, eat their dinners and move out again for the pub. The few that stayed sat in the dining room which was also our sitting-room. If White and I were there at the same time we usually became involved in an intense argument about politics, or kicked off one of our equally fiercely competitive games of drafts. He liked the pub too, but I saw he wasn't addicted and was an independent minded individual.

As the weeks pass, although I'm fairly happy here, I realise I'll be so much better off if I can find a place of my own. For the truth was I only visited this little sitting-room so as not to appear a complete recluse. I much preferred to stay in the bedroom and read one of my library books. When in the bedroom, Matt stayed with me – just lying on his bed and smoking. He never read and to my certain knowledge he never received a letter or wrote one. At a certain point, I'd stop reading and suggest what I knew he was waiting all night to hear-

"Will we pay a visit to the watering hole?"

Many years later, looking back, I'd feel pangs of sadness for Matt. He was always so quiet and with that certain aloneness about him. He never talked of family or relations. I realised he was probably genuinely alone and was looking to me for friendship and perhaps even support or leadership.

But at that time, the thought that I of all people could fulfil this role was inconceivable. So a major turning point has come. I'll find my own flat or digs and give up my job as a high roller.

The origin of this word *digs* is interesting. It originated with Canadian and American gold prospectors in the nineteenth century. They lived, worked and slept where they were digging - their digs. The best source when searching for either accommodation or jobs was the local paper: "The Express and Star".

The Express and Star ran pages and pages of jobs. The rebuilding after the war was reaching a peak. Unfortunately for me, most of the jobs required some skill or training I didn't possess, so I decided to become a bus conductor. This job would perhaps give me two or three evenings a week to attend the college. In a matter of days, I found some accommodation where I was the sole boarder. My new home is on Great Hampton Street and I'd be living with a woman of about forty-five and her eight year-old son. It's an old house and I only realised after I moved in that the toilet and washing facilities were out the back. This hardly mattered. My room is my own and this good woman makes a great fuss about what exactly I like for my meals. On my own, I feel liberated, like I'm released from prison. Now I can come and go where and when I want to. All that concerns me is that my friend Matt will understand.

In the bus transport office, I fill in the usual forms and repeat the lie about my age. I must to do this because these details will be on other papers from Goodyear's. I'm told I can start my two weeks training immediately. I'm handed a bulky, heavy parcel containing two uniforms and given a time to report for duty. I remember so well taking on a somewhat superior attitude as I admired myself in my perfectly fitting uniform complete with badges and shiny buttons. I almost expected a salute from passers-by as I paraded through the streets. Almost half the conductors are women, known then as clippies and about a fifth of the staff are Irish. Over the next two weeks, I underwent a very gentle introduction to the not so gentle world of the bus conductor and judging by the turnover in staff, not a happy one either.

As a new staffer, each day I am allocated a different duty. I may start any time between 4:30 a.m. and 4:00 p.m. and on any route - but mainly trolley bus routes. For the first four or five weeks, I was so busy that no time during the day did I ever know in a geographical sense just where I was. From inside the bus, peering out through wet steamed up windows, or a brief glance from the platform, all I saw was endless streets and roads - all looking exactly the same and queues and queues of people waiting at every stop. And you may well say, for someone with a strong aversion to buses and a tendency to motion sickness, this was not a smart career choice.

To this day, I still marvel at the number of people using this bus service. Each morning between seven and nine-thirty, it was as if the entire population was fleeing in panic from an imminent catastrophe. They pushed, shoved and barged onto these buses in their thousands. I remember thinking at the time that perhaps some fundamental natural or social law operated which decreed that going to work actually meant you travelled a minimum of five miles from where you lived. And from the point where you found work, everyone who lives there travelled back to where you lived for their jobs.

A more extreme version of this law was that for three hours each morning and each night thousands were doomed to travel endlessly because they never arrived at their hoped-for destination. They would stampede on and off trolley buses cleaning their boots on the conductor as they trampled on him while charging frantically to join another queue. They didn't need to check where the buses were going because the imperative was just to travel, Where too was of no consequence, Anywhere would do. So these busses had destinations like anywhere, somewhere, or nowhere, or perhaps just somewhere via nowhere. If it happened there was no queue to join, then these people would instinctively and intuitively coalesce into a queue and a bus would materialise out of nowhere to bring them anywhere or somewhere as the case might be. The result is the travel frenzy is unceasing.

When I departed New Hampton Road East, I didn't tell Mrs Evans or anyone else where I was moving to. I didn't want any on-going contact with my old friends. This would be a complete break: a fresh start, new accommodation, and new job.

Some days after moving to my new place, I returned, hoping to collect my mail. Mrs Evans said there was no mail on the Hall stand for me. Disappointed, I left it until the weekend and tried again. Mrs Evans repeated there was nothing with my name on it. Each morning, whoever was first to the front door picked up all the mail and popped it on the hall table. She wondered if I'd asked Matt McKiernan or anyone else to look after my mail for me. You, dear reader, may be thinking why not pick up the phone. Indeed, but so few people had phones. For urgent matters, it was a telegram. Otherwise, it was letters.

Into the second week, still no letter from Mary. Whereas at first I thought I must dash of a letter enquiring why she hadn't written - what was wrong? I didn't. My demons have taken over, my outward veneer of normality has cracked open and I've dropped into a familiar chasm of insecurity and rejection, and with this comes the emotion that is most damaging - what psychologists call overcompensation. Not a reasoned a reasonable response, but jumping to the most extreme conclusion.

Mary has, without explanation and for no reason, decided to kill off what I thought was so special. How can she do this? How can she betray my total, innocent, childlike trust in her? And the many moments of delight we shared. And without a word, discard it all, throw it away as if all that happened was worthless and of no consequence.

Hurt, angry and depressed, I sleepwalked through the next few weeks in my new job. I'm fixated on how right I was. I had written last. What had happened was all Mary's fault. Why should I write again? Meanwhile, I'd spoken to my sister Bridgie on the phone to congratulate her to on the birth of her second child - a son. It was an opportunity to enquire about Mary. Yes, she said, Mary had visited and would be home with her parents soon again. Her summer job was ending. Day and night, a multitude of ideas played endlessly in my dizzy head as to why Mary didn't answer my last letter. The thought that troubled me most was that I never arranged for her to come to England. This must have hurt and disappointed her. The truth was I had gone cold on the idea. At home in Howth, and living near her parents, I knew she was safe and happy. My experience in the UK so far was of a much coarser way of life. In my romantic idolising of Mary, I felt sure in this place she would lose her innocent, unaffected, happy personality.

The weeks pass and no letter is sent or received. My new career is demanding in the physical sense. These buses are always full. Travelling east from Wolverhampton, you can travel forty miles and never see a patch of green. One million people live within a radius of five miles of the town centre. For eight hours each day, my bus passes up and down endless dreary streets and roads through vast cavernous estates and forests of high rise flats. I only knew where I was when the shift finished. Throughout the day, it was like driving around a vast maze and never finding the way out.

But all this is an aside. My immediate and urgent need is to get home to see Mary. Experienced Irish people in the transport department advised that my best hope was to request compassionate leave. Not a black lie they said, just a memo pleading "difficulty at home". I got four days without question. I was home on Friday night of this particular weekend. If I didn't see Mary at Mass on Sunday, I would go round to her home. My brother Peter, who lived and worked in Shercock, was also home on Saturday afternoon. Peter had been a technician for some years and he always had some old jalopy he'd fixed up from scrap. Saturday evening, he suggests we drive into Carrickmacross. Carrick was a lively, busy place on Saturday nights. We parked on the main street. After sitting for a little while, watching the passing scene, Peter said he'd go up the street and buy us two hot dogs. As we sat there munching and chatting, he says,

"Did you know Patsy Keenan has a brand-new car?"

This was the expression used at the time. There were so few car owners - this was sensational news. Owning a car then was synonymous with wealth and status, especially status. Only the doctor and the priest drove new cars.

"It's parked just up the street." He continues.

I was keen to see this new car, but not to meet Keenan. I knew him, but not all that well. We attended the same school, although he graduated long before me. I figured he was at least six years older than me. I asked Peter if Keenan was in the car.

"No." He says. Then the bombshell.

"Mary Burns is sitting in the passenger seat."

I choked on my hot dog. My munching stopped as if I'd been stricken with lockjaw. Peter wouldn't know about my interest in Mary Burns and had no inkling of the drama ignited in my head. Regaining a little composure, I said I must see this new car. That Mary was in this man's car mattered, but could be just coincidence. They were neighbours and at the time you could not, dare not, pass someone on the road or the street and not give them a lift. A little way up the street, conspicuous on its own, sits a gleaming new black Ford Popular. And sitting in front, her glorious hair illuminated by the street lighting - Mary. After bravely walking up the street, just as I see her a few paces away, my stomach starts churning. It feels as if I'm walking the plank and the next half minute will decide my fate.

The car is facing into the street and I'm on the footpath behind. I move slowly, fearfully towards the window where she is sitting. I say a subdued, nervous hello. Mary, startled, glances up for an instant. Then with her head down on one hand covering her eyes she says,

"Jesus, how, where did you spring from?"

"Mary, you didn't answer my last letter?" I say.

"But I did. I did." She says with emotion and a hint of anger in her voice. "And you never replied. And then two weeks later I wrote again and you didn't answer that one either."

I feel like a sledgehammer has hit me. So convinced was I all along that she was entirely to blame.

"I didn't get your letters, Mary." I'm pleading. "I was sure I wrote last."

"But you didn't, you didn't, and you promised to bring me over." She then glances toward the street as if to warn me. She says Patsy is in Reids Hardware shop just across the street.

"When you didn't answer my letters and you didn't ask me over, I knew you'd given up."

Again, I make my feeble plea. How pained and disappointed I was not getting a letter. She's inside the car looking up at me standing outside. Sadness and hurt are etched in her lovely eyes and breaking voice. All my experience of her was of a happy, laughing, joyful presence - as if being let down, or being disappointed, or any other human failing was unknown, even alien to her. I desperately want to comfort her, but it's impossible here as now and then she glances towards street. I'm overwhelmed by guilt at not trusting her and writing when I first missed her letter. All my feeble protests must sound like lies to her. I'm the cause of her pain. I'm the cause of that tearful agonised look that drew me to her a few years earlier in the poetry class. It's a look I can't bear. It tears my heart out. I want to take her in my arms and promise her my life. I've been standing there just a couple of minutes and in those few minutes it feels like I've lost the one thing in my life that I've cherished. Mary looks up and says Patsy is coming. I can see him crossing from the far side of this wide street. In despair, sick with guilt and remorse, I just stumble away from the car and up the street to where I can hide in the darkness.

How am I to deal with what I've just heard? From hoping to discover why Mary stopped writing, in a matter of minutes I've learned I'm the architect of my own misfortune. I've trampled on my life-sustaining dream and ground it into the dirt. I accept the truth of all Mary has said. I haven't the tiniest doubt. I know she's incapable of deceit. But where oh where are her letters?

Only then did I realise how careless I was with my mail. I've lived at three different addresses in three months and left no forwarding address at my last digs. Since they didn't know where I was, my letters would be returned as address unknown. After that, who knows? Tomorrow is Sunday and I should be travelling back to England, but at that moment I thought I must stay and see Mary happy and laughing again.

All that night, the more I thought of staying at home the more I realised it was impossible. There would simply be nothing at all to do and in Dublin it wouldn't be much better. I thought of the humiliation of going around like a beggar again and having to accept a barely subsistence level existence. In England, I quite simply had a life. It's autumn now and I will be enrolling in the College of Technology for the new academic year, taking full advantage of the library and when I'm not in the library I'll be in the swimming pool. The following day, I found myself on the boat back to England.

So I have all this money, a place of my own, I love the college and my transport duties get easier all the time as I learn the town, routes and fares. But I'm a complete slave to my emotions and one emotion dominates. How will I resolve the torturing dilemma of what happened with my sweetheart? This dilemma is a tsunami that washes over and drowns everything else.

And yet despite what's happened, I don't fear I've lost her. I'm sure she'll believe I genuinely did not receive her letters. And I have this confidence that we have shared so many beautiful, innocent memories and from such an early age, I felt so sure our future was predestined. And I know she will feel the power of these memories just as I do. And when she remembers, she will enter the domain of the magical. When she does, it's only me she'll find there. And she'll know only someone who loves her as I do, could inhabit this special place.

It's now the autumn of 1955. I walk in to the College of Technology to unroll. But which course? At the time, I thought a Bachelor of Science degree was the ultimate. A little innocently, I thought I would be off to a flying start on this course after spending so much time in the library reading "Scientific American", "The Science Journal" and "Nature". When I stood at the desk with my application form, I was disgusted when the young woman explained that before I could enrol, I would have to do a preparatory two to three year course. And as I tried for other courses, the same story. My educational background left me far short of the standard required for starting any of my preferred courses. Anyway, I was a bit naive in thinking I could be successful in any of them because with the hours I worked, I'd miss two out of every three lectures. But I could enrol in the Gymnastics class and German for beginners. And I did.

I felt good about my physical fitness at the time and the gym routine went well. I was thinking what a good gymnast I might be. When the first routine ended and it was strenuous, the trainer calls out,

"OK chaps, that's it for tonight – showers."

In less time than it takes to tell, all the class had stripped and were in the showers. But not me. Sixty years later for you, dear reader, it may be difficult to understand my extreme attitude to nakedness. In Ireland at the time, it only happened, if at all, in the most discreet and private circumstances - never in company. I had never seen anyone else naked. I had hardly ever seen myself naked. The swimming baths had rows of individual changing cubicles. Nakedness in Ireland was regarded as gross and indecent. It was associated with sin and obscenity. You might wonder how the biological function ever happened in Ireland at the time. The instructor wondered why I wasn't joining the others in the showers. I told him I had to rush away early to catch a bus. I used this and other silly excuses for several weeks. Eventually, I gave up the gymnastics class because I couldn't bring myself to strip with others present. However, I was still a keen student in the German class. At the time, in the Central Library, I was struggling to read Hitler's book "Mein Kampf" - in

German.

At this stage in our story, the truly all-important aspect of my life was I'd acquired so much money and didn't know what to do with it. Each week, I'd send some to mama via the post office in Shercock. I liked to imagine her delight when she was in town collecting what for her would be a bonanza, then to go shopping and not to deny herself or be concerned about the cost of her favourite jams, cakes or biscuits. She might even, in a moment of wanton sinfulness, descend to the limits of decadence and buy herself a pair of sheer nylon stockings. They appeared in the shops in the early Fifties in Ireland for the first time

Chapter 27 - First Aid for the Injured

One of the more unusual aspects of the bus man's life is that rarely will starting and finishing time be the same on two consecutive days. A few buses leave the depot very early in the morning - say 4:30 a.m. The service will peak at 7:45 a.m. and stay at this level until 9:30 a.m. With the rush-hour now over, most of the buses will head back to the depot. Something similar will take place in the afternoon. So each day there are two peaks and two troughs. This means many duties cover this rise and fall in demand. My starting time could be 5:00 a.m. and finishing at 9:30 a.m. and then resume from 3:00 p.m. until 7:00 p.m. in the evening. Most mornings, after finishing one of these split duties; I'd walk with my driver to the transport staff canteen. Meals were very good and it was always packed. This particular morning, I bought my sausage roll and tea and joined a very quiet concentrating huddle of spectators around a table where a chess match was taking place. This match has an international flavour. It's between a Polish man and a German - one of the considerable number of ex-prisoners of war who have settled in Britain. The rivalry is fierce and intense - even hostile. As I stood there, straining to catch a glimpse of the chessboard through this dense huddle, a smiling plump lady of about forty asked me if she could speak to me in her office. She introduced herself as Miss Tustin. I never heard her Christian name - it was just Miss Tustin on her office door.

She told me she was the Transport Department Welfare Officer. She knew I'd started just a short while ago and her job was to do everything in her power to ensure I was happy bus-man. She enquired if I had any difficulty at all and especially if I was happy with my accommodation. If not, she held a list of excellent landladies I could choose from, if the need arose. Our little meeting continued in a happy friendly way as she enquired about my background, family and what ambition I had. A s I rose to leave, she asked if I had any interest in first aid . I said I knew what it was and that was all. She told me the Transport Department had an excellent first aid team, but one member had left and she needed a replacement. Would I consider joining? What a compliment, I thought, even an honour. I'm being asked to join a team. And she's so encouraging - telling me how marvellous it will be if I fill this vacant position. I tried to control my enthusiasm as I said I would indeed join the first aid team, immediately, if not sooner.

In no time, Miss Tustin arranged a course for me and I started attending team practices and eventually refresher courses. And yet more courses that focussed on particular aspects of the first aid skill, such as artificial respiration. After a few months I'd attended so many courses I thought I might study medicine.

There was a noticeboard inside the canteen door and Miss Tustin frequently pinned little notes on it such as:

'Patrick, please speak. M.T.'

Thus began on-going leg pulling by the canteen tea ladies.

"You're seeing a lot of Miss Tustin, Patrick? We know what's going on. Can we expect a happy announcement soon? I hope we'll be the first to know, Patrick"

I felt awkward and immature not being able to fall in with this good-natured banter. I usually responded with something serious,

"Oh no, it's not like that, we're just arranging a course or a competition."

They all enjoyed a great laugh at my seriousness.

"Ah yes, that's what you tell us, first aid he calls it girls, did you hear that? - First aid. We know what's going on. A single lady with a good salary and a lovely house up Goldthorn Hill, you know which side your bread is buttered on all right Patrick".

Meanwhile, we attended competitions and a bit later were competing ourselves. I believe I was a good team player. It fulfilled some deep inner need. And when you're on the road all day and especially at night, there were so many opportunities to practice my new skills.

One day, I'm standing at the back of my bus waiting for a queue to board. Remember - none of these buses had doors – just an open platform at the rear. I see this elderly man on the far side of this very busy road trying to cross over. I was just about to dash over to help him when he steps into the road. A car hits him. He's down, out, unconscious. I folded my jacket and placed it under his head. My driver runs to a phone box to call an ambulance and I direct one of the small crowd that has now assembled to call a doctor from a nearby clinic. The unfortunate man, so sickeningly obvious, has suffered a fractured skull. I make sure his tongue hasn't fallen backwards which would cause him to suffocate. Afterwards, very gently, I turn his head slightly to one side in case he vomits with the same result. I want to get him into the recovery position as soon as possible, but can't yet because his back may be damaged or he may have serious leg or other fractures. As I examine his legs, someone has appeared out of this crowd, kneels down and turns his head back into the upright position. I angrily advised this individual to turn his head back.

"I've done the courses," I said "I know what I'm doing".

"Good man," he says, "I've done courses as well, I'm also the doctor you sent for."

Chapter 28 - First aid for the uninjured

Miss Tustin has unbounded pride in her first aid team and she's arranging for us to compete in ever more serious competitions. We've won at different levels and our next test is the really big one, in St George's Hall in Liverpool. For us, this is the Olympics and the World Cup wrapped into one - and I'm team leader. This great Hall is one of the finest neo classical buildings in Europe. From the outside, it resembled one of the prodigious buildings Albert Speer had designed for Hitler's Germania. A great squat multi pillared monstrosity, but inside it's all glittering chandeliers and gilded plaster work. Over the years, it's hosted many grand state occasions. Ours is a comparatively modest event.

Four teams were competing. We would go last, so there are anxious hours to pass. But could we be in a more relaxing or inspiring place? Luminaries who had graced this great hall, such as Sir John Barbirolli, Arturo Toscanini and Herbert von Karajan, looked down reassuringly on us from where they adorned the walls. Did they fret and worry before a grand concert? Did they bite their nails, perhaps, as they agonised over the finer detail of a complex musical score? No doubt, their artistic genius provided sublime pleasure to people, but we were not overawed - our skill could save a life. As we wait our turn, anxiety is building up. The place is so quiet we wonder if the organisers have forgotten us.

Frantic footsteps that come hammering down the corridor outside shatter the stillness. A breathless voice said a catastrophe had occurred outside. He demanded we come immediately.

"But we are competing!" I stammered. "We are due on any minute". "Competing," he mocked. "This is a matter of life or death."

We charged down the corridor after him and outside to a scene of mayhem. A wall had collapsed. Bricks, blocks and scaffolding were scattered about as if by an explosion. From a tangle of planks and masonry came moans and cries for help. The street light piercing the February gloom revealed four casualties. When we recovered from the initial shock, the needs of the injured galvanised us into action. A policeman arrived and I asked him if he'd called the emergency services. He said he would. A light rain was falling, so our first priority was to provide shelter for our patients. In response to a polite request, people with umbrellas at a bus stop responded with good-humoured, even gleeful enthusiasm. Two of our patients had fractures, so we created improvised splints. Some people, as if by magic, had just what we needed. We are now in complete control and felt were doing really well, although a little disappointed we had missed the competition. All our patients were now comfortable. Fractures immobilised, wounds dressed and the two in shock are getting on-going attention. I asked the police officer about the ambulance.

"All in good time, laddie, all in good time." He said.

And then, as if on cue, we heard the siren - but no ambulance arraived. In the same instant, the rain stopped and suddenly the place is flooded in light. To our amazement, we only then realised we were on a very elaborate set - a building site. Bystanders reached out to congratulate us. Applause rose from the main hall, which had been in complete darkness and obscured from us by the brilliant set lights. One of our patients with a fractured kneecap, ashen faced, in shock, started pulling at his splints. Still disbelieving, I rushed to stop him. As he joked about it, the truth hit us. The realism of the set, the make-up and the mock wounds had us convinced we were treating real patients. None of the other competitions, or even Miss Tustin, had prepared us for this.

At the prize-giving ceremony, "we were runners up" the doctor adjudicating said our team was deserving of the highest commendation for the urgency with which we went about our work. Our sense of duty, care and compassion for our patients was exemplary. No more could be expected from us even if it had been a real incident. Little did he know?

Chapter 29 - Harry Lime

You'll remember when I first started work in Rush, on one pound a week, there was very little money remaining after living expenses. Even in Blackrock College, I didn't have sufficient surplus to venture out on a clothes buying spree. In Goodyear's, and now as a bus conductor, my income is the same as a married man with a family - there was no graduated or incremental scale. But I have neither family nor expensive girlfriend. After my weekly donation to mama I still have a substantial surplus. And can I confess, just to you, I'm vain. I'm very self-conscious of my appearance and I want to improve it as much as I can. First of all, I thought I'd go to the eye clinic in town to see if I could do without my glasses permanently. This clinic had an international reputation. A surgeon there, a Dr Hirtenstein, claimed a world first - giving sight to someone blind from birth.

He explained that my glasses did little or nothing for my eyes. My brain only interpreted the best image, that from my left eye and therefore the only way to get my lazy right eye working was to wear a patch over my good eye. I threw away my glasses for good. I bought a black patch and wore it over my left eye when not in work. At Burtons, the best tailor in town, I bought a smart made-to-measure suit, followed by my crowning glory - a trench coat and hat. The cut and style of these trench coats was based on the British military officers' attire and included imitation epaulettes on the shoulders and an extra-long belt.

The military style and what it represented had great appeal for me and there was also the influence of the film '*The Third Man*'. This is one of the great classics of the cinema and was enjoying a rerun at the time, with unforgettable theme music which leaves you sad, happy and melancholy all at the same time. It's always fresh – always as if you're hearing it for the first time. The bright cheerful tones of the Mandolin linger on and on in the memory. The film's main character was Harry Lime played by Orson Welles. I'm modelling myself on him.

It's now the winter of 1954 and when I finish my transport duties I change out of my uniform and into my finely cut suit, place white handkerchief in breast pocket, slide on my trench coat, belt knotted loosely. This knotting rather than normal buckling demonstrated my no nonsense tough credentials. Now with collar turned right up, black eye patch over left eye, finally check most carefully in the mirror that my trilby is at precisely the right angle à la Orson Welles, before heading back into town. On the way I'll chat to the clippie and get great satisfaction out of being unrecognisable. I don't have any reason at all for going back into town. I just fancy a sashay around the town centre. In this gear I feel completely anonymous. I remember I attracted some attention, even admiring glances. So soon after the war, in military style trench coat and black eye patch, perhaps this is a gallant officer wounded in battle, blinded in one eye. He's always on his own, perhaps the after-effects of shell shock and he doesn't speak to anyone. I didn't want to speak to anyone. I avoided all possibility of recognition. If I was recognised, the act, the role, the make-believe would be discovered and I'd be back to being me. A me I hated. This would be the new me, tall, debonair, confident. I would discard the old me like a dirty infected rag. It was just an empty shell anyway, hollowed out, ashamed, a nonentity. I was fearful the tiniest connection with the old me might infect my new self like a plague bacillus. If I was in a café and took my hat off I felt half naked, wakened, my new glamorous persona slipping away. Still I was fairly sure in time my new personality would become permanent.

During this time, I didn't have a friend – either male or female. I didn't socialise. I didn't go to pubs, clubs, or anywhere people meet. There was an excellent transport social club and it was very well attended. I was frequently asked why I didn't go. I didn't ever start a conversation with anyone. I think I could be judged as excessively shy and withdrawn – with zero self-confidence and self-worth.

Chapter 30 – Another romance!

After about five or six months as a conductor, I applied for the driving course. The Transport Department consider me twenty-five, but in reality I'm nineteen. At the time, it was a serious offence to drive a public service vehicle under the age of twenty-one. I'm worried. Anyway, I passed the test and like all new conductors and drivers, I'm assigned duties everyone detests. On my first week as a trolley bus driver, I'm scheduled to take the first morning bus - the four-thirty out of a small satellite depot at a place called Bilston, five miles from Wolverhampton.

Each morning of that first week, I walk from my digs on the other side of the town, passed the entrance to the Wolverhampton depot and on to Bilston. And at each of the nine or ten miles as I walk, I cursed my luck and wonder what on God's holy earth I'd let myself in for. How long will this last? Happily, over the next month or so, my duties in Bilston come to a stop and I was assigned a permanent route in Wolverhampton.

On the first morning on my new route, feeling good, even a little proud, I looked up the schedules to see who might my conductor be. There, opposite my name, written large, was one Vincent O'Connor.

I checked out all the likely suspects -young fair skinned individuals. None of these respond to the name. I was told it was a Jamaican man. I asked him about his name he said this was his ancestor's slave master's name and all slaves in his control had to take the name O'Connor.

The route I'm assigned is Pennfields. It's the shortest route. Twelve minutes each way – roughly twenty trips per shift. Therefore, at least a hundred times each week, I leave Chubb Street, just off Victoria Square, pass through the town centre and out to Pennfields. On the return leg, I approach the town centre by way of Worcester St. It's quite a steep climb before I turn hard right into Queens Square. Immediately in front of me now and taking up one of the most prominent positions in town, is the hippodrome - commonly called a variety theatre. My landlady referred to it as a den of iniquity. I was genuinely intrigued by this last description and I would have to say the clues were there. The advertising of the shows was on a grand scale and took up the entire front of the building. On top, in huge lettering,

Girls! Girls! Girls!

- combined with life-size figures of dancing girls, more or less topless. In the middle of the advertising, would be something about a juggler maybe or a trapeze artist. *"Come and see the great Luigi Canasari mesmerise you with his juggling! Don't miss the incredible Dmitri Shostakovich straight from the Moscow State Circus with his death-defying high wire act."*

And then at the bottom, more Girls, Girls, Girls - and yes, you've guessed it, pretty much bottomless. And each time I pass, and I'm passing forty times a day, I'm ever more curious and ever more tempted. Whatever about Canazari and Shostakovich, it was what the girls promised, and especially my landlady's description, that so intrigued me. I felt I couldn't resist very much longer. It's important to point out here that if sin ever existed in England, it has long since been abolished. But it was still a powerful and potent force in the Irish psyche and would remain so for a good while yet.

And remember, I could commit a sin in four ways, by thought, word, deed or omission. I'm already guilty of one deadly sin just thinking about going and I would be dammed to eternity in Hell fire for this. How much more punishment would be due if in going I committed another deadly sin? Would I spend twice eternity in Hell? While I conjured with the intellectual challenge of twice eternity, I wondered how come everyone else seemed to be enjoying their sins, while I was doleful and sad resisting.

And all the time I'm thinking of mama's warning about 'the dangers I faced in the pagan land where "the people had lost the faith". Sinful ways and evil temptations would beset me everywhere, she said. Still, she was confident that with my armoury of spiritual defences, the black forces of evil would surely perish.

I wore the brown scapular round my neck, as well as a miraculous medal, and a Sacred Heart badge on my lapel, and sewn into the lining of my coat was a St Jude medal, mama had reminded me frequently he was the patron saint of hopeless cases. But surely poor mama couldn't have realised how hard and austere virtue could be and how pleasurable and attractive sin was.

The months pass and the shows came and went. My imagination is now at fever pitch. I can't resist any longer. But my guilt was such I would have to plan carefully for this most challenging, even terrifying, event, which I knew would land me at the very gates of hell. And I wouldn't be able to bear the shame of anyone I knew seeing me, an innocent Catholic lad, inside the four walls of the hippodrome. But then I thought if anyone I knew did see me, the great Canizari would be my salvation, for I'd say I had suddenly developed an all-consuming interest in juggling and was there just to see the master at work.

At the top of the steps, on my way in, I took a last nervous look back to see if there was anyone I knew about. On I went and bought my ticket at the box office. Soon I would be overwhelmed by the forces of darkness. But I would keep my St. Jude coat on so perhaps I could still be saved. I was early, so I took the best seat right in front of the stage. The show opened with a dance routine by a troop of scantily clad girls.

The same girls in different costumes and dance routines arrived at the start and end of each act - right throughout the show. One girl who seemed to have a leading role entranced me. In her make-up and scanty red and pink costume, I could not take my eyes off her. And then it happened, to my delight and astonishment she was returning my gaze - she was looking straight at me as she performed. I couldn't wait for the following night to come and back I went to the same show. Now I was in no doubt, at every opportunity, she smiled at me. And as she and the other girls danced off the stage, she waved, and there was that certain long lingering look along with another coy little wave from behind the curtain.

After the show on the third night, I waited by the rear exit from the stage. From my reconnaissance I knew where the girls and the other performers departed the theatre when the show was over. The girls billowed out, most with stage make-up still on and in long dresses. Party time I suppose, after the show. Their happy giggling and glamorous evening wear lighting up the dreary winter night. The fantasy and magic of the theatre overflowing with them and lingering on in their presence outside. As they flow out, names and greetings are called out as they recognise boyfriends or companions waiting for them in the small crowd outside. Then, arm in arm, they melt away into the night. Any moment now she must appear. With each new face at the doorway, I think my heart will explode in my chest.

I'm more nervous than Shostakovich on the high wire, my senses madly see-sawing between agony and ecstasy. The tension and the sense of expectancy are unbearable. Now illuminated by the mellow colourful stage lights in the background, I see her beautiful silhouette in the doorway. She hesitates - she is scanning the little group. Then, with arms reaching out she runs forward. I'm standing there half-paralysed and struggling to react, as she runs past and into the open arms of a man just behind me. I see them embrace, and head nestling on his chest, I watch them disappear into the night. The place is now completely -deserted. I'm standing there, alone, feeling all that had happened was unreal, a fleeting illusion - a very brief dream. And now I'm back to reality. Forlorn and dejected, I hear the stage door bang shut. The bolts slam into place. One by one, the lights go out. What a moment or so ago was a cradle of dreams, is now just a dark dreary loading bay. Feeling rejected and sorry for myself, but perhaps a little wiser, I trudged through the lonely streets back to my digs in the rain.

Chapter 31 – Violence, Vandalism and a Stalker

On nights when I'm not working or doing my Harry Lime act, I keep up the German language course and spend at least one night a week in the college library. Perhaps once a fortnight, I venture out to one of the very large cinemas. The television revolution hasn't yet happened. These cinemas were always packed with great long queues forming outside. The Central Library and the swimming baths are all that interest me during the day. The manager in the baths has christened me "Paddy not a hair out of place."

Each day I arrive, hair in perfect shape, go up and down for an hour or so with one foot on the floor, pretending to swim. Then leave the water, hair still perfect. This hair thing became an obsession and when I removed my Harry Lime hat Id search for a mirror right away to make sure I haven't disturbed my hair.

After I learned to swim, I became very determined to do well. I attended the baths five or six days a week, concentrating on the breaststroke and swimming half a mile each visit. I wanted to record a good time for this distance before I joined the local club. I was putting huge time and effort into trying to achieve a reasonable level. But that was that. Ever since, I have been convinced that for a great many aspiring athletes, training and effort will achieve so much, but beyond that further investment in time and energy is futile. I would spend hours practising the racing dive, yet after a while I seemed to be going backwards. One day, putting in a mighty effort, as I hit the water I sensed that certain sudden, terrifying looseness around my waist. My trunks are down around my ankles. I turned and made a frantic flailing attempt to retrieve them, but can't, as I watched them wafting about and sinking slowly down out of reach. I came back up, I'm naked. I'm under the high diving board and its fifteen feet down so it's desperation time. A great gulp of air and down I go again. I can see my trunks - I'm almost there.

Then I feel some monster putting me in a headlock from behind and I'm being sculled backwards to the side. With my head bobbing in and out of the water, I'm spluttering my frantic protestations to this eejit.

He keeps repeating "You're safe, you're safe, I've got you. Stop struggling, stop struggling, I've got you." At the side, he is heaving me with all his strength up the steps, while I fight with all my strength to stay under the water. I told him what happened. He said "When I saw you go down that last time I was sure you were a goner." On my next dive I would get my trunks - otherwise I would stay down.

Hardly can there be a better vantage point for seeing and learning about a place than from sitting inside the cab of a bus. One thing I saw that left a deep and lasting impression was a notice outside a works saying "No Irish need apply."

The Irish had a bad name in Wolverhampton at the time and often for good reason, and as always is the case, that trouble came from a very small minority. But these few were guaranteed banner headlines in the local paper "The Express and Star".

"Irish men arrested after pub brawl."

"Irish men in court for disturbing the peace."

"Irish man in court for threatening behaviour."

Now and then, my landlady, glancing at the paper in the evening would say,

"Look here Patrick, I see they're at it again".

And now dear reader, ignominy of ignominies, I'm about to make my personal contribution. Coming into town one morning, it's the peak of the rush-hour – 8:45 a.m. and my bus is loaded to the gills with workers and schoolchildren. There is a car moving slowly in front of me as I approach the school stop. Just short of the stop, I'm checking my rear-view mirror to see if there is any danger a child might fall off the platform as they jostle to be the first away. In that moment, the eejit in front of me has stopped right at the bus stop. There is a minor shunting collision. The driver of the car is an off duty police officer. This got great emphasis in Court as well as in "The Express and Star". And so it declared in large lettering, Patrick Joseph Coyle, the driver of the bus, was fined for driving without due care and attention.

Time passes, and this Saturday night shortly after eleven, the last buses are loading up with weekend revellers. Several routes pick up here, so there is a good deal of jostling and milling about, no one wants to miss the last bus. I'm standing at the front of my bus chatting to the conductor. Three individuals are coming towards us.

From a distance, their condition was plain to see. Shirts half in half out of trousers and open right down to the waist. Long, lanky, wet hair, hanging over clay smudged faces. They are taking a straight line for me - and they're Irish. Sensing trouble, my conductor has the good sense to get out of the way. One of the three asks me for directions somewhere, just as I tell him, I'm suddenly seeing stars and indeed fireworks - I've been knocked back against the bus. I have my hands over my face being momentarily blinded. Re-gaining my sight, the lad who hit me is standing there – mouthing - not a word from the other two. I was truly in a tight corner and as a natural born coward I'd run if I could, especially with the other two either side of me. I didn't. Then remembering the importance of good balance for leverage from my gymnasium class, with all the power I had at the time, reinforced with a substantial measure of venom - I retaliated. The mouth is now on his back in the street. I can't believe I'm doing this, I just can't believe it. In the same instant, the other two vanish. But not for long - all three were taken into custody. And so the inevitable court case and *The Express and Star* banner headlines:

"Irish men in court for assaulting bus driver".

Two got off with a fine, the mouth got three months for threatening behaviour and assault.

You may might think that's the end of it. Well no, I'm determined to keep the bad name of the Irish on the front page.

Driving to Willenhall one night, the bell rings inside my cab - an incessant, frantic ringing. Brakes full on, I peep back through the little window behind me. I hear mad pounding footsteps stampeding down the stairwell - all my passengers are piling off onto the footpath, looking at me and pointing and gesturing towards the back of the bus. I climb out of the cab and am confronted by this man with a pen knife he's telling my conductor what he is going to do to him. And yes, he's so obviously Irish. One way or another, I ask him not to bother the conductor. I'm Irish too, I said. I'm not concerned about your fare. I'll drive you to wherever you want to go. Luck is on my side - he wants to go on to the town centre. Going back to my cab, I ask some of my ex-passengers to call ahead to the police station. I drive right to the station door and an unexpected reception for our knifeman.

Another day in Wolverhampton magistrates Court - another headline for the newspaper and Patrick Joseph Coyle. He got six months. As well as a knife, he was in possession of a lavatory chain. Yes, dear reader, laughably - a lavatory chain. All the toilets at the time were built with high-level cisterns, so a chain hanging down was essential for flushing. It was classified at the time as an offensive weapon because like-minded individuals would wrap it around their fists to attack an opponent. Standing on the steps outside the courtroom, I was abused and threatened by it would seem one of our knifeman's cronies. He's coming down the steps behind me, leaning over, physically breathing down my neck,

"You're some expletive, expletive Irishman, getting one of your own sent down. Six months - six expletive months. For wha? For wha ? You'll expletive pay for this. Boy, from now on you just watch out, you just watch out."

I felt sorry for the lad on the bus but this thing was spitting viciousness. I did look out, a lot, especially walking home late at night. From the depot, I'd walk along Pipers' Row to Victoria Square, then up Lichfield Street to Queen Square. On the way, I'd stop frequently to check out the latest sports cars and scan the scene to see who is about. Individuals - I ignored. Two or more men, anywhere in sight, I'd mope about studying shop windows until they vanished. On one particular night, I've left Queen Square, heading for Darlington Street. I'm now in power walk mode for home. As I turn right from Darlington Street onto Waterloo Road, I look back. In the distance is a figure striding out strongly behind me. No matter, he won't turn into Waterloo Road. He did. There wasn't another soul about. If there was I'd stop and ask for a light. This was very common as everyone smoked. We pass some side roads off Waterloo Road - he doesn't turn off. Next, I turn off Waterloo Road onto New Hampton Road East. My Stalker follows. He's around a hundred yards behind. In the quiet of the night, his fast, incessant drumming footsteps sound out a warning. I'm beginning to think the threats on the steps of the courthouse are to be carried out. Four hundred yards to go to great Hampton Street - my digs. I'm walking as fast as I can. If he turns into great Hampton Street, I'll continue past my digs and around the next corner.

Maybe he wants to see where I live? Beyond my digs is a warren of dark backstreets. I'm not going there, I have to stop somewhere. A sharp look around confirms he's in Great Hampton Street and getting closer. I turn onto the next street, passed my digs. The doors of these houses open directly onto the footpath. My pulse is racing - my heart drumming in my ears. I'm thinking of the bitter nastiness of the individual on the courthouse steps. My mouth is dry and my breathing is heavy. This is no act. This is Harry Lime for real. I flatten myself in a dark doorway - I'll be all but invisible in my black uniform. The weak low street lights, originally gas lamps, shine little pools of light directly underneath, in between almost complete darkness. The quiet stillness of the deserted streets adds menace to the staccato rap of his footsteps on the cobblestone footpath. He is slowing as he approaching the corner, I'm a few paces away. Being only half hidden in the doorway, I'll see him as soon as he turns the corner. It's not possible, it's just not possible he'll turn here as well. He does. I spring from the doorway, I'm right in his face. If he has a weapon, he'd have no time to react. Just as we collide he lunges onto the road with an incoherent choked shout of astonishment and apology. He stumbles sideways along the road, looking back all the time, almost as if expecting an assault and perhaps unnerved by being unable to see me in the darkness. I stayed tight, motionless against the wall, still stricken by a mixture of fear and relief, still disbelieving that from the town centre, after all the side roads and turns, this stranger following me could be mere coincidence.

I watch him into the distance, move between the pools of light and darkness. In the light, I see him peering back into the gloom no doubt badly shaken and trying to comprehend what possessed the lunatic in the black uniform into frightening the life out of him on a dark backstreet in the dead of night.

Now, I'm sure you're thinking I've done my bit to spread the bad news. Not entirely, one little trick remains. This time, I'll be a little devious, I'll use a proxy. At mass on Sundays in St Peter's and Paul's, I meet another Coyle family. The father's name was Danny. He had twin teenage sons, one of whom was also Patrick Joseph. This evening, sometime after my last court case, I'm browsing the pages of "The Express and Star". I'm relaxed and at ease, knowing I won't be in the news. But wait. I turn over a page, at first I blink, wondering am I seeing things? The cringe factor goes off the scale. There, under a banner headline:

"Youth in court after orgy of vandalism."

and the name – Patrick Joseph Coyle. The following day, I am in the little shop up the street where for years I pick up various odds and ends. Coming out the door, the manager calls after me:

"Oh Patrick, I see you are in the news again. First it was violence on the buses, now I see you are trying your hand at a spot of vandalism."

Chapter 32 - Draft Dodger and the Curious Case
of the Flying Reptile

Happily, that was the end of violence and vandalism for me. However, there are shades of violence casting a shadow over everyone at this time. The Cold War is getting hotter by the day, with an on-going threat and counter threat of mutual annihilation between the Russians and the Americans. For years the acronym MAD was used to describe this situation, [Mutual assured destruction] Tanks are in the streets of Budapest and conscription is still in force for all young men in the UK. This includes me.

So often, young fellas I'd see about from time to time, just weren't there anymore. When I enquired, I was told they'd received their call up papers and this was something I could look forward to as well. This was an urgent, even frightening wakeup call, because whatever the consequences - I wasn't joining the British Army. When I spoke to a sympathetic official in the bus depot, he said three options were open to me: one, dodge – go from town to town and leave no trace; two - leave the country; three - volunteer. By volunteering, I could choose which service: army, navy or air force. The only snag for the volunteer was you had to serve five years. The first two options were out. It was panic time. I decided to volunteer for the RAF for five years. I could choose to train in any of a great range of highly-skilled trades. I'd be an artificer. I remember lying awake at night, agonising over the decision. Five years was a lifetime, I'd be an old man of twenty-four when I came out. There was no option - I'd join the RAF.

The RAF Recruiting Office was at the bottom end of Queen's Street at Piper's Row - one of the most attractive buildings in the town. Not in an architectural sense, more in the meticulous way it was painted in the light blue and white of the air force. If the outside was attractive, the inside was the most alluring and seductive honey trap.

Huge, mural-like, floor to ceiling posters promised a life of daring adventure and excitement. Soon, I'd be hurtling down ski slopes like an Olympian, hang-gliding, free-fall parachuting, or hanging on by my teeth rock climbing in the Cairngorms. After the mountains, I'd climb into the cockpit of a jet aircraft to roam the heavens with the most glamorous female officer as my navigator.

One giant poster in particular had me spellbound - it showed a moonlit sky, swarming with aircraft and troops and equipment parachuting to earth – night time covert operations behind enemy lines. All I'd seen so far, the skiing, hang-gliding, rock climbing and now these covert operations, this was the ultimate adventure. I couldn't wait.

I was already blowing up bridges, when the roar of "Next" lifted me out of my seat. The recruiting sergeant's questions came like rapid fire pistol shots.

"Name?", "Age?", "Date of Birth?", "Sex?"

That stopped me dead. I'm sitting there silent, shocked by the aggressive tone of this sergeant and wondering what he meant. He leaned right across the desk with his face a few inches from mine and snarls,

"Don't you know, Paddy?"

With the forms filled in, arrangements were made for my medical. I was confident this would be a most genteel and discreet affair, allowing for personal sensitivities. Reality dawned in a huge rough barn-like barrack room where I was corralled with about two hundred others. How would they manage these numbers, I wondered? Then this florid faced, moustachioed sergeant major appeared. He looks like he'd just clambered out of a First World War trench and had a very quick clean-up. His boots look two sizes too big, he had this rough, thumping, clunking walk. He knows there is no way out for the cowering mass before him. There's no choice. Conscription was the law. On day one, the dehumanising, depersonalising will begin. He looks as if he's going to enjoy humiliating this callow mass of youth before him. He struts up and down like a vulture eyeing up trapped helpless prey. Then in a rasping disjointed voice mid-way between a screech and a yell

"Aw-rite yo lot den. Yo know why you're 'ere! So to prepare ourselves for medical hex-am-in-ay-shun, we must first git all our kit orf. AND I MEAN ALL OUR KIT ORF!"

This was my deepest, darkest nightmare. I wouldn't take my jacket of in the bedroom at night unless the door was locked and the light switched off. Heavy jowls, continued to bark and prowl. Then, with chin jutting forward and swagger stick pointing straight at me where I cringed and cowered at the back, trying to be invisible.

"Do yo think yo came 'ere for a picnic? I will tolerate no further shilly-shallying. Yo will remove all your gear now, sharpish like, place it in the baskets and then take your places in the cubicles."

Ten cubicles were set up in a u-shaped formation. Each had a doctor who carried out a small part of the entire medical. After much squirming and embarrassed wriggling, I joined the mass of other naked bodies. Another barked order sent us shuffling forwards. Terrifying thoughts came to mind of other medicals that lead to gas chambers. And I was thinking of poor mama because I hadn't written to her the week before to tell her how well I was doing in England. With my hands firmly clamped over my genitals, and half crouching like a hunchback, I reached the first cubicle. Here, the doctor asked me to stand on one leg. I thought this was unusual but realised when I'd be skiing in the Alps, balance would be all important and there would be times when I'd only have one leg to stand on. Next, he asked me to hop up and down on each leg in turn. This was desperately difficult because no force on earth would get me to move my hands, but as I hopped up and down, I could not resist my hands flying out in order to keep my balance.

He then ordered me into the next cubicle, sneering,

"Your balance is quite good Coyle despite your deformity."

In the next cubicle, I underwent a hearing test and for this I was blindfolded, before tiny tinkling sounds were made that came from different directions. As the sounds became weaker and weaker, I was asked to point out precisely where I thought the sounds originated from.

I wondered about my being blindfolded for a hearing test. I realised, when I was on night time operations behind enemy lines, a female agent might lure me into a compromising situation. This would be an opportunity for the enemy to creep up on me, but with my razor sharp hearing, I would smite him down even with my eyes closed.

The eye test was next. And I thought if they blindfold me for a hearing test, I'll probably have to wear ear plugs for the sight test. For many years afterwards, when I went to an optician and started to undress, the receptionist had to tell me that I didn't need to take my trousers off for an eye test. Lastly, but not mercifully, I entered the final cubicle. A sign said,

'Please take glass to wash room and wait until you are called.'

But my waterworks were completely deaf to military orders. I hurriedly filled my glass from a hand-basin in the corner. Holding it up to the light, the bemused doctor asked if it was mine. All too clearly, I was lying.

"But it's cold man, it's cold," he said. "Or am I to believe you could be our first flying reptile? Get back out and see if you can prove otherwise."

Back out, I discover that the next lad in line has gone in and is now standing there smugly with his glass full. Naked and forlorn, clutching my empty glass, and now with a spectator, I surely have no hope of proving my warm-blooded nature. But as I turn back to meet my nemesis, a hand is reaching out to save me. The other lad's pouring gesture is unmistakable. I gladly accept half his life-saving sample. I held it aloft like a prize trophy, although I didn't kiss it. My nakedness forgotten, I swagger back to this surly doctor who announces,

"I'm greatly relieved, Coyle, it's warm, you may be a member of the human species after all., get back out and put your clothes on "NEXT

Anxious days and weeks followed as I waited for my call up papers. None came. I wondered why. My landlady, the transport department, as well as the Personnel Manager all wondered why. I hadn't the nerve to tell anyone about the urine sample. But I like to think that at certain decisive moments in our lives, the fates take a hand and something seemingly trivial, a tiny intervention, perhaps just below our level of awareness, changes our direction and with it our entire future.

For good or ill, who knows? To this day, I still don't know for sure why I didn't get my papers and those around wondered what I had done to escape. I do remember a short interview after the medical by a panel of three officers, and in particular, one question stood out: "Are you a de Valera man?" And I answered "Yes, in the same way you might be a Churchill man".

This was 1957; Sean South of Garryowen (an IRA leader at the time) was about his patriotic business making headlines in U.K. papers, so perhaps they were suspicious of the motives of an Irish volunteer?

Chapter 33 - Billy and Patsy

I'm in the middle of my Harry Lime role and the transport department hires two new recruits: Billy McCormick and Patsy McCabe. Billy, from Galway, was a striking young fellow with a mop of blonde hair and three years older than me. We became best friends and but for a brief hitch, remained so for life.

If Billy was a gregarious extravert, I was precisely the opposite. He was also a very smart dresser. We would socialise two to three times a week, always and only to the lounges of the best hotels. He's in a smart double breasted suit and I'm likewise but with a white handkerchief in my breast pocket and my black eye patch covering my good eye. Not forgetting Trilby hat and trench coat, weather permitting. Billy smoked a lot and the strongest cigarettes at the time, Afton Major, which in time would kill him. I stuck to my Peter Stuyvesant, just for show, you understand. After work, we'd meet around the town centre - both of us like we'd just come from a wedding. The imperative now is not to go next or near any of the pubs Irish men frequented. We'd stand around for a while pointing out to each other with derision and contempt our countrymen heading for these pubs. All looking as if they have stepped straight out of the trenches. And trench is the word. Gangs of Irish men with picks and shovels were digging one – all the way from Wolverhampton to Birmingham for British Telecom.

Our objective is a posh lounge where we will, dare I say it, pose. But also, along with the posing, is what Billy called *looking for talent*. Or sometimes he'd say *class talent*. In this endeavour, he thinks my gear - especially the eye patch - has irresistible cachet.

We'd enter a lounge, scan the scene, if there were single, unaccompanied girls inside, we'd stay. We now try to get close enough to get chatting. Ideally, there would be a free table nearby. I was the willing accomplice, while Billy usually led the conversation, and he always managed to think of something original.

One night in the lounge of the Star and Garter hotel, we found seats next to two girls. These two are dressed very expensively – class - to Billy. One girl held a miniature dog in her lap. I suppose you could call it a hand bag dog. But really, this thing is masquerading as a dog. It's just a handful of fluff with huge eyes, hardly any nose, and small child's teeth that it keeps baring from time to time with tiny, barely audible little snarls. We sat there for some time, pretending not the slightest interest. Then, at the right moment, Billy says to the one with the dog

"I never thought I'd ever envy a dog"

And now you're thinking, well what of all your posing and chatting? The truth is not very much. Sorry to disappoint you but not once did we leave with any of these girls.

The most entertaining aspect was when the girls asked what we worked at. We'd say 'we're 'in transport'. No lie there. 'In' was the word if you wanted to impress. Trying to suppress the urge to roar out loud laughing wasn't easy as Billy would proceed to explain our particular speciality was traffic management. This took us all over the place in our efforts to keep the system running smoothly. So we could push the flirting to the limit being so mobile there would be no exchange of addresses.

Billy and I would talk a lot about the relative merits of the young Irish women clippies. In particular, there was this one girl called Rose McElhone, from Derry, who was in her early twenties, smiling and chatty, pale face, jet black hair and always a red rose in her hair, along with some other small, red accessory. I had a serious interest in Rose. I didn't know it, but Billy did as well. Wouldn't you know it, he was first off the mark. With this, our relationship went from cool to cold, then ice. Each day, he'd be in the depot waiting for Rose to finish. Then he'd help make up her waybill (the tally of cash against tickets sold). For a while, Billy and Rose are inseparable. This night, I see Rose counting her cash. Billy's there, but not helping. He leaves the depot on his own. I left a little later. Billy was waiting outside. I stride away as if I didn't know him. Friendships and loyalty, especially loyalty, were seriously important to me.

Billy calls after me in his great, good humoured way,

"All's fair in love and war". I stopped and waited. "I'm finished with Rose," he says. "Oh," I said, "what happened?" in a false tone, pretending sympathy.

"I think ya know, you knew all along, didn't ya? You know about Monica don't ya?"

I said, "I don't know anyone called Monica, and anyway, what has this Monica got to do with your interest in Rose?"

"Monica is Rose's three year old daughter."

It wasn't very long however before Billy was romancing again and this time, it was serious and for good. And I was his best man. Into the scene now, arrives my other lifelong friend, Patsy McCabe, from Dublin. At the time, I had a seriously prejudiced opinion of Dubs. He relieved me entirely and in full of that burden. Patsy convinced me I should abandon orange juice and drink beer or whisky and Canada dry ginger like a man, play snooker and stay up all night playing cards for big stakes, like a man. And this we did, like men. But I mustn't give an exaggerated impression of this card playing and drinking. The drinking was seldom, if ever, excessive - and all night drinking and card playing orgies only ever happened a few times. This occurred in a small, terraced house we bought on Willenhall Road in our joint names. It was in a very poor state but with youth on our side, we soon had it in excellent shape. It seemed ideal at first, but we hadn't considered the time it takes to shop, cook and clean.

Another brief interval and back at the Marriage Bureau, aka the Bus Depot, Patsy is romancing seriously. And since I was happy with us drinking and playing cards like men, I resented these intruding females. Still, the path to the altar was irresistible. And I was his best man.

Standing on the railway platform, seeing Patsy and Mary off on their honeymoon, he asked me my age. I told him. He said "I knew we were about the same age". I asked him what month and he said March, and so we discovered we were both born on St Patrick's Day, 1936.

Chapter 34 – A Romantic interlude at midnight
in a sewage works

While all about me are romancing and getting married, I'm advancing my career. I pass the Public Service Vehicle Driving Test, which is highly regarded in driving circles and qualifies me to drive almost all vehicles on the road. These are the buses with engines as opposed to the electric trolley buses. Telling you about the test vehicle and the test is worth a few lines. The test vehicle was a double decker bus with what was referred to then as a crash-type gear box. Also, the engine is set up so as to replicate maximum load conditions. All gear changes involve a double clutch action. Going up, gear changes are easy enough.

Changing down, not so. As you started up a hill with the engine governed as it was, it would start to die even on a slight incline, so you must select a lower gear. First, you clutch, into neutral, now very quickly, you use your accelerator to increase the engine revs to match the road speed in the lower gear. Finally, you clutch again to engage the lower gear. There is considerable skill in completing such a gear change and if you don't get it right, considerable embarrassment and gear box damage is the result. With the test bus, you have to change down from fourth to first a lot. If you crash the gears, or stall, as well as a red face, you'll fail.

My first motor bus route takes me to an estate where the town boundary meets a green belt. As the days and weeks pass, I get to know people who get on and off at the same stop at the same time each day. So there are lots of little waves and salutes. This day, I wave to people I know and they respond, but I also get a shy little wave and a smile from this girl in the queue. As the days pass, the smiling and waving gets more enthusiastic. And there is a lot of wide, bright-eyed, eyelash flashing between us. I also realise that on the homeward trip, she waited specially for my bus. And when she got off at her stop, she trotted forward hurriedly to smile and wave before I move on again. On arriving in town, after each trip, I usually step out of my cab for a stretch. I'll stand at the back, watch my passengers board and share a few words with some I know well.

This particular evening, I know my girl will be in the queue. The smiling and waving has run its course. I've been in a torment trying to find the courage to speak to her. It seemed an almost insurmountable challenge. I had started diving off the ten metre board in the baths. Many a time, I looked down and then gave up, feeling I'd never do it. This was the same feeling, except more difficult. I'm standing to one side and I can see my smiling girl at the back. I'm hoping that as the queue moves forward, she'll leave the queue and join me. The moment arrives, she's just a pace away now, she steps eagerly and confidently out of the queue to where I am standing with a wide, beaming smile. I've been rehearsing this so I say,

"I've been looking forward to speaking to you."

And she says excitedly "Oh, have you? That's nice, and I've been looking forward to speaking to you". All my passengers are now on the bus and I should be in my cab. Her name is Audrey Wood. I ask if she would like to come with me to the cinema later on. "Oh yes, please" she said.

That night, we visited the Odeon cinema to see the musical "Oklahoma". The following week, we saw it again. And later still, we went to Birmingham twice to see South Pacific. The two greatest musicals of all time. Sometime afterwards, Audrey invited me to meet her parents. I resisted this for some time. When I eventually relented, I remember her father giving me a minor interrogation and staying remote. In keeping with the time, he was letting his prejudices show, or maybe he was just being protective. Audrey wasn't just their only daughter, she was their only child. The way they both spoke, especially her mother, defined their social level - not a trace of the very distinctive Black Country dialect. It was all very nicely rounded vowel sounds. In the most class conscious country in the world: posh, middle or lower middle class. As I'm in the hallway leaving, the father stayed in the living room. The mother, who has been so welcoming and courteous, says,

"Thank you for coming, Patrick, and it has been so nice meeting you."

I was so overwhelmed by this wonderful compliment. It's one of those moments you never forget, a moment when you want to disappear. Standing there, silent, with my mouth open, while the lovely Mrs Wood waits for my reply, I say

"Was it?"

Despite my lack of social grace, I'm being invited to her parent's and her friends' houses. These people are all very prosperous: one had a tennis court, outdoor swimming pool and paddocks with ponies for the children. I feel complimented being there but there is no enjoyment. I'm tense and serious. Everyone is having a roaring time, but it's all passing me by. I'm a bit like the poor hobbled goat that sees a bunch of the most enticing fresh, green shoots. She's longing for them and struggles desperately but she is so disabled she just can't reach them.

At one of these parties, Audrey introduces me to her friend who is getting married and has asked her to be her bridesmaid. Naturally, I'll be there with Audrey. They would be married in a Methodist church. This was a concern for me because I was forbidden to go to a non-Catholic church, much less be involved in the service. I think I must have placed my dilemma in the hands of St Jude because after attending I didn't feel my time in hell would be extended beyond eternity.

The scene now moves to the hotel reception. We are all lined up outside the main door. I wasn't near enough to see what was happening so I asked Audrey what was going on. She explained the guests were being introduced to the happy couple and she said I would have my opportunity to embrace and kiss the bride and even the groom, if I wanted to.

Now, to people who kiss, were kissed, or are being kissed, this wouldn't be worth mentioning and you may feel I am stretching credibility when I tell you this prospect is little short of terrifying. In a cold, non-kissing, affection starved, loveless culture, this kind of intimate contact with a strange adult female is awesome, and there is a huge crowd looking on.

I am going to try every trick I can to avoid this, short of leaving my lovely Audrey in all her grandeur and huge bouquet, standing there on her own. She persuades me to give up my attempts to escape. Now we are at the door. She introduces me. I shake hands and congratulate them and wish them well. Now, that desperate, empty moment when I should have moved but didn't. I felt like saying something really scintillating like

"Grand spell of weather we're having altogether, thank God."

The hungry crowd outside are getting restless. In desperation, the poor bride leans forward to kiss me. I pull back as if repelled. I feel Audrey grip the back of my jacket. Thinking she is about to drag me away, I decide it's now or never. But as I go forward, Audrey is also giving me a great shove towards the bride. Result: a clash of heads and probably a unique case of the bride blushing because a peck on the cheek leaves her with a black eye.

Sometimes, when we were out late, we'd miss the last bus that took us close to Audrey's home. When this happened, there was another service we could take but it left us with a long walk along a dark, country road. Knowing the area so well, I could see that if we crossed a big field, we'd cut off about two miles from our journey.

From the cab of my bus, all I could see was a row of Lombardy poplar trees (the very tall, thin wavy ones) between this field and the road passing Audrey's house. Anyway, this night, we took the alternative service and then we, or maybe I, decided to cross the field instead of walking the full journey along the road. Together, we tripped and stumbled along in the dark, but we can see the lights on the road getting brighter all the time as they glint through the branches of the swaying trees.

I'm thinking what a smart, decisive man I am and how impressed Audrey will be. With only another twenty to thirty metres to go, what came looming out of the darkness, starkly outlined by the street lights behind, only a high spiked railing? We stand there staring at it, while only a hundred metres beyond the trees lies Audrey's home. Then, in a fit of bravado or stupidity and at considerable risk to my manhood, I scramble over this railing. I don't know what I had in mind, perhaps just a bit of midnight madness or to amaze Audrey with my physical prowess. Now inside this railing, I thought I'd explore for other obstacles. I'm moving towards the trees. I hear swishing sounds, a lot of bubbling, gurgling, flowing water. A little nearer and with the light from the street, to my horror, I can see I have climbed into a sewage works. I trudge back to Audrey and even in the darkness; my face must have been glowing with embarrassment. I am standing there, holding the bars, with my head resting against them. Dear God, Jesus Almighty, how do I get out of this fix?

Audrey stands in the field peering in at me through the bars. She's making fun of the whole thing, trying to ease my embarrassment. After a little while, she asks me to excuse her. I'm thinking what an unusual way for boy to meet girl. It's midnight. He's inside a sewage works behind a high spiked railing. She's in a field on the other side.

Audrey has been away for a minute or two when I hear this gentle mocking Black Country voice behind me, "Does you come here often den? There's a gate along there and it's open" she says.

After some time driving my bus along Audrey's route, a vacancy occurs on one of the Corporation's most attractive routes. If I get it, I'll be very fortunate indeed. To my astonishment and delight, I'm allocated this slot. This scenic route takes me well away from the town's traffic, calling at two collieries and two outlying villages. This is as good as a bus driver's life can be: plenty of time, little traffic and great variety of interest along this meandering run on the boundary between the town and the countryside. I enjoy this route so much, I am elated and tempting lively thoughts sparkle in my head of a lifetime as a bus driver.

A pleasant, enjoyable summer passes. Winter arrives, and a little incident I must tell you about. Following a hard frost overnight, and these roads aren't gritted, I set off from the village of Sedgely, and then on to another village called Lower Gornal, and lower is the operative word here. It involves driving down a gentle descent for a couple of miles, with the last five to six hundred metres being dangerously steep. Starting down this section, because of the icy surface and the steep camber, my bus slides tight against the kerb and knocks the top of a street light.

Inching forward, I can't get off the kerb. I am going to damage a lot of street lamps. But nothing I try frees me from the kerb – there's just no grip. Upstairs are a group of minors. I spring from the cab and ask them if they will try pushing me off the kerb. They succeed with such ease and enthusiasm they shove me right across the road and now I'm stuck tight against the kerb on the other side. My only interest is in keeping my bus straight. This hill is so steep, the tiniest movement of the front or the back of the bus from dead straight would be a disaster, it would topple over. I'm stuck on this kerb, on the wrong side of the road, in the lowest gear, inching down the hill. Drivers trying to climb the hill are abandoning their cars in terror. There's a Kamikazi bus driver on the wrong side bearing down on them, along with car traffic on the right side.

In the fifties, a bus driver's second horror was smog. This was before any clean air and smokeless fuel Acts. If I tell you that in bad smog, visibility may be zero, can you believe that? I've been sitting on a trolley bus taking me home. It's going so slow I walk in front to help the driver, using the footpath as a guide. At one point, I lose sight of the kerb and wander blindly towards the centre of the road. The driver follows and loses contact with the overhead power lines. It's unforgiveable. The bus is sitting there in the middle of the road like a giant toy, utterly helpless and immobile. I remember smog so bad, I've stood at a neighbour's door, fiddling with my key trying to get in, thinking it was my digs. If you opened a window, the house filled with it and when you coughed, you had a spit that was black as soot.

At night-time, in this throbbing industrial community, the tempo eases. And for a period between 7.30 p.m. and 10.30 p.m., the roads are remarkably quiet. People are resting after the frenzy of the day. Bus crews take time to visit cafes or the canteen and join other jolly jabbering crews for tea and chat. Drivers' nerves can settle and heal after hours of traffic conflict and trying to keep good time. Conductors can sit, ease tired legs, remove the ticket machine and achingly heavy leather bag of coins from around their necks. All afternoon, they will have battled to control the numbers charging on and off at every stop. It will be standing room only most of the time, so just moving through the bus to collect the fares is a real challenge. And often at the very worst moment, the overworked ticket machine will jam. These buses have no doors. In winter, the conductors will feel the cold, especially when the traffic eases and there is no racing up and down stairs.

My cab is always warm because the engine is right beside me, my left leg rests against the casing. At night-time, when it is quiet, I'll fold my arms over the steering wheel and rest my head on them. I am thinking of home, mama, Mary Burns, and how things might have been so different. I am dreaming of the little fields that I love and hate, the lakes where we used to fish and the little roads like threads weaving their way through the hills. I have regrets. I worry I have lost my way. I've gone sleepwalking from one situation to the next. I've lost my sweetheart. Instead of hobnobbing with the Duke of Norfolk, I was keeping the darts score in the Checker Ball, and to cap it all I'm not attending college.

One night, almost in panic, I'm thinking of my interview in Goodyear's and the verdict,

"No skill, training, or qualification".

It's a Damascene moment, an epiphany. I've wasted, lost, six vital years. And there is an even more pressing reason why I must get out of my present position. If I look through the little window from my cab, I see my clippie at the back. Her name is Barbara Latham and she's been with me since I started on this route over a year ago. If she's not counting and bagging her cash, she'll come round to the front of the bus and we stand there close together with our backs to the hot engine. We are about the same age, and yes, she's married. Her husband's name is Keith. Perhaps twice a week, when we are on nights, he'll bring a flask of hot, sweet coffee to Barbara. I always know when Keith is coming. Barbara will stay at the back as a warning to me not to move from the darkness of my cab. When he goes, she'll invite me to join her for a cup of this hot, delicious, sweet coffee. At no time did I meet him and I often wondered what he imagined the relationship might be between his irresistibly attractive wife and the young fellow in the cab. Remember, we are together fifty hours a week and in a multitude of small ways, instinctively, I am helping her. And as time passes, so much of what I do or say, and she says, is unknowingly forbidden fruit. The attraction is mutual, but I am striving to keep a distance, conscious of the unthinkable consequences - not least the deadly sin of covetousness. Was this what mama meant by "sinful ways and evil temptations?"

And all the time, I am wondering can Barbara be so innocent? She doesn't know what she is doing, because lately, alarmingly, she is using the word "Love". In the Midlands, it is an expression of endearment commonly used between husbands and wives, intimate friends and children. Never between a married woman and a single man,

"Goodnight Patrick, see you tomorrow love". And at certain opportune moments, "My machine has jammed again, love".

I open it up and can't see anything that's jamming it. And I am sure she knows that I know this. Sometimes, when she uses 'love', the atmosphere is so charged that I am completely in her hands - just a touch, a word away from the tipping point, beyond which there is no coming back.

So it's back to the "Sits Vac". I'll accept any job that leaves me free at night to attend college. I'll take any job such as bread/milk delivery. I was lucky. The first or second night, I see a display-type advert: Applications are invited - It was the Engineering Department of what was then, the Department of Posts and Telegraphs. My interview was in Wolverhampton Telephone Exchange. I didn't go as Harry Lime. It was blue blazer and grey trousers with blue and red striped tie. I remember this so well because my interviewer asked what college it represented.

He told me I'd be starting at the bottom, as he did, and it was entirely up to me how far and how fast I advanced.

Chapter 35 - The Last Romance, Geoff Rock, and Power to the People

It's 1960, I am 24, but as you will recall the record says I am 30. I'm at Mass in St Peter and Paul's. I happen to be in a seat next to twin girls that I knew to see but had never spoken to. I'd been kneeling there just a minute or so when a jab from a bony elbow stabs into my side, along with a look of severe censure from the one next to me as she passes me her rosary beads. She wouldn't have known that I was already damned and beyond salvation. I go through the motions with her beads, pretending to be just as religious as she genuinely was. The service over, I return the beads with a short, clipped "Thank you".

My nose was streaming from a cold. There would be no light-hearted socialising. I didn't know where the girls lived, but as I turned down Whadam's Hill, heading for the bus stop, I saw them ahead of me. Now on Waterloo Road, we're waiting at the same bus stop. It was dreary, wet, cold morning and they're in a huddle, half hidden under an umbrella. I'm standing a few paces away, in two minds whether to wait for the bus or not. With the reduced Sunday morning service, I might walk home before the bus arrives at the stop. And that's what I did. After a few quick strides, a call rings out "The bus is coming".

The twins board and sit on the bench seat, just inside the door. I asked where they lived and discover we're getting off at the same stop. They live in a flat nearby. There are a few words on the footpath when we got off and I'm invited up for a hot drink. The flat was small but warm and homely. As I sip my hot drink, the chat warms up as well and my mood is changing. I'm making my hot drink last. Thoughts are forming in my head, yes, some, forbidden ones. They are attractive and in this cosy setting, if there was only one, then who knows? I'll be leaving in a minute. I'm thinking I'll invite myself back.

I rise to go, thanking them enthusiastically and start down the stairs. I'm surprised when one of them follows me down the two flights to the front door. They'd told me their names earlier, now twenty minutes later, I can't tell one from the other as they are identical. I don't know who's on the stairs with me. However, my mind is made up; I'm going to ask her out. At the door, I ask her name again - it's Sheila. She's in slippers and as I look down at her, I'm thinking she is small, looks frail, and is looking up at me with a sad, lost, slightly pained look in her eyes. Her voice is gentle and reserved. All this so aroused my protective instinct, it was easy to ask if we could meet again. We did. And so that call back to the bus stop meant the meeting would go on for at least another fifty years.

The following Monday, my new career begins with a memorable job title – I'm a quasi-temporary labourer and I am assigned to a Major Works Gang. As the only Irish person in the place, I think I was expected to play a certain role - not to act too smart, be fair play for a laugh and generally, not to have an opinion or know much about anything. But I was reading widely, was a bit opinionated and had a lively interest in politics. So I disappointed some but got on well with most. A lot of the work was rough and demanding, but always interesting in that one day we might be cabling inside an office block and the next day in the heart of a mighty steelworks. The scale of the engineering in some of these places was wondrous to behold. The actual making of steel involves engineering on the most massive scale. Afterwards, it's turned into an infinite range of products mainly to support the other heavy engineering works that are all over this part of England. One day, I watched the making of an anchor chain, each link weighing 250lbs.

We needed to access the most inaccessible places to repair faults and install new line plant. Looking back, it's hard to believe how the telephony system ever worked. Suspended, insulated cable had just arrived on the scene. Previously, we were working with bare cadmium copper wire, strung from poles, sixty to seventy feet in the air. And no protective gear of any kind was issued, such as gloves or helmets. Cuts and gashes were an everyday occurrence from broken insulators and rusting bolts and wires.

With my nights free, I can be a proper student in the College of Technology. I planned to do a City and Guilds Telecommunications course, after the two year preparatory course. Therefore, it's Workshop Science, General Science, Maths and Engineering Drawing. The rest of my time, it's romancing, the library and swimming. There's no stopping me now. Only a few months have passed and I receive a memo from my manager telling me I'm a quasi no more. I'm being upgraded to the honourable and noble rank of labourer. Another six months and I'm told to go to our Headquarters in Birmingham where I fill in some forms and sign the Official Secrets Act. Did I feel important? I'm now a fully-fledged Civil Servant, and with this went promotion to the rank of Fitter and driving a medium sized van with a mate. Compared to the gang work, you could say this was glamorous.

Meanwhile, I'm romancing as much as time allows and one Sunday afternoon, on the beach in Rhyll, north Wales, I proposed to Sheila. Eight months later on June 28th 1962, we were married. While we were engaged, we were making plans and had many earnest talks planning our future together. The key to all our planning was that we wouldn't start a family until our mortgage was paid off. Next, we'd buy a car and then a family in that order.

I promise you, on any honour I might have, not a single word passed between us on how this might happen. It wasn't until our third and last child was born, did we discover the cause of all our trouble. Back at the office, I picked up an advice note to cease a telephone line and recover a phone from 18, Newbridge Street. The house was for sale. Compared to new houses we had looked at, this place was a delight, with its south facing great curving bay windows, high ceilings and spacious rooms. In a matter of days, I paid the deposit and arranged a mortgage. This was our first home.

As I continued with City and Guilds courses, I figured I'd have better promotional opportunities, working on the purely technical side. With this in mind, I arranged for a transfer into Wolverhampton's Telephone Exchange. Here, I met the Communications Workers Union Secretary - Geoff Rock. There was great agitation on the British political scene at the time. Much unease about the hundreds and thousands of coloured people arriving from the Caribbean. The Communist Party was strong and creating a lot of unrest. Edward Heath was trying to negotiate the U.K.'s entry to the European Common Market. And the Japanese and Germans are killing off some of Britain's great traditional industries such as ship building and car manufacturing. All of this provided a great range of topics for fierce debate around the tables in the canteen. The staff were very politically aware and we had ample time for argument with breaks at 10 o'clock, 12.30 and again at 3:00 p.m. in the afternoon.

My friend Geoff was on the outer fringe of the Labour Party. I felt seriously attracted to the Communist ideal. This ideal, as I thought is encapsulated in the Marxist expression: "From each according to their ability - to each according to their needs."

This was regarded as bringing the maximum happiness to the greatest number. I also thought these few words enshrined the essence of Christian doctrine – "The Beatitudes ,the commandments ,and indeed St. Pauls second letter to the people of Corinth, and the best that could be expected from the socialist doctrine of the time. I was doing serious reading of "Das Capital" and "Marx on Economics". And each morning, I picked up a copy of the Communist Party newspaper – "The Morning Star."

My favourite politician was Aneurin Bevin and I was well acquainted with his book "In Place Of Fear". Geoff considered me a torch bearer for the coming revolution and from time to time would seek me out to tell me in quiet, grave tones of certain meetings I should attend. These meetings, never advertised were for the advance guard only, and always held in the most unusual and obscure places with never more than nine or ten people present. I'd knock on a door and be asked who I was and who advised my attendance.

The tone of the agenda was always the same. The corruption and decadence of the hated Capitalist system, the vile exploitation of the working man, and how comrades and brothers could unite in solidarity to bring the whole, rotten edifice crashing down. No-one else could achieve this. Society depended on us, the workers, to sweep away the hated Bourgeoisie so we could get off our knees, break free of our chains and establish once and for all our utopia, a model society ruled by the Proletariat.

On one occasion, Geoff said, the speaker at one of these meetings would be a fire-brand from Dublin. He gave me directions and told me to knock on a certain door in Piper's Lane at the back of the main Post Office, say who I was, and give his name. I thought this really is it, our moment has come. Tonight, the touch paper would be lit and the reverberations would travel around the world. This, for us, was the equivalent of Vladimir LLyich Ulyanov's (Lenin) journey in a sealed train across Germany to lead the Russian October Revolution of 1917.

The "fire-brand" spoke with a genuine and original Dublin accent, and should have brought an interpreter with him. He used two words continuously and monotonously that only I and he would understand. These two words were "foisted" which he pronounced "fausthed". The second word was "ousted" which he pronounced "austhet".

Working people had this, that and every conceivable injustice "fausthed" on them by their tyrannical masters. He outlined the many ways they could be "austhet" and brought to their knees. As I watched my fellow revolutionaries look at each other in puzzlement, I was certain this speech would not inspire them to man the barricades. Equally, I knew I wouldn't be lying down in the street anytime soon.

While the debates rage as we plan the downfall of Capitalism, the work scene is fine but for one major faux pas. This particular weekend, all British Rail's telephone numbers in the town are being changed. I've done the work and set up a recording, advising callers of the change. On the stroke of five on Friday, as I leave the building I should have flicked a little switch putting the recording out on all British Rail lines. I forgot. So over the weekend, no-one could contact British Rail. On Monday morning, I was handed a stern note from the manager and a "please explain" form to fill in. I'm seriously embarrassed because we get on famously. I'm sitting there at his desk, looking at this question on the form: please state the reasons etc. After a long pause, I start to write: this was regrettable and careless. The manager says,

"No, no, you'll have to learn how this system works" he says "pressure of work, man, pressure of work, an oversight due to pressure of work".

Chapter 36 - The Shark Fishers

Every year, the Engineering staff enjoyed an annual low budget outing. This year, I am nominated to make the arrangements. Because the image of the Paddy was so low, I am obsessed - paranoid - that this should be a great success. I am sure, rightly or wrongly, that everyone expects a disaster. I'm aiming high. I decided we'd go on a shark fishing trip to Looe in Cornwall. We'd travel in a self-drive mini-bus and stay overnight in tents, bringing our own food and refreshments (beer). I asked each member of the group to take responsibility for just one item, such as one type of sandwich, or one kind of confectionary such as tarts and cakes.

That morning on the pier side in Looe, onlookers would think we were heading out on a transatlantic voyage as we loaded boxes of food and several crates of beer. The crew consisted of a skipper and mate who told us the fishing area was three hours offshore. In the little harbour all is quiet and peaceful. We settle into rough seats. There is plenty of room but it is more a big tub with an engine than a boat.

With a lot of smoke and the stench of diesel, we chug-chug out into the open sea. At first it was choppy, but as we venture farther out, the swells rise and the troughs deepen.

If you've ever suffered a moment in your life when you felt your demise was imminent, this was it for me. I'm standing, holding on to a timber post by the tiny wheelhouse. Time after time, the boat rises onto a crest, then an uncontrollable lurching, stomach churning dive into the trough. As it dives, our eyes are stinging as the salty spray lashes our faces. Each dive I think is our last. Not a word is spoken. No fun, no laughter, faces anxious and fearful. From their seats, a few are already hanging over the sides. I'm still ok - but for how long.

About thirty miles out, the noisy stinking engine is switched off. Nets full of bloody offal are launched over the sides. There are three seats forward into which our fishermen will be strapped and at their feet is a fixing point for the rod. While the boat was more or less going in a certain direction, I and most of the others are still on our feet. Now with the engine stopped, the boat is swinging, twisting and corkscrewing, utterly at the mercy of the raging waves. In seconds, all the jolly, happy, shark fishers are emptying their guts into the foaming waves. I recall just hanging helplessly over the side. I can see a dorsal fin, slicing patterns in the waves near the boat. I thought what a mercy it would be if it dragged me overboard and into the depths.

Everyone now quite ill, it feels like a coffin ship. We make our silent, despondent way back to port. Not one bite has been eaten, not a single sip swallowed. To our real shame – no shark landed. Each day back at port, there was a prize for the biggest fish. Returning to the pier, I see a line of people waiting to see ours. But all they saw was a group of staggering, wobbly legged, bedraggled young men with long, white faces.

We slope off in the direction of the nearest pub, hoping to revive weakened bodies and very depressed spirits. By closing time, spirits have revived but we had lost control of our bodies. There was a lot of lurching about as we staggered up this very steep hill to the field where we had pitched two tents. The atmosphere between us wasn't bad, but there were some angry words of blame for our failure to land a shark and a few have told me how sick they were in the boat but not half as sick as sitting in the pub afterwards listening to me singing repeated renditions of *Kevin Barry*. Mama taught me this ballad. It was one of my favourite pieces at the Christmas party in school.

Kevin Barry

In Mountjoy Jail one Monday morning,
High upon the gallows tree,
Kevin Barry gave his young life
For the cause of liberty.
Just a lad of eighteen summers,
Yet no one can deny,
As he walked to death that morning
He proudly held his head on high.

Just before he faced the hangman,
In his dreary prison cell,
British soldiers tortured Barry
Just because he would not tell
The names of his brave comrades,
And other things they wished to know,
'Turn informer or we'll kill you!'
Kevin Barry answered 'No!'

Calmly standing to attention,
As he bade his last farewell
To his broken-hearted mother,
Whose sad grief no one can tell,
For the cause he proudly cherished
This sad parting had to be;
Then to death walked, softly smiling,
That old Ireland might be free.

Another martyr for old Ireland,
Another murder for the crown,
Whose brutal laws may kill the Irish,
But can't keep their spirit down.
Lads like Barry are no cowards,
From the foe they will not fly;
Lads like Barry will free Ireland,
For her sake they'll live and die.

Now begins the grand climax to our shark fishing adventure. With a light hanging from the roof of the ten, and each with a good supply of their favourite refreshment, lying half in and half out of our sleeping bags, we settle in to play cards for the remainder of the night.

Chapter 37 - Birth of Anne

Time passes relentlessly and on the morning of 31st July 1963, the most momentous event in anyone's life, our first child was born - our darling daughter Anne. Inside the maternity home, the fathers line up behind a glass partition. Ahead of me, I can see each father cooing and making silly noises as they admire their babies. It leaves me cold, even repelled because all I saw was knarled, twisted, crunched up, cringing little faces. Imagine my delight when a nurse brought Anne. I'm overwhelmed with pride and admiration witnessing such beauty and perfection. I floated home in a trance, thanking God, how lucky I was to be the father of such a heaven–sent little parcel of delight and feeling so sorry for the unfortunate fathers of those ugly babies.

We have our home, our first child and I'm in permanent, pensionable employment and more promotion than I want. I noticed a huge turnover of staff in my previous jobs, whereas here, no-one leaves. All those around me started working as sixteen or seventeen year olds trainees. They knew they were going to have careers for life. For them, the thought of leaving for something else was laughable. Nothing could beat this. And I was told the position of the permanent civil servant in law was such that it was all but impossible to be sacked. With all this, what do you think I am planning? I'm leaving.

Two issues force this decision. The first and most pressing is as follows: from the time I started work in the Exchange, my physical well-being has been well below normal - rheumatoid-like pains in my joints are getting worse and most days I have the energy and liveliness of a wet rag. I force myself to get my work done. Whereas I used to enjoy a walk home in the evening, lately, with my knees on fire, I take the bus. Come Sunday, and especially in the swimming pool, my energy recovers and the joint pains ease noticeably. I've reached the firm but soundly based conclusion: the Exchange is a sick building.

The great expanse of floor I work on is packed from floor to ceiling with electro-mechanical switching equipment. An atmosphere pervades everything.

As I walk in the door, it hits me. The air is incredibly dry, seems oxygen deficient and at times I half expect spontaneous electrical flashes to leap in front of me - it's that charged with electrical energy. The very floor throbs and resonates as thousands of relays, switches and various generators hum and chatter in response to billions of electrical impulses. I believe the entire building is carrying a powerful positive ion charge and I'm extra sensitive to it. But even without this difficulty, my second reason would be sufficient for my leaving.

Chapter 38 - The Fortune Seeker

In the forties and fifties, we didn't emigrate simply to find work. The real dream was to make our fortunes. Then to return home in swaggering triumph, like fake Yanks in flashy suits and gaudy ties – all set to buy a farm or a pub. Therefore, although I am well paid and have a good standard of living, I'll never build up a sufficient surplus to show off at home. And come what may, I won't be spending the rest of my life here - our children will never, ever grow up in England. But each day, I feel drawn ever deeper into the web that I fear will imprison me. A web I am busy spinning for myself. All that I do and say about my work, relationships, the union, the manager, and Geoff Rock would leave no doubt this indeed was, and would, be my life. The truth is - it's all a great, self-destroying lie. I'm in denial.

I'm giving myself wholeheartedly to a kind of voluntary enslavement, even wondering if my lying to myself is linked to my physical condition. Remember, examination of conscience was still very much part of my Catholic make-up. And in the rare moments it happens, the truth is revealed: so much of what I am, or appear to be, is false. I'm not being true to myself. I can't continue with the lie. I can't ignore what my conscience is telling me. I don't need to be, or have to live up to, whatever Geoff Rock or anyone else wants or expects me to be. I don't need to be fearful that the tiniest, most trivial mistake will lose the perfect image I believe the manager has of me.

If I stay, I'll end up more of a robot than the men on the machines in Goodyear's. I can't continue to ignore conscience, personal integrity and most especially heart. Years ago, this job, the status but most importantly, the acceptance was a dream fulfilled. I craved it as if my life depended on it and in a way it did. Heart and conscience will now be my guide, but my heart is at home in Ireland somewhere- lost in a mist of memories and dreams. Still, returning to Ireland is now my quest, but first I must go seeking my fortune.

How? It would need to be a business of some kind. No wage earner, even people on the highest salaries, accumulated much surplus. One Saturday afternoon, I am browsing in W H Smith's bookshop on Lichfield Street, when arrives one of those moments I truly believe contains something more than coincidence. Call it serendipity if you like a combination of unusual circumstances - that mysterious something that prompts a life changing decision. I'm searching for anything in science, astronomy or the natural world.

I fish out this book only because I can't see the title on the spine. It's a trade magazine - completely misplaced. It should be with its counterparts back near the door. I open it, thinking maybe it was a catalogue of the books in this section. It's not. It's entirely about manufacturers, wholesalers and distributors from all over Europe who are looking for agents for their products.

As I read through it at home, ideas sparked in my head about mail order. On page one, a well-known French perfume company was advertising for applications to franchise the marketing of its product in the West Midlands. The urge to do this was powerful. Me - an importer and distributor of the finest, most expensive French perfume – surely the ultimate in sophistication. A tiny snag – I'd need to invest an amount equal to twice the value of our house. And yet, all is not lost - there are hundreds of other possibilities. A Danish manufacturer of guess what? Needle threaders and magnetic soap holders are searching for a UK agent. No indication was given of the investment required for sole rights within the UK. What I do have is a name and a telephone number and ample opportunity to make calls at work. What have I to lose? Memory fails me here on detail, but broadly, if I imported a given number they would guarantee me the sole distribution rights in the UK. All I can be sure of was the total amount was not prohibitive.

My head is buzzing with dreams of starting my own mail order business. Sheila was excellent at shorthand and typing, I'd telephone the newspapers for the cost of advertising, calculate the cost of a post office franking machine for postage as well as jiffy bags and a big stapler – packaging solved. The only real challenge was an address, a letter box, say, for my customers. This doesn't hold the same appeal of expensive French perfume, but it will do for a start.

I visited the various estate agents, looking for suitable premises and spotted one that was ideal - serendipity again. Half a mile from home, small, but big enough and cheap - I'm in business.

I've spent a lot of hours on the phone at work, setting this up, and all in complete secrecy. I'm worried someone will overhear me. One day, I'm sitting at my desk discussing the cost of 'bargain squares' in the Sunday People, the biggest selling newspaper at the time. As I'm haggling with this individual for better terms, I happen to glance down to my right, and half behind me I spot a pair of brown size elevens - unmistakably the manager. I drop the phone and stand up, waiting for him to demand an explanation. Even if he'd only arrived a few seconds earlier, he couldn't help but overhear. I am pleasantly surprised when there isn't a mention of my business dealings with Sunday newspapers.

As if things weren't busy enough, I was also working part-time in the pub at the top of our street. I used to visit this place from time to time with my father-in-law. One way or another, the landlord, Roy Capper, persuaded me to help out three evenings each week. I didn't like it and I didn't want to do it. Still, he got me behind that bar. I think he wanted me to deal with his troublesome Irish customers - and he had his share of them all right. The other barman was called Norman Frost. He was perhaps ten years older than me, married, with no family.

Little by little, I discover Norman is not a happy man at home. The later the clearing up at night, the more it suited Norman and no matter how late it was when we eventually finished, he wanted to chat. But we got on wonderfully well and he was in every respect a gentleman. He lived near my new business premises – a small lockup shop on Hordern Road. He had noticed my coming and going and naturally he was curious so I told him what I was up to. He thought it an inspired idea. He was so enthusiastic and encouraging I already had vivid images of myself showing off at home. The beauty of it is that I can organise all the start-up detail while keeping my job in the Exchange. The advertising is expensive, that's the only sizable outlay. That's ok because I'll have customer's money flowing through the letter box before payment is due. Discounting our labour, breakeven point is quite low, so the amount of money at risk is comparatively small.

The momentous day dawns and my advert appears in what were referred to as the "bargain squares" section of the newspaper. Ok, I'll tell you what was advertised here. It was a lot of knick knacks, just as mine are. Still, such was the excitement and anticipation of the eagerly awaited response it could have been expensive French perfume.

Travelling home from the Exchange in the evening, my first call is to the little lock-up on Hordern Road. No doubt, I'd judge from the resistance to me pushing open the door exactly how much mail was behind it. The volume wasn't great, but it kept coming throughout the week. The work involved was minimal: jiffy bag, some advertising, a Pitney Bowes franking machine for cost of postage, staple, address label. Norman insisted on helping free gratis, while Sheila had by far the biggest task - typing the address labels.

As far as I can recall, my first consignment of knick knacks sold out after three weeks. My second order was for a much bigger number with a pro rata discount. I also increased the advertising space. Over the next three to four weeks, the accompanying increase in sales was minimal. Then sales levelled off, then tailed off. But I was ignorant of the law of Diminishing Returns and so advertised some more - to no effect. With this business model, my dreams of horses, foals and paddocks are dimming a bit. Having said that, I have gained a good knowledge of how mail order works so the learning curve from now on will be less steep. I'm still at the day job and can't wait to try something more substantial than my knick-knacks.

In the Exchange, apart from Geoff Rock, there was just one other individual I would call a friend - a Welsh lad by the name of David Howells. At the time, we were working closely together on manual switchboard maintenance. With all the phone calls I needed to make each day, I couldn't keep my secret any longer. I let David in on what I was doing, making him promise not to breathe a word. Imagine the shame, the disgrace, if Geoff Rock learned his protégée, whom he trusted to lead the revolution, had sunk to the ranks of the lowest level of capitalist lowlife - the despised money grubbing, gombeen men? David is also enthusiastic and eager to get involved, but we have nothing to sell. If I took account of labour, with the trade I am doing now, it wasn't worthwhile.

Nevertheless, human nature as it is, when you're riding a wave of enthusiasm, the target can be set high and the decisions aren't difficult. Norman's day job is salesman with John Brown's Spares - one of the biggest wholesale car spares companies in the UK. The evidence from what research we did pointed to a vast market for the supply of car spares by mail order. The money involved is serious. Together, Norman, David and I agree to create a limited company. The name I came up with was Costell: 'Co' from Coyle, 'st' from Frost, and 'ell' from Howells. Companies House accepted and registered this name, as well as the trademark Norman designed. We were aiming high. We are now a company with limited liability, a registered trademark, and the grand claim to be importers, exporters and mail order suppliers.

The news from Norman and other sources was that relined brake shoes and clutches drove the biggest sales. Norman worked on the counter in Brown's and as none of us had any knowledge of how the relining was actually carried out, it's time for a little industrial espionage. Remember, I could dress up! Early one morning, I arrived on the steps at Brown's. Norman introduces me as a major new customer and proceeds to take me around the places of special interest. I make a note of the processes and especially the machine needed for the relining of the brakes and clutches. Our little lock-up had no free space for machines. Instead, I installed the most important piece of equipment - a Stenor Riveting Machine - in the garden shed (one must never underestimate the industrial potential of one's garden shed). Money! That's what it's all about and I haven't mentioned it yet. Norman is a great addition to the team, but hasn't a penny to invest. Initially, as the prime mover, I owned the majority of the shares and wanted to keep it that way. David also had money to invest. I simply can't recall figures, except to say the money invested was small. Indeed, this was our main weakness from the very start - most of our capital was loaned from the bank.

The scene is now set, curtain up - the advertising goes out for a complete range of spares and accessories. The response wasn't dramatic, just encouraging. Around the third month, it's at the point where I can't cope part-time, a momentous day has come. I'm resigning my permanent, pensionable un-sackable position as a civil servant.

The manager asks for a written explanation. A day or so later, I am called to his office. He and two others put me through a minor interrogation, examining the wisdom of my decision and finish by saying regulations allowed a grace period of three months - to learn the error of my ways. If and when Id changed my mind I would be reinstated without loss of rank, seniority or benefits.

Now the serious work begins. I'm responsible for a young family and not one but two mortgages. When the house next to ours went on sale, we bought it with a mortgage from another company and I converted our home into two self-contained flats. It was a hell of a busy time, in the little shop all day, close up in the evening, bringing home all the old clutches and brake shoes for relining, then work late at night, taking off the old linings, cleaning and repainting them to look like new and finally, relining. Sheila is working even later, her work starts with the children in bed, typing letters and address labels.

By and by, I learn from Norman that wholesalers get much better terms from distributors than retailers. I figured - why not establish a second company to act as wholesalers? Norman and David are still in their jobs. All of this, like so much in life, has its own momentum. There is inevitability about each move. It seems unstoppable.

With all the preparatory work complete, including purchasing a substantial new premises, Norman and David resign. Now that we are wholesalers, we can go straight to the manufacturers for our supplies. Our main supplier was a company called Quinton Hazel. This company supplied 95% of the huge range of car parts and accessories we stocked. For your three aspiring tycoons, it's a hard working, exciting time. This wholesale business however, differs from retail in one major point. Retail is cash in hand. Wholesale involves credit and terms depending on the amount involved, with payment up to three months away. It was this aspect we had difficulty with, and which would eventually sink us.

Dealing effectively with cash flow, we weren't so much three musketeers as three naïve innocents at large. No difficulty finding customers and shifting plenty of merchandise off the shelves. But no skill, knowledge, or know how on collecting payment for it. At the time, it was beyond our understanding or belief that so many customers would simply not pay, or would drag out the paying process to exasperating limits.

Still, we battle on for two years and were getting a handle on the cash flow problem when the British Chancellor at the time, Selwyn Lloyd, introduced his notorious credit squeeze.

Our customers owe us. We owe the bank, and they, along with Quinton Hazel are demanding payment. Our house was collateral for my bank loan. I remember the fateful morning well. I was shaving in the bathroom upstairs. Suddenly - an impatient hammering on the front door. It felt like the house might be on fire. It was the postman – I had to sign for this letter, he said. It was the bank telling me to pay before this date or they would foreclose on our mortgage.

Geoff Rock would have enjoyed this. Patrick has abandoned all his principles. He has made money his God, but now he has offended grievously, committed the one unforgivable sin: failure. The Capitalist gods won't be denied. Your personal situation or circumstances count for nothing. They will have their due.

Our accountant advised voluntary liquidation. In the hierarchy of traumas that we all experience, I believe business failure figures highly. This one did. Apart from the money, such an immense investment of time, energy and effort, all ending in complete failure - and gone with it my dreams of horses, foals and paddocks. As a footnote, the final act contained a certain grim irony. Sometime after reclaiming his stock, Sir Quinton Hazell (he has been knighted), was involved in a major scandal. Unaccounted for, unpaid for, container loads of spare parts had been turning up at his depots. So effectively, he had forced us out of business because we weren't selling enough of his stolen goods.

Chapter 39 - Roofers and Choirboys

With two mortgages to pay and the business gone, there is an urgent need for income. Into the breach steps my brother in law, Peter Kennedy. Peter worked for an Irish roofing contractor called "A & T McNulty Ltd". on Henwood Road, Wolverhampton. He made the necessary enquiries and no doubt recommended me. Remember, as John Bunion said, "He that is down need fear no fall." I haven't been down long and already I'm on my way up again, well, physically, at least. Peter said, "The industrial roofing could be rough but the craic was ninety."

Ninety, it seemed, was the upper limit on the craic scale. My future workmates informed me the money was especially good on the lump jobs. As that name implies, McNulty agreed a total fixed amount paid out on completion of particular jobs (a lump sum). It was then left to the men to arrange everything for themselves. These jobs always involved a lot of travelling and also presented abnormal difficulties. The lump job though was a whole different caper. Keep to the day work for a good while before you even think of taking on a lump job, they warned me.

I remember my first morning standing on a roof. I know its pretentious but you could say - how have the mighty fallen? I'm depressed. It genuinely felt like a bereavement.

I was also bothered that my new colleagues might think I was putting it on a bit. It wasn't false, but over the previous few years I had adjusted my tone a bit. Standing there trying to look, act and talk like a roofer, my mind turned to mama. One day, when Michael and I arrived home from school, she told us our neighbour's thatched roof had fallen in on them during a storm while they had slept. Pete, Maggie and Katie lived there with their mother. Mama said a neighbour found them semi-conscious under a foot thick duvet of sodden straw.

"Jesus, Mary and Joseph, weren't they horrid lucky, "she said. "But for the Grace of God, they would all have been kilt". So I suppose I'm lucky. Business wise, the roof has fallen in, but at least I am alive.

The lump jobs suited the main contractors fine because it absolved them of any responsibility for their workers' safety or welfare. This was especially the case on firewall jobs. A firewall was about encasing all the main structural steel elements of a building in two inch pure asbestos sheeting in order to slow down or negate the effects of a fire. It involved non-stop cutting and drilling of this deadly material. The particles produced by the asbestos were so fine and light, they remained suspended in the air and looked and behaved very much like talcum powder.

We worked all day and had our meal breaks in that lethal atmosphere. When we left in the evening, we looked like we had crawled out of a vat of flour – white as ghosts. The ultra-fine particles stuck to the hair on our faces, eyebrows and even our eyelashes. Not once did I hear a word about protection. A few years later, anyone near even a suspected source of asbestos had to wear a spacesuit. The risks and dangers were known at the time, but perhaps not to the same extent they are now. And there was no all-powerful Health and Safety body to enforce any kind of regulations.

Among McNulty's happy band of roofers is a Polish man - one Jan Morovski. Morris was the name he insisted on being called. He arrived in Britain after the war via Italy, and most especially Monte Casino, where he served with the Polish Brigade. Monte Casino would rank as one of the great set piece battles of all time and we would have deep conversations about this and other aspects of Poland's unfortunate history.

After a few handy weeks on day work, Morris asked me to go with him to Sheffield on a lump job. I was wary of this lump job, remembering the warning I got. Morris told me the contract price. He said if we left early, we would complete the job in a day and be home for supper. Enough said. In my financial situation, suddenly I'm an enthusiastic lumper.

Next day, while the rest of civilisation slept, we drove the 90 miles to Sheffield. Sheffield on the Don, city of steel and cradle of the Industrial Revolution, Its centre prosperous and chic but this clean face hides a grimy industrial heritage.

We passed through monotonous tunnels of red brick houses, which eventually gave way to the red of rust and an endless vista of grey - the deadening grey of one hundred and fifty years of industrial grime. Steel was born here and the afterbirth and effects of an ugly childhood are all about: the endless clanging of shunting railway wagons laden with coal and iron ore, the earth trembling as the mighty rolling mills give shape and form to the molten steel, and hanging overall - an obnoxious pall of smoke as yellow fire and fumes spurt from blast furnace retorts.

Our destination lay at the end of a rattling, growling, smoking canyon of buildings. In huge lettering - *Sanderson's Die Casting Works*. Our job was to replace damaged asbestos sheets and glazing on the roof. From the start, the omens were bad. I'd conquered a few drumlins , but this was Everest on a bad day. The roof was steep enough to challenge a mountain goat. And a biting, sleety rain lashing our faces gave the coup de grace to my sinking morale. My predicament was further complicated when I realised Morris didn't believe in even the most basic safety measures.

When I highlighted this to him, I got a blunt, uncompromising lesson on the lump job. We could decide to do nothing while it rained, but then overnight accommodation would cost us, and the weather could be worse tomorrow. On safety, it would take a day to put all the elements in place and another day to dismantle them when we finished. Then with a note of scorn in his deep gruff voice,

"Anyway Patrick, if you are to die here you will, safety or no safety. Whatever you do, you have no say in your ultimate destiny. At Monte Casino, thousands of my countrymen died - all my friends, one by one, over three months of rocket, artillery and machine gunfire, yet I haven't a scratch to show my children".

Morris was not only a battle-hardened soldier, after twenty years of his trade he was inured to the hazards. Then with one last deep draw on his fag,

"Patrick, I teenk we start".

His words were like a death knell. I want to be anywhere but here - anywhere else on earth. I am in mortal dread that I will not survive a day on this roof. Oh God, why didn't I stay at the day work? Maybe Morris had a death wish as the only survivor of his brigade? After the final desperate assault at Casino did he feel he had betrayed his comrades? Fully aware of the horrors inflicted on his countrymen by the Nazis, did he feel guilty that he did not also forfeit his life.

Our longest ladder was too short to reach the roof, so a second was lashed to it. It was like climbing a swinging, vertical rope bridge. As I followed Morris up, I felt as if I was an innocent victim being led to the gallows by a hangman. Each step up that swaying, straining combination was a step closer to my doom. On a wet, crumbling, asbestos and glass roof, without a vestige of safety precautions, this was more a suicide than a hanging. Morris had his Monte Casino, this would be mine - and it would be a baptism not only fire, but of bone chilling fear and fumes as well.

With the removal of the first damaged sheet, a blast of hot gases from the furnaces below left us choking. As the underside was exposed, bone-dry grime built up over generations swirled all about us leaving us half blinded and as black as coalminers. This was a battlefield alright and the fear just as real. I saw it in Morris's face as well, though he would deny it. The drawn ashen look, the grim set of his jaw, the staring intense gaze as he balanced on a wet, three inch wide glazing bar while struggling to balance a heavy sheet of glass. Down through the cavernous hole at our feet lay a terrifying view of hell, as fiery, incandescent crucibles of molten steel poured into moulds as they passed along on a conveyor belt.

The firmament all around a fireworks display as molecules of water vapour exploded in the volcanic heat, generating a thousand pinpoints of light. Morris would squat down and lean forward, defying gravity and the fates he believed in, to place the glass sheet into position. I would remove the damaged sheet, teeter down the icy slope, praying fervently that I would stop on the brink of oblivion, before pitching it down to the skip 50 feet below. I would have felt safer in a minefield.

Next, down the ladder again for a new sheet while Morris removed a damaged one. Each time out of his sight, I mustered every ounce of reserves to control and hide my fear. Another reckless climb: I step up with my left foot, the ladders lurch to the left, up with the right foot, a lurch to the right. At the point where the two makeshift ladders are lashed together, they bend under my weight so that the second ladder is now rising almost vertically. The sheet of asbestos or glass is balanced in my right hand with the top edge resting against my head. Whatever happens I can't drop it because the exact number needed will have been supplied. The step from the ladder onto the roof is fraught with danger because the decaying roof is covered with wet moss. Without a catwalk to step onto or a guardrail, I am indeed on thin ice. I'm riven with fear - breathing in short shallow gasps. My bottom lip is quivering like a child who is tired of crying yet doesn't want to stop. I place the sheet down on one edge to help me balance and hide my trembling legs. Morris mocks my efforts.

"Come on - my old Granny in Krakow would be quicker. At this rate we will be here till Christmas."

Once, when my head appears over the top, he isn't ready and we both end up on our bellies struggling desperately to remove a particularly difficult sheet. We pause for breath. The rain and sleet is beating down and our eyes and throats are stinging as acrid fumes and smuts pour up from below. A vision of heaven fills my mind - it is a smallish homely room with a smiling open fire. Three babbling, gleeful children shriek with laughter as they struggle playfully with each other for their father's cuddles and goodnight kisses. In an alcove formed by the chimneybreast sits a tropical fish tank. The radiant ivory's pinks and greens of the multifaceted coral, and the easy, lazy grace of the exotic fish lend an air of tranquillity to the scene.

"Oh God, don't let me die on this god forsaken roof. Please, please let me survive just one more day. I will never, ever, ever set foot on another roof."

As dusk closes in, the grim battle ends and we descend to safety. Physically exhausted and emotionally drained, no time is taken to even wash our hands. Near the city centre the weary silence of our homeward journey is broken when Morris announces,

"Patrick, I teenk we stop for a drink."

My God, he wants to stop for a drink? I'm on my way to heaven but this mad Pole wants a drink.

"No, no and no again. With the decrepit filthy state we're in, no self-respecting pub will let us in, or if they do they'd surely have us carted off to a place for those in distress or in need of humanitarian assistance. A promise and a compromise - "Just one, and we'll try to get it at the outdoor serving hatch for takeaways." I'm looking at Morris and wondering could I possibly look as bad as he does? Long, wet, grey hair hanging down over a face that's mostly black but with streaks and smudges where he has wiped off sweat and rain with his hand.

We're slouched by a serving hatch at the end of a corridor trying to be invisible. People pass, averting their eyes, giving us a wide berth. A faint but distinct sound of music wafts down from a door at the other end. I try not to believe my senses but Morris is clearing his throat. "Patrick, we join the sing song for a minute while we have our drink." My protests are drowned out by his heavy-booted, clumping footsteps down the corridor. Anyway, I thought whatever the musicians think about our appearance, at least it can't be life threatening.

Morris opened the door and we are transfixed for an instant like rabbits in headlights. This was no smoke filled singing lounge. It's a brightly lit room, air clean and pure - with delicate, fragrant hints of perfume. Not a cigarette or a glass is in sight.

We were in the presence of about 30 men and women in evening wear (women in long dresses) - all very elegant. They were seated in intimate semi-circles around a piano on a dais. The singing was very orderly and disciplined, with the voices clear and resonant. Before we had a chance to bolt we were ushered quietly and most courteously to two front seats. In extreme fatigue, I thought maybe I'm hallucinating. Maybe I died on that stinking hellhole of a roof and these lovely people were angels proclaiming their joy at my entrance into Valhalla? Indeed, it must be so, since their singing was a soaring anthem of ecstasy and joy to God and his angels.

When the music stopped we were overwhelmed by the welcome heaped upon us. The choirmaster said how impressed he was at us coming straight from work to join in. We had gate crashed a 'Primitive Methodist' choir practice. The conductor announced the next hymn.

Come, sing out your joy to the Lord".

I did so with conviction and sincerity, since a little earlier hadn't I been humbly beseeching him for my life? The conductor, a slight, dainty figure, face and hands delicate and pale, with skin like Ming porcelain, raises the baton. Fragile, child-like fingers coaxing, shaping, prompting, encouraging, demanding, drawing out the most subtle nuances of the music from artists and roofers alike.

At times, he bends down to his new recruits to whisper rapidly the next line when he saw we were stumbling. The smiling pianist turns towards us and nods her encouragement. Not the slightest sign of irony at the two dirty, unkempt figures, so conspicuous in the front row with pints of beer gripped in their grimy, black hands, surrounded by such genteel refinement. Morris and I, as genuine aspiring choirboys might do, placed the beer on the floor and responded with all the enthusiasm we could muster - staying on right to the end. We were not let leave until we faithfully promised to return the following Thursday. Alas a promise we could not keep, this would be our only opportunity to be choirboys.

A thousand times since, that scene has flowed quietly, calmly, gently, back into my mind and a wave of affection for these people overwhelms me. We were in such a terrible state in the middle of the front semi-circle that anyone looking in the door and seeing us would convulse in hysterical laughter. And yet, we were so welcomed. And that dainty, artistic conductor, along with the lady on the piano smiling at us all the time. If there is a life hereafter, I'll join a Primitive Methodist choir for eternity.

The Sheffield lump job was a baptism of fire, but I would learn over the next few years that roofing jobs would present many challenges in terms of health and safety. After some time, however, you become inured to the hazards knowing there is no choice but to get the work done, one way or another.

On one occasion, I arrived with three others at a site in Gloucester. The other three already had their working gear on. By the time I was ready, my workmates were nowhere in sight. I looked up, way, way up - perhaps two hundred feet up, this was the highest yet. All three were on the top deck of many levels of scaffolding, waving at me to join them. How? I searched for any possible means of climbing from one deck to the next. There wasn't any. Now they are roaring and waving. One of the three, clinging to the scaffolding poles, climbs halfway down and shouts at me to follow him. It was like asking a bird to fly with a broken wing. Everyone round about was staring at me. I glanced back to my car thinking of home and safety. If I do that I'll be looking for another job tomorrow. Clinging to each pole with a grimness born of mortal fear, I clamber upwards and eventually reach the top. After about an hour someone shouts,

"Jaysus lads, it's ten o'clock." Tea time.

All three were over the top rail and down out of sight before I'd even considered getting down. And looking to see how I do this is more terrifying than looking up. Below, I can see them with their flasks and sandwiches and there is a tired, resigned gesture for me to join them. The entire site has gone quiet. A minute ago, the place shook and rattled with the din of several trades building, bolting, welding, riveting, drilling and fixing. I'm standing there like the very last fledging. I've seen the others do it but I know flying is impossible. I thought of my first time on the high diving board and it helped - never, ever look down. With a mixture of some embarrassment, but especially in utter desperation, I heaved myself over the top rail and down - to great acclaim from below.

Chapter 40 - Civil Rights and Uncivil Reactions

It's now 1969/70 and the Northern Ireland troubles have literally exploded, And I've poached some of McNulty's staff and started stealing his work. The McNulty Brothers were well established sub-contractors with about twenty staff. But sub-contractors they were. They submitted a contract price (tender) to the main contractor for roofing and cladding work as it came up. With some of the men, I proposed the idea of taking on jobs entirely on our own account. As the feedback was generally positive, I approached the main contractors and requested drawings and details of upcoming jobs with a view to tendering for them. I allowed ten per cent on the price for the expected haggle. There wasn't any. My first price was accepted in full. Apart from the increased money, the benefit is no more firewalls for me. The downside is people with me will expect to be paid every week. I'll need to be on my toes to keep the work flowing. All went well, but there was a lot of travelling and I'm still working in the pub. Several times, I quit. A few weeks later, Roy would be at the door again. Back I'd go. This went on for years. Most of his Irish customers behaved. Others were an embarrassing nuisance and a disgrace.

As the trouble in the North boiled over, so did my interest. This interest though, was initially kindled at about age fourteen reading about the nationalist's situation in the North and the difficulties of Cahir Healy, and later, Eddie McAteer and their nemesis Basil Brookes.

One night at the pub, a steady Irish customer asked me if I read the letters in the Express and Star. I didn't. I simply thought – what possible interest would local views on local issues have for me? He advised me to take a look. Every evening, a couple of letters would appear with a barely concealed racist, religiously biased, anti-Irish theme. I read these letters every night for a couple of weeks and wondered why there wasn't a single response from anyone Irish or English – something to at least give the letters page some semblance of balance. I concluded people were responding but the Express and Star wasn't printing their letters so I'd have no chance. Anyway I had never written anything. I thought people who wrote letters to an editor would have an excellent knowledge of the subject and the facts, as well as some scholarly knowledge of English grammar and syntax. I didn't, so I thought I'd look foolish.

At weekends, our newspaper was the Irish Sunday Press. I started reading its letters page. This week, I spot a letter from one Captain Lawrence Orr, cutting rapidly to the chase, from what I'd read, I didn't like Captain Orr. He was a Unionist MP. He was also a shallow hypocrite. In the Commons he would be addressed as 'my right honourable friend the gallant captain'. I didn't think of him as either honourable or gallant. His letter was just too much. I'm going to reply. My response had anger and attitude.

The following Sunday I couldn't believe it, my response was published in full, precisely as I had written it. Not a line, not a single word changed or omitted. Seeing this as an unparalleled, intellectual triumph, why not carry the battle to the Express and Star? And I still haven't seen a single response to the bigots. A week or so after my first letter appeared, there was a sudden increase in our mail. One evening when I came home, I found Sheila in distress. All our extra post was unaddressed, unsigned, abusive and threatening. They were all variations on a theme of pigs, scum, rats, rabbits, the living conditions and breeding of. A few were outstanding along the lines – they knew we lived with our pigs in Ireland also how we killed them, so wouldn't this be good enough for us? The actual language was much more explicit, not for a refined, gentle soul like you dear reader.

Naturally, you are thinking, how vicious and extreme. But consider this - one of the bestselling magazines at the time was Punch. It was famous for great humour and carried serious news along with satire. Any issues I saw always had an Irish angle - invariably portrayed as a pigs in the parlour uncivilised, stupid race. The caricatures portrayed the Irish as wild, dirty and ape-like, even well-known Irish politicians might be shown well-dressed but with beetle browed Simian heads. Maybe it's hard to believe it now, but in Britain at the time the Irish are very much fair game for a laugh and a sneer.

Back at the office, the solution to the hate mail is poetically simple. Each and every letter with a local postmark and unrecognisable handwriting is dumped.

A few weeks later on, one quiet and holy Sunday afternoon, I hear a knock on the door. I hesitated at first, it was a favoured time for children to knock and run. I peeped out and saw no-one. I stepped out onto the footpath and standing out of sight was John White. We first met him fifteen years earlier in digs in Newhampton Road West. I was surprised to see him as we weren't great friends and this was the first time I had seen him in all that time. But with the developing situation in the North, there was plenty to talk about. He'd seen my letters and discovered my address. He asked if I was interested in forming some kind of organisation in support of the Catholic/Nationalist people in the North. I emphatically was, but wary of White.

Living in a flat beside us with his wife and child was a man called Pat Mullen from Derry. Pat worked for me so we had often talked about how little or no voice the Irish community had in England. We decided we'd contact White to see what ideas he may have. It turned out he had some contact with a group in Birmingham known as the Campaign for Social Justice in Northern Ireland. A public meeting was arranged to form a branch in Wolverhampton. The attendance was remarkably good. White was acting chairman and subsequently elected. I proposed my friend Pat for Secretary. He was elected. But he had warned me beforehand, not to propose him. Then a Treasurer and committee were elected.

In preparing for our second meeting, Pat told me he simply could not write up the minutes, he asked me to do it. And at the second meeting, he proposed me for the job. I was duly elected. And so was born the Wolverhampton branch of the CSJNI (Campaign for Social Justice NI).

We grew to a steady membership of forty to fifty and met every week. White had confidence and was a surprisingly good chairman. At first, all anyone wanted was the Secretary to write to just about every politician, the Prime Minister and the Opposition, the Taoiseach, the northern Nationalist leaders, Irish associations in the UK and the US including Ted Kennedy, just about everyone who it was thought supported the Irish Nationalist case. As well as dealing with our friends in "The Express and Star".

You may well ask, what is the basis, the source or the authority for me to present the Irish position? Well, principally, it was a long standing, passionate interest. And I knew where to look for information. My most important source was a small pamphlet called the "Plain Truth" produced by the McCluskey family in Dungannon. The husband and wife team, both doctors, began sending me this pamphlet. The information it contained was unchallengeable, incontestable, the objective facts on the political situation in the North.

The central library also had an updated copy of Hansard, the verbatim account of every syllable uttered in the House of Commons. From this, I understood both sides of the argument. I also homed onto any kind of survey, academic work or study about the place. So I felt on very safe ground. I could debate on a one to one basis and write about it with complete confidence. But I couldn't stand before an audience and speak. When it came to public speaking, I was shackled, hobbled and hamstrung all at the same time. My first experience of this was when I was the CWU delegate to the local trades council. At meetings, the minimum expected of me was to stand up and give my name and who I represented. I couldn't do it. My second experience was more serious. I had written to John Hume and he agreed to come to speak at a public meeting. A local MP, Peter Archer, who I knew was sympathetic, would be the other speaker. I was still in the college and had spoken to the Student's Union Secretary and booked the spacious common room which had a stage. White was leaving this entirely to me and I thought the college as a venue which now had university status would enhance our credibility. As the date approached, my paralysing fear grew - my fear of being dumbstruck at this very important meeting. At the last minute, I cancelled.

Despite my failure, we arranged for a succession of NI politicians to speak at public meetings including Gerry Fitt, Paddy Devlin, Frank McManus and other names I can't recall.

With little or no experience, White chaired these meetings very well. At the time, the Conservative party was linked to the Unionist party so Labour MPs were our natural allies. From our contacts with them, we were advised that the most effective method to generate action was to lobby at Westminster. We were agitating for a 'bill of rights' so we decided we would a-lobbying-go. For this idea to have any hope of success and to lend weight to it, we needed to show widespread, public support for it. The only way to do this was to collect signatures, so in co-operation with the Connolly Association and the Birmingham branch, we started collecting. These signatures would then be presented at Number Ten, Downing Street. Our target was 50,000 and when we reached it, we were ready to take Westminster by storm.

In the early 60's, the convention was you could only lobby your own MP. We lived in the Wolverhampton south-west constituency so our MP was the Right Honourable Enoch Powell, MBE, writer, poet, classical scholar, double first from Cambridge, youngest brigadier in the history of the British army, youngest professor ever of ancient Greek and the second youngest professor in history. His secretary told me I should first write by way of introducing myself and then follow this up with a phone call to him the day before the lobby. On that day, I was doing some roofing work on a building site in Derby. Hard to believe now, but making a phone call will pose some difficulty.

The only phone anywhere about is inside the site office, a very busy place. I need a few minutes privacy to make this call. My workmate is Alf Connolly, in his sixties – should have retired from this job long ago. He wasn't great at it, but he was one hell of a talker.

We're watching for the men to leave the site office after the morning tea break. This will be my best chance. Alf loiters about some distance outside. He'll ambush anyone coming back. I call Powell's constituency office, his secretary isn't there. My only hope now is his Westminster office. Watching out the door, I see the Project Manager striding earnestly back towards the office. Alf's on station and moves to ambush. He's puffing on his cigarette, talking at mile a minute and waving his arms. They both start to walk away. Powell's office answers –

"Mr Powell will see you in the Commons tomorrow."

I ask Alf what he said to the manager. "The one thing he didn't want to hear," he said "we turned down another job and travelled sixty miles to take this one and now we may have to leave as the material supplied isn't right. I told him you'd gone crazy but if you had a few minutes on the phone you might work something out."

I was looking forward to Westminster but not to meeting Powell. I was in thrall of his reputation. Every spare minute I spent researching Northern Ireland history, legislation, the case for a bill of rights, his speeches on the subject and his book 'Freedom and Reality'.

But such was his reputation, I thought no matter how well prepared I am, with forensic skill, he'll dismantle my case little by little and show me up for the rank amateur I am. Still, I know his week points - he was an ultra-nationalist and in all his speeches in the Commons he preached equal rights for all citizens, so how could he possibly defend the denial of these basic rights to nationalist people in Northern Ireland?

Powell had a forbidding even threatening appearance. Always dressed in black, black umbrella hanging on his left arm, gloves in hand. Topping this uniform was a big black wide brimmed hat. His face is pale almost white with a thin moustache and there is this wild look in his bright wide eyes.

I would never miss an opportunity to hear or see him on radio or television, always hoping there would be someone who takes him on in debate. It never happened, he wiped the floor with all comers.

Despite his genius his political legacy is infamous. He will forever be defined by what is remembered as his rivers of blood speech in Birmingham in 1968. He used words to this effect to describe what would happen on British streets if coloured people continued to pour into Britain form the West Indies.

On arrival at Westminster, we were met by a Labour peer, Lord Fennor Brockway. He referred to himself as 'Bwockway'. In the lobby between the Lords and the Commons, he briefed us on how the system worked. "Fill in a green card, pass it to the Sergeant-at-arms and he'll locate your MP". I filled in my card and waited nervously, very nervously. Looking back, I'm a little embarrassed admitting I could be in such awe of another human being. After some time, the Sergeant-at-arms reappears with the comment "Mr Powell will not be in the Commons today". I mentioned my arrangement with his secretary. Mr Powell was not in the House and that was that. I was perhaps more relieved than disappointed, though many years later, I thought what an opportunity missed.

I'm not able to tell our children or our grandchildren that I had a heated political argument with the second youngest professor in all history, beaten only by the renowned philosopher Frederic Nietzsche of "what doesn't destroy me makes me stronger" fame. Whilst the others lobby - what do I do? I cross to another sergeant-at-arms and asked him for another green card. On it, I put down one of a number of MPs who I knew supported us and when I got a reassurance of their support, I filled in another green card. So I spoke to Jock Stallard, Stan Orme, Roy Hattersly and Maurice Foley. These all had strong

Irish connections. In Foley's case, he was born in the UK but his wife was Irish as were his parents.

We had our lunch in the Common's bar sitting at a table with George Brown, deputy leader of the Labour party. George was always about half drunk. He wanted a United Ireland as much as we did and he voiced this loudly if a little slurred. And "in a few short years, it would be a reality as the EU swept away all borders partition would be a footnote in history."

After lunch, Lord Brockway escorted us to Downing Street to hand in our weighty bundles of signatures. As we formed up outside number ten, pictures were taken. Later when I enquired, nobody had any photos. We hadn't arranged for a photographer and nobody knew who the photographers were. No doubt, special branch did.

From Downing Street, it was back to the Commons, Mr Brockway vetting each of us past security into the lobby. A vivid memory of that day is how politicians love crowds. Like pop stars surrounded by their fans, as they came out of the Commons they'd join us as if we were a band of their supporters. And since we want to gain their support for our cause, we cluster around like bees on a honeycomb. Amazingly, Captain Terence O'Neill stayed to chat. He was most extraordinary mild mannered, soft spoken man, with a soothing tone, like speaking to a child. Such a contrast to the loud mouthed mob orator Paisley who was eventually the architect of O'Neill's downfall.

We stayed until nine that night and while all the others left one by one, Foley remained. Before we left, he asked me if I'd join him on the upcoming election canvas in his constituency. I was astonished and intrigued. He was a rising star, tipped as a future leader of the Labour Party. Surely, he'd have a legion of the party faithful working for him? I wasn't even a member. I suppose he must have thought I could make a convincing case for him and the Labour policies to his constituents. His constituency was West Bromwich, ten to twelve miles from Wolverhampton so I won't have far to travel. Secretly though and in the quiet confidentiality between pen and paper here tonight, I fancied myself as his PPS (parliamentary private secretary). That would really put the sight crossways in Alf Connolly and my other roofing mates when I told them.

I arrived at the Labour Party club in West Bromwich. I'm his chauffeur. Off we go in his car to a housing estate. He's very like Packy McEnaney. I've suddenly transmogrified from roofer to ardent Labour Party worker. I'm not sure, but he knows I can do it. He doesn't even come to the first house with me. Around midday, we went back to the Labour club for a sandwich. After that, out again, going from door to door. When he asked me back a second day, I thought surely it's PPS or nothing for me. How innocent I was. He thanked me and assured me of his support. "And be sure to get in touch when we planned our next Westminster jaunt." Indeed, there was another one but I wasn't on it. I'd already taken more time than I can afford off work.

As the situation in the North developed with the success of the Civil Rights movement, the abolition of the B Specials and then Stormont, our initial purpose was rapidly overtaken by these events. And changes at home and in my head are happening as well. Our children are growing up and each day I hear them use words and sounds in the local accent I detest. We must make the decision soon – either stay in England permanently or return home. My wife Sheila is entirely practical and wonders and worries about how we'll make a living.

I'm a dreamer. My reasoning is emotional and sentimental - the head doesn't intervene at all. If we stay, our children will grow up to be Black Country Brits. They'll be strangers to us. They won't identify or feel any connection or emotional attachment to Ireland and I can't live the rest of my life permanently separated from the fields, the infinitely varied landscape, the wildlife and the winding boreenns with a surprise round every bend .But most importantly that certain powerful indefinable feeling of something lost .And for life's sake I must return and endeavour to find it.

My head is swimming in thoughts and dreams from childhood that I just long to recapture – such as Michael and me lying in the grass on a summer's day. Teddy, our dog is between us, dozing - his head resting on his front paws. We're gazing at cotton wool clouds as they chase across the sky. The only sound is the breeze whispering in the long grass. A few yards away, a lark catapults upwards, rising vertically and pouring its heart out. It's as if it's struck with the sudden realisation that there was so little time remaining and it had so much to say and all living things had to hear it while there was still time. No other sound intrudes. It seems all the earth is listening. Forty to fifty feet up in the air, it hovers for a moment or two - its singing is urgent and intense. As it rises in these vertical hops, its singing grows in intensity. The tiny creature is now lost out of sight in a vast blue ocean of sky but we can still hear it. After its lung bursting effort to proclaim its message, complete silence follows. It drops like a stone down to its nest in a little tuft of dead grass.

And the curlew, how I long to hear it again. Just as darkness falls and you are near our bog or any marshy wet place, the curlew will announce its presence and its message couldn't be more different from the larks. His is a lonely, drawn out, haunting cry. Any sadness or despair you may feel or have ever felt is expressed by the curlew's mournful plaintive lament. It's a warning. The lark told you of life's brief joys, and it's full of hope. The curlew reminds you of the coming, inevitable darkness and its loss. You may be nearby but its call always seems to come from somewhere far, far away - somewhere beyond human habitation but it's carried on the wind to all places however remote so everyone will hear.

But most importantly, I need to connect again with the people I loved as a child. Overall, it felt like something of vital importance is missing, something lost in the past. What am I to do? Finding it is all that matters. It can only happen if I am home in Ireland. I have to go, even if we live in a tent on a hill.

The decision is made. We're selling up. It doesn't help that the housing market is in one of its inevitable, recurring dips. And the process was so slow; we returned leaving a lot of loose ends.

Chapter 41 - Home again, and the Mysterious Case of the Mutilated Mail

August 1974 and our new home is number 9, Dublin Road, Drogheda. My younger brother Michael owned this house and luckily for us it was vacant so we moved in. What followed was the most frustrating, disturbing and infuriating period of our lives, due almost entirely to what was happening to our mail.

From the first day, no item of our mail was delivered to our new address, on time or intact. At first, when we didn't get any mail, we thought it was down to the process of relocation. Meanwhile Sheila attended the Lourdes hospital for a job interview. After two weeks, thinking she had been passed over, she decided to phone the hospital to enquire. She was told she'd been accepted for a position in the Children's ward and the letter had gone out the day following her interview. Several phone calls to the Post Office over the next few days only compounded our anger and frustration. I wrote to the Postmaster. Three weeks after the Lourdes Hospital letter was posted, it popped through our letterbox. The envelope had been ripped in such a crude way, it couldn't possibly be accidental. And it's so difficult to understand how any post people dealing with it could deliver it in such a state.

After weeks of waiting, my new road tax certificate and disc hadn't arrived. More phone calls followed and another letter to the Postmaster. Some days later, a Garda knocks on our door, saying he found this letter in the road - my road tax documents. Repeated letters to our solicitor in England received no response. This was urgent and serious. Our house had been sold but we hadn't been paid. One afternoon, I stood in Brian Taylor's (our solicitor) office in Drogheda waiting for him to confirm that our solicitor in Wolverhampton hasn't made off with our money. Brian Taylor confirms that the cheque for our house was posted weeks ago.

In most cases, it was so obvious our mail was intercepted because the letters were stamped with two postmarks. The first and original date and time could be seen over stamped by a later date and time, days or weeks later. Over a period of about two months, our mail was delivered in such a tatty state it was so obvious it had been opened, and what was so incredible no attempt was made to conceal this fact. This was genuine and original hacking. It was a difficult situation to deal with because we were both so preoccupied dealing with a multitude of things as we restarted a new life. This meant being out all day, and in my case, away from home hunting for work.

The problem with our mail along with other incidents at home and before we left Wolverhampton leads to one conclusion.

Given the political situation at the time, the Brits must have made contact with An Garda Siochana or the Irish Special Branch and they, in the crudest imaginable way, decided to take an interest in us.

Chapter 42 - Strike Breaker and All Work and No Pay

My first job back in Ireland was on Little Island, in Cork Harbour. I sourced the work from a company called Burke, Higgins and McNulty who were based in Clonmel. The main contractors were Mitsui (Japanese) and Denman (British). It was the biggest project in Ireland at the time and was for the manufacture of Manganese Sesquioxide. My three trusty colleagues and I were delighted about this contract because it looked as if we'd have work for months. My first two invoices were paid in full. The third one, only partial payment - which always looks bad. We are working long hours and are two weeks ahead of what we are paid for.

About the fourth or fifth week, a shop steward tells me a meeting will be called to decide what action to take over a dispute involving some welders. I attend, but don't hear anything by way of a decision. Nevertheless, a few days later, a strike is called. It's 'down tools' and this huge site falls silent. All the trades people tramp despondently out the gate. This is terrible for us. If everyone else stops work, we have no option. We watch from our perch on the roof and are the last out the gate. The entire site is closed off with chain link fencing, six feet high. So here we are, perhaps six to seven hundred men, loitering about outside this boundary. As I chatted to people over the next few days, all without exception were angry with the decision to call an all-out strike over a dispute involving a few welders.

I also learned that it's a typical industrial standoff - the union convenor won't approach management to talk. Instead, he demands they come to him. They, on the other hand, are waiting for the union leadership to come to them.

Each day, the mood grows more sullen and angry, and we're furious as we haven't been paid. All our living expenses need to be paid, and now of all things, this damn strike. About the fourth or fifth day, the dam breaks - I'm going to the site manager's hut - we can't afford to be idle. We are going home. As I walk through the gate, I expected to be restrained or at least verbally abused. The very mildest response would be a roaring chorus of the strike-breaker's anthem: "Scab, scab, scab."

There wasn't a peep from anyone. I'm a short distance inside the site, feeling exposed and isolated, and at any moment expecting to be dragged back to the nearest hanging tree. This is a huge site and it's a long, long walk to the management office on the far side. I look back and see hundreds of faces peering at me through this chain link fencing - forlorn, sad faces. Some appear to be clinging to it as if I had made a successful bid for freedom and they are desperate to follow me. They look like camp inmates or prisoners and I'm the only one escaping to freedom.

Images flash in my head of pictures taken by Russian troops just as they approached Auschwitz. Or am I hallucinating? Maybe the stress and anger of the recent past was taking effect.

As I near the manager's office, I'm thinking how much worse it is going to be on the way back. The door opens, and I am greeted like the long lost child - beaming, smiling faces are all I see, with hands reaching out with the warmest greeting. There is the most effusive thanks for my initiative in making the first move to speak to them.

"This whole business of a strike was so pointless and unnecessary." The manager said. "Now, it can all be settled so easily". I am completely bemused, and as I was about to spoil it all by mumbling something about going home, I realised what was going on. I am now accompanied by three or four of the management team in a very happy mood, who tell me the Mitsui manager was in a state. It was a great dishonour and humiliation for him to report a work stoppage on his site to Head Office - something completely unknown in Japan. As we arrive back at the gate, there was a brief exchange, then a flood of people back on to the site.

Over the next few days or so, I had a very gratifying but embarrassing number of people thanking me for what they thought was my decisive strike breaking initiative. We continued for another week without payment. Phone calls and visits to the Company's office ensued, all a waste of time, so we came home. Later we would learn that before this job was completed two of the roofing crew who replaced us fell to their deaths.

Before travelling down to Little Island, Sheila and I had been checking out the estate agent's lists of houses for sale. Late one Sunday afternoon, we were at the end of our list. The last house had been struck out by the estate agent because he said it had been withdrawn. Still, we were on the road nearby, so we thought we'd take a look anyway. The owner, George Ledingham, said it wasn't supposed to be l on the list but he still wanted to sell. He asked me in. From inside, looking out I see something truly magnificent. The house is on a high bank, not visible from the road, and in the valley below at the back of the house, a great sheet of water stretches into the distance. This is the river Nanny and the tide floods the river right up past the house. Swans glide along in their easy, lazy graceful way, hardly making a ripple on the still, glass-like surface. On the far bank, great clumps of glowing yellow furze and stands of trees, and in the fields, horses and sheep graze. The slanting rays of the late evening sun floods the entire scene with a glorious pinkish, yellow light. Speaking to Mr Leadingham I had difficulty trying to hide my delight. This place is priceless.

Ledingham names his price. We haggle. We agreed. We shook hands - a gentleman's agreement. Back from Little Island the following weekend, the agent informs me Ledingham has changed his mind. He's gazumped another £500. We haggle, again. We agree. We shake hands, again. It can't happen a second time. It does. The agent hatches an ambush where he'll have Ledingham, me and our solicitor lined up to sign off on the deal within the hour - except Ledingham and I won't be in his office at the same time. A bit like the fox, the goose and the bag of corn. The house is ours.

Chapter 43 - My Day in the Four Courts

We have our new home, it's perfect – infinitely better than a tent on a hill. After Little Island, I managed to wrangle another small contract in the Dublin area - place and company instantly forgettable, and it's a repeat of the Little Island story. The first invoice paid, then a declining scale. By this time, I had decided this contract would be my swansong as a roofer. We completed the job and I had the site manager sign that all works had been completed to his satisfaction. Then into Brian Taylor's office. One morning in the Four Courts, I was the plaintiff in two separate actions: Burke, Higgins and McNulty and this last company. Standing in the brilliant light under its mighty dome, the barrister retained by Brian Taylor told me Burke, Higgins and McNulty had been declared bankrupt. The other company paid in full. It was a great anti-climax. I was hoping the case would be heard and I'd have an opportunity to say something about how these would-be business people operated. Perhaps the judge might even don the black cap and hang some of them.

My trouble with these two companies caused severe financial embarrassment at home. The worst we ever had. One Saturday morning in the supermarket, Sheila and I found we had 20p between us. Sheila presumed I'd been paid. We had no credit card and no bank account at the time.

Father-in-law rode to the rescue. To this day, I don't know of a more humbling experience. Many years later in circumstances I can't recall, Sheila and I went walkabout in the back streets between Dame Street and Westmoreland Street. We were checking out pawnshops to put a value on Sheila's few pieces of jewellery. We came home disgusted and angry at what they offered for what to us was equivalent to the Crown Jewels.

Chapter 44 - Back To The Future

My abject failure as a businessman was now fully reinforced by my failure as a roofing contractor, what have I to lose? I thought I'd see if the Department of Posts and Telegraphs would take a chance on me. They did. Guess my job title? I'm a quasi-temporary labourer. Back to where I was, twenty five years earlier. My British Telecom rank and training along with my City and Guilds' certificates count for nothing. I thought my driving credentials would impress. No use to them, I was told. Exactly what was said to me when I showed my Irish driving licence in the UK. I'm ordered to go to Navan for a driving test which would allow me to drive a small van, the same category as a car. Later, when I volunteered to drive the much bigger gang truck for the extra allowance, my British PSV/HGV licence wasn't acceptable. I would need to complete the P&T driving course and test. In total, from my original course in Dublin in 1954, I have now successfully completed five driving courses and five tests. On my first morning in the Pheonix Park, my tutor saw I could drive so for the next two weeks I travelled to Dublin on high substitution, travelling time and travelling expenses. Each day, we toured Dublin from Howth to Rathfarnham, from Bray to Swords, and visited all the places we both wanted to see.

Leaving the world of self-employment and joining the Department of Posts and Telegraphs was a leap both dramatic and traumatic. Self-employment is about working long hard hours, being alert to every opportunity to improve your position, and taking full advantage of any opening that comes your way. In the P&T, any suggestion, opportunity or possibility for change or improvement was alien. Any act that delayed progress, obstructed work, wasted time (including sabotage) was commended. As far as flexibility, adaptability and adjusting to change goes, for me, my new life in the P&T. was the final frontier. And the truth is, I never quite made it.

But "quite" is the operative word here because it is not entirely a tale of woe. But first the bad bit. For many employees, work was an obscene four-letter word, and I, in trying to convince myself I wasn't a complete moral coward, never stopped trying to prove otherwise. For these people, I was a freak of nature that must be resisted. This meant rows were common. But to be fair, there were also some excellent people and I did have friends.

Rules, regulations, procedures and form-filling were precisely the same as in the UK and there were so many people I met each day who were clones of people I knew in British Telecom. Overall taking a positive view, my income, low though it was, was never in doubt. Half a loaf etc.

Chapter 45 - Scouts and Community Council

By this time, we are well settled in to our new home in Laytown, County Meath, and had made friends locally, and what most struck me was their belief in self-help. The economy was in a state and national morale could hardly have been lower, but there was a great interest in doing or creating something, especially for young people.

So in the autumn of 1976, I and a group of like-minded people met in Pat Collins house where we decided to form Scout and Girl Guide troops. As we got organised, the numbers wanting to join was much higher than anticipated, so we ended up with two large scout groups as well as cubs, brownies and girl guides. We were all very happy with this as we had ample adult volunteers.

While this kind of community activity is highly motivational, even inspirational, it's all needed because of the great demands it makes on volunteers' time. A programme needs to be prepared for each weekly meeting. Then planning for, and taking part in a lot of outdoor activities such as treks and hikes over weekends, annual camps and even an international jamboree.

At the same time, I'd joined the Civil Defence and was attending night classes in Drogheda. With the outdoor activities, the emphasis was on survival skills. This meant lighting a fire, no matter the weather. The challenge always was – get a fire going, so we can cook something. It was sacrilegious for anyone to suggest we'd carry any means of cooking. Even in the worst weather we lit our fires in the open and sat around them eating what we had cooked, and sang our scout songs. As the wind whipped stinging wood smoke and ash in our faces. Anyone returning home without watery, red bloodshot eyes and a good strong, smell of wood smoke was unworthy of the title "scout"

In today's world, most of what we were about would be regarded as reckless and endangering young peoples' lives. I remember one weekend, when we decided to cross the Cooley peninsula from Ravensdale, near Dundalk, to the Youth Hostel on Carlingford lough, on the northern side. The all-important point of this exercise was to prove to ourselves that compass bearings would take us to precisely where we wanted to get to, and we would follow these bearings faithfully, as the crow flies. No easy way for us, no strolling along well-known pathways. The trouble with this was that it took us along some really difficult, indeed hazardous terrain. And then at the last minute, the other leader who was to accompany me, dropped out. I found myself alone with 25-30 boys, aged between ten and fourteen.

We started by scrambling up through some woodland which was easy enough but as we got higher, moving forward became increasingly more difficult. Above the tree line, we found ourselves battering through a dense thicket of heather, bracken and whin. Next, lay treacherous patches of marsh and bog, which though difficult enough, we were coping with it. The real danger was the camouflaged deep gulleys and narrow ravines that were everywhere. The entire mountain side was a series of traps for us.

After a few hours of climbing, stumbling and falling, we stopped, lit our fires, and ate our sausages, beans and toast. Each boy found a comfortable spot in the heather. It's time for me to count heads, and all the time close to panic, thinking how simple it would be for any one of the boys to tumble into one of the deep gulleys. I am one short. I count again. There's one missing. I know who it is - it's Myles - the smallest in the troop. He's carrying the same pack as bigger boys so this adventure is more difficult for him and he is scarred by more than his share of cuts and grazes – but not once did he complain. Still, I am increasingly concerned. He may not make it and if our little warrior doesn't, none of us will. I roar at the other boys to find Myles. I'll never forget the feeling of euphoria replacing my fear and alarm as we find him just a short distance away on his own. There he is tucking into his sausage and beans but completely hidden by the heather and bracken.

We continue tripping and falling on this compass bearing for another four hours. The boys are tired and starting to complain, and my morale is sinking. As we reach the top of each high point, all we see ahead of us is an even higher ridge. Well into the afternoon, I start to worry. When will we see Carlingford Lough? Are we going to make it before dark? At last, at long last, after one final anxious, energy sapping scramble over a ridge, we are looking down instead of up.

Looking down far below is a sight which I promise surpasses anything I've ever seen. The sun is sinking behind us, so we are in the deep, almost dark shade of the mountain. The lake far below, long and narrow, like a fjord is bathed in brilliant late evening sunlight. It is a glorious afternoon and there are many sailing boats with brightly coloured white and red sails, looking like giant butterflies resting on the still shimmering surface. On the other side, the perfect backdrop - rising steeply to the sky are the green wooded slopes around Rostrevor, County Down. It's a giant painting. There is a fringe of houses along the lakeshore and more dot the hillsides. It's a brilliantly lit natural amphitheatre, on a vast scale. What a welcoming spectacle this was, and best of all, we had proven the compass worked. Our last bearing took us right onto a bridge over a small stream at the foot of the mountain.

On another scout trip, we decided on a weekend in the Youth Hostel in Glendalough, County Wicklow. We caught a bus from Dublin to Ashford. Soon after taking our seats, it started to snow. When we got off the bus in Ashford, the snow was perhaps ten inches deep, and still snowing, although not as heavily as earlier. Our original plan was to take the old mountain road to Glendalough. But this snow is a challenge. Will we hike along the main road? It's much shorter and less risky. Or will we take the old road through the hills? Our intrepid young warriors are not for taking the easy route, we took to the hills. Each one has a backpack which is a significant burden on a long hike.

Trekking from Ashford, the road climbs steadily and the higher we got, the deeper the snow becomes - it's now twelve to fifteen inches deep. Through the hills, there isn't a sign of life. Livestock have been taken indoors so the fields are empty. We haven't seen a living soul in hours. We have the road entirely to ourselves. Trampling along, single file, those in front will ache most as they sink into the deep snow, then drag each foot out for the next step. Progress was slow and after several energy sapping hours, everyone was tired and hungry. At one point, we stopped by a hay barn near a farmyard and were tempted to make our beds there. This appealed to some, but for others, hay barns and pleasant dreams did not go together.

We finally arrived in Glendalough, just after dark, aching and exhausted. The Youth Hostel held a surprise for us. The scout troop that were due to leave, to make way for us, were marooned by the deep snow and ice. That night, there wasn't the physical space for us all to lie down. All the beds and bunks, the bedroom floors, along the corridors, even the kitchen floor, were a mass of bodies. But after our epic endurance test, in Wicklow's Arctic snowfields, no-one had any trouble sleeping.

The years pass, all our scouts grew up and leave Laytown. Frequently I wondered what impressions, if any, their experiences in the Scout troop made on them. Did they gain or benefit in any way? Indeed, I worried they might be resentful, some of our exploits took place in harsh - even atrocious - weather conditions. At times, I felt guilty about some of the situations we found ourselves in.

Over time, the call of home brought them back, and one by one I met them again - at the local church, in the street, the last one just stepped out of a crowd in the supermarket. Each one, without exception, recalled the exploits and reminded me with such sincerity and enthusiasm all that happened on our camps and hikes and telling me these were some of the most interesting things they'd ever experienced.

The youth group's success lifts spirits locally and optimism grows that we can do even more for ourselves. The talk now is of forming a community council. So after the usual endless toing-and-froing, meetings and secret conclaves, Laytown and Bettystown Community Council was born, lustily, in the Autumn of 1981. It was maintained by the same constitution and organisational framework as similar bodies elsewhere. The locality was divided into fourteen identifiable segments with two representatives elected from each one. From the point of view of self-help, this is the perfect model and could hardly have come at a better time. Unemployment was high and rising rapidly. By 1984, it would reach 17.2% and we were paying 17% interest on our mortgage. My job as PRO was to promote the best possible image of the Community Council. To achieve this, I became involved in the various environmental issues locally such as anti-litter campaigns, but my two most important projects were tree-planting and the neighbourhood watch scheme.

Our tree-planting started each year with a day designated as 'Arbor Day'. The plan was for people to adopt a tree. A tree would be planted outside someone's house, and they, in turn, would commit to look after it. Our first year's planting, however, was along the boundary of our local school. All our plans were finalised. Trees delivered, many spades and shovels promised and at the ready. On the Saturday when this climactic event was to take place, no-one turned up. The promised spades and shovels didn't show.

Into the breach, stepped the Coyle clan - that is my teenage children, Anne, James and Paul. I was told nothing would grow in this area so we planted several species in the border along the road fronting the school – Silver Birches, Oak, Scots Pine and Rowan. All grew to magnificent maturity. Unfortunately, many years later in the interests of "Health and Safety" when the road was being re-aligned to provide bus bays and a drop off zone, they were all cut down.

From this bad start, enthusiasm did grow and over the years we planted several hundred trees all over the area: Beach Park, Beach Grove, in the centre of Laytown village, the Golf Course, St Nicholas Village, Marion Villas along the railway line, amongst others.

The neighbourhood watch scheme would surely be one of the best crime prevention measures available to people, and for so little trouble and expense. All you had to do was talk to your neighbour and have an arrangement to look out for each other. We provided stickers for windows that warned would-be thieves and we had a stencilling service so that people could mark all their valuables with their own secret identification code.

This Community Council is dynamic and ambitious and we started producing a newsletter called the Link. It's the best possible way to promote what you hope to achieve. There was a monthly print of a thousand copies which we distributed to the 980 odd households in the Laytown and Bettystown area. At the time of writing, it is roughly four times this number.

Without doubt, each year's highlight was Festival Week. We had a grand opening parade from Bettystown Square to Laytown with bands playing and flags waving, followed by our colourful, proud Scout troops and Cubs, Girl Guides and Brownies. On the green in Laytown there was a funfair with traditional music and dancing. Then throughout a great range of events, sports, arts and crafts, plays in the Parochial Hall, pub entertainment, pub quizzes, pitch and putt, fashion shows and perhaps most entertaining: round the houses cycling races, while on the beach: football competitions, mini marathons, and mountain bike obstacle races.

Our AGMs were always a great source of amusement, strife and argument.

It seemed to me that an AGM was where many people who would do nothing assembled to attack those who were trying. At the time, I used to go out for a walk every night. At one meeting, I was attacked for patrolling in my own area at night – but not bothering about where other people lived.

So many people thought that Neighbourhood Watch had a vigilante aspect to it, but I was simply enjoying my nightly stroll.

The year I was elected Secretary, my good friend, Mossy McKenna, who was Chairman, arrived in the Neptune Hotel with the Minute Book which he had picked up from our outgoing Secretary. A few minutes before we started, I opened it to check the minutes of the previous AGM. There weren't any. Time for a quick decision. I did a spirited reading of the minutes of the AGM two years earlier, no-one noticed.

In the winter of 1991, two of my brothers died within two months of each other. That marked the end of the Community Council for me. At the time, I thought it was the end of me.

Chapter 46 - Strike Maker

Over time, I moved up the P&T grades and I've graduated to a Renault 4 van. My job is the maintenance of seven manual exchanges within a seven mile radius of Kells. I would repair any fault condition I could. Otherwise, report back to HQ what stores and manpower was needed for all other faults. It was a big area to cover, and a hell of a busy schedule. My Renault 4 was singing on a high note all the time. On my first morning, I left Virginia exchange with sparks flying out of the road to my next call – Oldcastle, five miles away. In no time, I'm there. "What an interesting town" I thought - built around this great, wide, open square. I cruised around looking for the Post Office because the manual exchange will be in the same building. To my consternation, I saw it: Ballyjamesduff Post Office. At first, I thought the girls were playing a hoax, I'm not supposed to be here. It's not on my circuit and over all the years, hearing so many songs about it and all the times we planned to visit, I find myself here by accident. Though I hadn't the time to check out Paddy Reilly, or the stone sat outside Dan Murphy's door.

One morning, before leaving Drogheda in my race to Navan, one of my few friends suggested I should go forward as Communication Worker's Union (CWU) Secretary at the upcoming AGM.

I asked was there one other individual besides himself who would vote for me. He said he knew otherwise. At the meeting, to my astonishment and great sense of guilt, thinking so badly of my colleagues, I was elected.

I'd been on the committee for some time so had some idea of what went on, and as a natural approval seeker, you may now feel, this is a genuine and original masochist. The frying pan isn't good enough - he wants to be roasted alive on the spit. Years earlier, I had read John Fitzgerald Kennedy's book "Profiles in Courage" so my life's mission was to prove to myself that I wasn't the world's greatest moral coward.

The following may provide you with a little window on what customs and practices were routine in the department at the time: a lunch allowance (subsistence) was paid when our worksite was three miles or more from our headquarters. This tax-free allowance went up as the distance from headquarters increased. Everyone invented the most creative devices to gain a greater allowance.

One of these was as follows: if an item was not available in your local stores, you were entitled to travel perhaps twenty or thirty miles to another headquarters to fetch it, and so gain the higher lunch allowance.

In practice, people didn't telephone the remote headquarters before going. So they travelled to the remote headquarters, not knowing if the goods were there or not, just to gain the higher allowance.

At my first meeting with management, along with other union secretaries from neighbouring counties, management had this topic top of their agenda. As mama would say, "Dear God Almighty in heaven above, I just can't defend this." You say, it's easy, this is so blatant. But customs and habits became so established over time, that any change, especially to people's disadvantage, produces seismic reactions, as I was to discover. I'm the new boy and everybody knows I'm a freak. I played all innocent and naïve as if I didn't know anything about this practice. I piped up, "Surely, the sensible thing was to phone ahead before travelling? How could we defend ourselves if this became public?"

There followed a tense, clearing of throats kind of silence, as my union colleagues speared me with withering, murderous looks. No-one said a word. Management were obviously very pleased. It was agreed. In future, no travelling until it was established the stores needed were available.

A few days later, I wheeled off the main road at high speed and shot through the entrance of Navan's headquarters. Two individuals with placards dived to either side. Inside, I asked someone "What the two eejits were doing with the strike placards?"

He said it was a strike picket to prevent me collecting stores. A meeting had been held the previous evening and the men were incensed at my "pro-management attitude". By all accounts, I was taking money out of their pockets and food from their children's mouths. They thought I was a genuine and original trouble maker, especially now having run down the picket at the entrance.

When I spoke to the Navan secretary, he said a majority voted for this, and there was nothing he could do. I went to the stores to book out what I needed, not in the least expecting that a reception was prepared for me. The men had all gathered there, like in a Wild West saloon. As I opened the door, I was greeted by an icy sullen silence. A dozen pairs of eyes drilling into me. It was as if I had just released my holster straps, loosened my six shooters and was ready to open fire and blast anything that moved. The baddie had arrived in town so they would show him he wasn't welcome. Some I spoke to didn't respond.

The group self-reinforcing mentality has taken hold. All of them couldn't possibly be wrong. All agreed I had committed a foul deed, a hanging offence, and I must pay for it. I began reading my list to the store man, "Batteries?"

"No."

"Switchboard cords?"

"No."

"Bulbs?"

"No".

I departed the stores for the canteen and phoned around the other Branch secretaries. All said the picket on the gate and the store man's attitude was mad. All the men had now left the yard for their worksites. I went back to the stores. I can confront the store man now he's on his own. He brought me in to check his stock cards. He genuinely didn't have what I wanted.

As I burned the rubber going out the gate in my rally car, I mean Renault 4, I was feeling quite pleased. An hour ago, I thought my tenure as secretary would be short. Now that the other branches support me, it's not Thermopylae - yet it's a small victory for reason.

Although a bit battered, I survived my first year. The next AGM comes up and I put my name forward again, not out of any sense of duty, mind, only to prove my moral courage. I was half hoping I'd be defeated. Wonder of wonders, I'm re-elected and history of another kind is being made. The functions of the combined Departments of Posts and Telegraphs are being split into two entirely separate semi-state bodies: "Telegraghs" becomes "Telecom Eireann", while "Posts" becomes "An Post".

In the midst of all the excitement and euphoria, Telecom Eireann announces it will publish a monthly magazine and invites applications from its 21,000 employees for the position of Environmental Correspondent. The application would be in the form of an article of less than a thousand words. I sent in my piece and got the job. The going rate was 10p a word - not an insignificant amount at the time.

A shortened Version of My Winning Article:

The environment is where we all live, work and play. It's the air we breathe, the water we drink and the food we eat. Our environment therefore, very largely determines our quality of life and the state of our health and well-being. Yet, any widespread interest in an issue so vitally important to us all is of fairly recent origin. This dawning awareness of the close relationship between man and his environment is timely because much can still be done to learn from and correct past mistakes. And so ensure a healthier future for the generations to come.

One area where great harm has been done in the past and still continues is water pollution. Nature has endowed us with an ample supply of clean water and since it is so vital to life, it must be regarded as a precious natural resource. Yet the streams and rivers which supply us with 75% of our water, we also use as drains and carriers of all kinds of wastes and frequently as dumps. In 1989, there were 111 fish kills and what kills fish and gets into the food chain in this way also threatens human health. The remaining 25% of our water comes from underground sources, known as aquifers. There is serious pollution here also, mainly from nitrates and chemicals due to intensive farming methods. But also, and increasingly so, due to sewage leaching from the country's 100,000 septic tanks.

So increasingly in people's minds is anxiety about which is worse, the disease or the cure. Because as our water becomes more polluted, so greater quantities of chemicals are used to clean and disinfect it – more carbon, chlorine, lime, aluminium, sulphate, fluorine etc. Bottled water is not treated with these chemicals, hence the market for a product that would have been a joke a few years ago.

Whilst I personally believe our health is at risk, either from the polluting or cleansing chemicals in our water, the picture is less clear with chemicals in our food. But as with water, there is a level of fear that all is not well. This is due to fairly widespread knowledge of what takes place with intensive growing methods. An apple tree for example, will be spayed several times annually for pests and diseases. Chemicals will also be used to promote growth, improve the colour and shelf life of the fruit. So people are turning to organically grown produce in the well-founded belief that their health is at risk otherwise. There is also mounting evidence that the whole process of intensive farming is self-defeating anyway because the excessive use of chemical fertilisers creates ecological imbalances that result in enormous increases in pests and crop diseases. Farmers counteract this by spraying ever larger doses of pesticides. But losses due to insects have not decreased, indeed they have greatly increased as they become immune to the chemical sprays.

What we get in packaged food is also an area of great concern. So many of the ingredients listed leave us very perplexed. The synthetic, chemical additives are given an E number and are classified as preservatives, colourings, and flavouring agents. There are seventeen synthetic food dyes in use in Ireland; there are 3,200 flavouring substances without any regulation or control. Some countries ban these colourings completely. So clearly, they believe there is some risk involved in their use.

Our environment is steadily getting more complex, so increased vigilance is required of the relevant authorities if we are to prevent long-lasting damage to our delicate habitat. Remember products such as DDT which were so highly promoted for thirty years are now banned. The story is the same with asbestos which we are now told may remain dormant for 25 years.

As the above issues with a worldwide dimension make headline news, nearer home we have major environmental problems of our own. We have widespread public disregard for the laws on pollution. And a litter problem which is a national disgrace. Last year, only nineteen of all the beaches in the country earned a Blue Flag, the symbol of recognition that minimum standards laid down by the EEC were met and this list goes on and on.

As a major public utility we have a direct impact on our environment. Yet it is indicative of our own level of awareness that we have nothing to offer for "European Year of the Environment" which ended in March 1988.

Let's remind ourselves that we are the communicators especially so with regards to the means. Awareness of the damage caused to our quality of life is lacking and Telecom has immense potential to inform, enlighten and influence change company wise, nationally and individually. This can be done by utilising all our existing channels of communication with the community at large. We must show that a high quality environment compliments and enhances finely tuned technology and highly developed business acumen.

Many benefits would accrue to us all by our taking on this extra dimension to our role in serving the community. We must not ignore this area of vital national concern. A start must be made. Now is the opportune time.

A Sample Article I Wrote Published In the Telecom Magazine:

The Ancient Art of Water Divining

"Behold I will stand there before thee, upon the rock Horeb and thou shalt strike the rock with the rod and water will come out of it, that the people may drink".

This quotation from Exodus would appear to give some credence to the belief that Moses was the first water diviner and that this art was divinely ordained. Further reading however, tells of drawings from early Egypt showing figures in strange headgear carrying at arm's length in front of them – a forked stick. And Emperor Kwang Su of China is depicted in a statue dated 2,200 BC carrying an identical object. Both it seems were in search of water.

The forked stick cut from a tree such as hazel, rowan or willow and held out in front of the body parallel to the ground is the classical method of dowsing or water divining. When a source is located the stick moves in various ways and from these movements the diviner can tell the depth and quantity of water present. Other instruments in use include metal rods, copper wire, walking sticks, pitchforks, pendulums and Tom Graves in his Dowser's Workbook advises the beginner to start with two L shaped sections cut from your common or garden wire coat hanger.

While finding water is what diviners are best known for, they also claim to be able to find just about anything and are frequently called in by the authorities to help locate missing persons, buried treasure, criminals and even dead bodies. In Vietnam, the US army used diviners to find booby traps and buried shells and in Russia they prospect for lead, gold and zinc deposits, underground cables, pipelines and of course water.

In helping to locate missing persons or bodies the diviners will use a large scale map of the area, a tiny pendulum with a hollow bob at the end of which will contain some item or personal belonging of the person to be found, he will track back and forth across the map very slowly and meticulously until the pendulum is drawn to or circles the spot where the search should take place.

In Ireland the diviner is first on the scene when there is a water supply problem; the hydrologist from the geological survey would be a poor second. Years ago at home in County Monaghan, I remember the diviner arriving on a particularly wet day. The preceding days had also been very wet. The countryside was awash as this man patrolled back and forth for some considerable time through streams and rivers of rainwater. A sceptic could be forgiven for thinking that all this was in the area of sheer farce. How could he possibly locate our much prayed for well in the midst of so much water? Eventually he settled on a spot just behind the hen house and there just like Moses we struck the rock, only we used crowbars, sledges and steel wedges. Twelve feet down, we found an excellent supply that has stood the test of time and right through the driest summers when our neighbour's wells ran dry.

The literature on the subject abounds with examples of the diviner's success and they are employed worldwide by major water companies. How it works, however, is very much an open question. Tests show that no matter how carefully screened the diviner is, with steel plates or lead armour, the rods will respond. Powerful magnets strapped on operator's backs have no effect, although rubber and leather gloves kills the response altogether. It is suggested that whatever the force may be, it cannot work on the rod alone. A human being has to act as middleman/woman (women have a 40% higher success rate than men). The response is much greater if the underground water is moving and since our bodies are 80% water, it is said that a reaction occurs when one moving body of water intersects another. There are also vague ideas on resonance and radiation. Nothing is known about what forces are at work where the diviner is using a map to locate missing persons. It seems that in this instance the force is all in the mind and is perhaps a case of not so much "seeing is believing" as believing strongly enough may indeed result in seeing.

Chapter 47 - A Quiet and Holy Life

In March 1966, I took early retirement from Telecom. With my future now behind me I had only one thought. No more, never again will I get involved with anyone, any group or organisation of any kind. This way I will avoid all possibility of rows, arguments or disputes. I would do the garden and just enjoy a quiet and holy life, "far from the madding crowd's ignoble strife". After a little while, niggling unsettling little thoughts came to mind of two things I'd wanted to do for some time. One was write something for Radio Eireann's "Sunday Miscellany" and the other was public speaking. So I joined a creative writing group in Drogheda and a Toastmaster's International Club in Malahide. I was confident there wasn't the remotest possibility of trouble among these gentle, self-effacing artists.

I thought I was joining a writing class – it wasn't. The group all aspiring writers met casually once a week in a Union office on the North Quay. A few had some success, others had experience in theatre and one was Young Playwright of the Year in 1994. The format was to write a piece on a theme chosen at each meeting. At the next meeting each would read out their work and anyone who wanted to or indeed nobody would give their personal evaluation of it. This worked for a time in a harmless, amusing sort of way. Eventually we came to the conclusion we should organise properly, raise money and then we could pay a tutor.

So we advertised a public meeting, our first AGM. I was ad hoc chairman, voting started. The first person elected, our new chairperson was someone I thought of as the group's alpha female. She was domineering. But then as the election of officers and committee was completed, there were would be alpha males amongst them and they fiercely resented our new chairperson. I kept well clear, I knew my place.

However, despite the trouble and strife major work was undertaken over the following year. Our biggest job was a short story and poetry competition offering thousands in prize money. We advertised in every newspaper and magazine published in Ireland. The response was overwhelming. We all had to give long hours in processing the entries. Meanwhile, we continued with our own work. Still we didn't get a tutor. But from time to time we had successful authors at our meetings who we all knew would guide and lead us along the road to greatness and undying fame and fortune, maybe even celebrity status. We also entered competitions and sent in our pieces to Sunday Miscellany. This created a spiteful rivalry among ourselves, each one striving to be first to get some little bit published or win something. A year passes and our alpha female exhausted by the endless struggles departed. Peace reigns, we have a new chairman, I'm secretary. We continue with our poetry and short story competitions, and then finally I get my hands on the reins of power. Now I'll be able to demonstrate the art of conciliation and compromise.

I nominate an excellent lady member and friend as secretary. She's elected. Five or six weeks later I get a phone call. It's our secretary. She's resigning, she's leaving a letter with the caretaker and I am to read it at our next committee meeting. She's asking me to volunteer to hang myself. In it she said she resented being gagged by me at meetings and not being allowed to speak her mind. She no longer wished to work with people who didn't believe in free speech!

That night I nominate another lady member I admired. She's elected. A few weeks later we had a public meeting at which we expect to recruit new members. We begin and I'm in full flow telling these strangers what a life transforming event it will be for them if they join. Just as I'm thinking how well I'm doing, this individual (one of our members) stands up and says he disagrees with something I've said. In keeping with Robert's rules of procedure as he gets up, I sat down. I thought what a crass and ignorant thing to do with the general public present. At the start of our next Committee meeting, I am well primed to retaliate. I ask him for an explanation. My new secretary, face flaming with anger accuses me of starting another row and storms out. You may well say losing one secretary is bad enough, losing two in as many months is downright careless and especially my own nominees!

As for the quiet life, it seems the more we strive for the perfect world, the greater will be our disappointment.

Chapter 48 – Sunday Miscellany

Short Story Submitted To RTE Radio 1 Sunday Miscellany Programme:

From Tobin's Cottage to O'Malley's Barn

It's early morning and I'm sitting at the kitchen table looking towards the east coast. Just off the beach perched precariously on a rocky outcrop I can see Tobin's Cottage. Small, thatched and whitewashed, it looks fragile and vulnerable behind its shield of giant boulders. If I look over my left shoulder, I can see the massive curves of O'Malley's red roofed barn. From barn to cottage is just 600m and yet this is the most incredible journey. A journey of 17,000 miles and travelling at a thousand miles per hour takes 17 hours to complete. Each day I am involved in this extraordinary event, knowing my life, my very existence depends on its successful completion.

It begins in the most inauspicious way. There is no rousing clarion call; no stirring roll of drums, no great crowd is gathered, waiting with bated breath. Those who by chance are near at hand who might be inspired, enthralled, stunned into quiet meditation or even silent prayer at the awesome moment that presages this epic journey, pass on their way hardly noticing.

Now quietly, silently but radiating fierce some power, an incandescent orb of fire appears just behind the cottage and for a few minutes, it disappears as if consumed in the dazzling inferno. Slowly, the cottage emerges and the sun is on its way once more on its epic journey westwards as it has for the past five billion years. We can plunder the lexicographer's store for superlatives to describe the sun or its place in our lives but our finest words barely hint at what is truly the source of all creation.

At a distance of 93 million miles and burning 600 million tons of hydrogen every second. This hell-like holocaust is the origin, the source and the sole progenitor of all life on planet earth, animal and vegetable and should the cataclysmic events that keep it burning, shut down for the briefest period, then our fragile little home would in a very short time become an utter wasteland of rock and ice, lost in the inky blackness of space. Should we wonder that all the great civilisations of old worshipped the sun? Or that the Mediterranean area was the cradle of today's science, philosophy and architecture? For anywhere blessed with its abundance, it not only creates, it enlivens and inspires.

Now as it clears the roof of Tobin's cottage, a rolling wave of radiant light sweeps inland. This is the quietest, the most gentle of wake-up calls, a call back to life for untold and uncounted living things. This is re-creation indeed. The night has passed and there is a new day to be celebrated.

The mysterious, the inexplicable but beautiful dance of life continues for at least one more day. The lowly, humble daisy smiles, the haughty osteospermum resplendent in magenta, not only opens it petals but keeps its face to the sun all day as it tracks it across the heavens, Likewise, the stately extravert sunflower.

As the radiation increases, so does the tempo of the dance. Creature's sensitive to light and heat are animated. Bees reacting to a single degree change become active at 54 degrees Fahrenheit. Humans are comfortable at 61. In the warmth of the sun, all life celebrates and proclaims its life. But in keeping with its timeless, cosmic rhythm the sun is now setting behind O'Malley's barn. Light, the lifeblood of all things drains away. There is an ominous stillness, a sense of foreboding. Is this darkness a harbinger of oblivion and doom? The sunflowers' glowing yellow petals turn inwards, hiding its purple heart. Its head is bowed and half turned away as if in sadness or is it fear and despair? Does it sense the impermanence of all things? The sun was born from the remnants of another exploded star.

Might this night be the last night? The start of eternal night? Or will another day come and the sun once more lead the dance with another glorious dawn?

Chapter 49 - Toastmasters:

So often I've wished I'd been a grandparent before being a parent. It seemed a great store of knowledge and wisdom in the art of childrearing had come thirty years too late.

It was a bit like this joining Toastmasters at sixty, learning skills that would have been crucially important indeed a major asset, forty years earlier. At sixty, I thought I'd be the granddaddy of the club. In Ireland with a young population, sixty isn't old, it's very old. But I wasn't old in my head, I had the same thoughts, feelings and beliefs I had at forty. Perhaps this is why nobody wants to die. Mentally, there isn't a tipping point in your head that signals "Your time has come, life no longer holds anything of the tiniest interest or value to you. Hope itself must now be abandoned." Other sixty year olds in the club were of the same mind. All bright-eyed and yes, even keener than the forty year olds to have a bash at this public speaking.

The membership was a cross section of the community, working and retired school teachers, working and retired business people, two doctors, a barrister and a diplomat. All had one thing in common, belief in the power of the spoken word along with a great fear of performing before an audience.

And each had a story of humiliating embarrassment before an audience, indeed a near death experience from the past and a horror it might happen again.

The experts say it's one of our worst fears. Many people confessing they'd rather die than speak in public. So I suppose you could say we were determined to cheat death by doing our speeches before we died or die in the attempt! And the word is not misplaced. It's used by all public performers to describe what happens during a performance when the mind goes completely blank. This is how it happened to me.

In public speaking good eye contact with your audience is vitally important. This night about a year after I joined I'm well into my speech. I'm going from face to face around the room. Now I turn to the top table where our President and Chairperson are sitting. The President is sitting next to me at the podium, the Chairperson, in order to see me is leaning back in her chair to see past the President. Turning from our President to her, I see a look of horror. Her bottom jaw has dropped, mouth wide open, wide-eyed as if terror stricken. I wanted my speech to create a powerful impact, but not as powerful as this! I stopped dead and I didn't say a word for the rest of the night. I looked out with a blank, blind stare to my audience, I knew why I was there but my speech and every last tiny clue of what is was about had vanished. I turned to my cue cards but saw nothing. All that I was capable of thinking was – how quiet the place was.

I'm up here on my own and everyone else down there is gawking up at me. I thought I'd rather be sitting down there with them, and that's what I did. I was told – it happens to everyone and that I'd get over it. Indeed you do, but never completely. The horror of it happening again lingers on.

I had one more embarrassing incident but not nearly as bad as the last. Each year, serious and humorous speech competitions are held. This year I was asked to enter the humorous speech competition. I won. And of the many things that have given wonderful satisfaction over the years, this ranks near the top. Writing and performing my own humorous speech was a challenge, something I'd never dreamt of doing, and then on the night, getting such a great reaction from the audience was magical. It had a profound effect. I started planning right away for the following year. The title of my speech was "Panic at the Podium". It was a send up of all the advice for women for calming nerves on speech night and applying it to men. I began with the advice of taking a few deeps breaths just before speaking. I said "the state of my nerves was such I thought a few deep breaths – good, a lot more, even better, so I started deep breathing early in the afternoon of the day of my speech. By the time I got to the club, I'd been hyperventilating for four hours! And so on but giving a twist on the advice for women to do with wardrobe, hair, make-up etc. and as it might apply to men! Judging by the audience's reaction to all the speeches, I was convinced I'd won. The chairperson announced the winners in reverse order.

With third and second gone, I'm just waiting for my name to be called. He announces "And so our winner tonight is…….long pause…….but too long! I'm on my feet, but it's not me, someone else is called.

Still this was a fairly minor faux pas. And I continued with the humorous speeches. My best effort was based on the RAF medical mentioned earlier. This won the area contest which comprises clubs in the North, County and Dublin city region.

I was in the club fifteen years, did all the various jobs and many speeches. And after all that time, I never felt I was getting anywhere near what is achievable. Irrespective of what job, career or profession you're in, you will gain hugely from being a more effective communicator. I know of no better way to do this than through the Toastmaster's programme.

Samples of My Humorous Toastmaster's Speeches:
Alternative Medicine

These days our Health Service is in the news a lot and there is endless debate about whether or not we have a two tier service. In the Monaghan of my childhood, we also had Health Service tiers but ours wasn't so much a two tier service, it was more a tearful service! This was because one of its main elements was castor oil. For mama, this was the ultimate cure-all; medicine's much sought after magic bullet.

After fifty years, I can still recall its nauseous taste and smell, yet its healing properties were remarkable if not miraculous. So often when someone complained, mama would say "Just you wait till I get the castor oil?". On hearing this, the cringing sufferer would cry out in a tone of barely suppressed horror that a complete cure had taken place that very instant. And we had a wonderful backup to castor oil to treat more severe conditions. This was our red-flannel treatment. This involved placing sections of red flannel over the affected area. However, as with modern drugs, this treatment could have unfortunate not to say embarrassing side effects. I discovered this one day at school, standing in front of the class reciting "The Village Schoolmaster". I had just got to the point where it says "Well had the boarding tremblers learned to trace the day's disasters in his morning face".

Well, my personal disaster was taking place and it would certainly show in my face. My red flannel had decided to migrate and was inching its tormenting way down the leg of my short trousers. I felt the warm, gentle agonising caress of each little slip until it fell in a crumpled little heap at my feet. My mortification was complete when my sweetheart said that my face was now as red as the flannel.

Now while castor oil was a simple remedy of the many conditions affecting a reluctant scholar, our cure for mumps was sophistication itself.

This procedure as you will see had to take place outside after dark and we didn't have electricity at the time. So mama had to light up the old smelly paraffin oil lantern. Then we all moved out into the dark farmyard. There, an asses hames would be placed around the sick child's neck and the rest of us would form up in a line behind – conga style. Now, with mama leading the child by the hames and holding up the blinking lantern that threatened to expire with the slightest breeze, we made our way to the pigsty, chanting:

Mucna, mucna, seo chugat do leicne,

Leicne, leicne, seo chugat do mhucna

We then circled the pigsty three times, now chanting in a much lower tone, since as the verse suggests we hoped to transfer the symptoms to them while they slept. But if there was some angry squealing, this could be taken as a sign that we were successful and they were showing their bitter resentment. It was always thought that aromatherapy was the most potent aspect of this cure and I think anyone here who has danced three times around a pigsty in semi-darkness would surely agree. And it was a very successful procedure because no one ever needed a repeat, at least they didn't ask for it anyway.

But perhaps the ultimate remedy for us was that fiery by-product of the humble potato-poteen. Not only was it used as a soothing rub for every ache and pain, it was taken as a medicine for all manner of conditions, then when you recovered it was the most potent of tipples with which to celebrate with your friends. And the best part was, if you took too much and got sick, well then you'd only have to take a little more, this time as a medicine mind, to make you well again.

However, some uses were just beyond its powers. Like the time when my father feeling in need of renewal discovered his life giving bottle almost empty. His consternation was relieved when mama said she'd been throwing a liberal skite of it over us each day as we went out to school. She thought it was her holy water! And I suppose in a way it was.

So each day as we strode out valiantly to school with castor oil in our bellies, red flannel on our chests, and with a good skite of poteen over us, we knew we were well fortified against anything the elements or the cruel world could throw at us!

What's In a Name?

It's the sweetest sound in all the world, our own name. And we are all very attached to our names. Rarely do we hear of anyone changing their names, no matter how odd, curious, or even comical names are, people will stick with them. On the other hand, for some their names could be a distinct advantage. Like the dentist called Phil McCavity, but perhaps not for the solicitor names Lawless. Hardly ever, does anyone admit to disliking their Christian name. But I had a girlfriend once who hated hers. Her name was Cynthia but people always shortened it to "Cyn". So I didn't like it much either, for that reason. People would refer all the time to me and Cyn. and socially they would say things like "Are you still with sin?" To which I'd answer "Well yes, but I am determined to mend my ways". I wouldn't mind so much but sin wasn't anything like as popular then as it is now. And all this went on to such an extent that me and sin were practically synonymous.

Then I was invited to meet her parents. Her father asked me what plans I had for the future. I said "Cyn had been such an important part of my life for so long, I simply couldn't contemplate the future without it, I mean her!" In the end though, we went our separate ways and I've been sinless ever since!

Now think of the author conjuring with names for characters. It's as if the name creates the character. We hear the name and then in our heads form a personality that goes with it. Now I wonder did Ian Fleming consider Irish names for his super agent James Bond or for his arch villains? Think of it this way, instead of Monsieur Scaramanga, could he have used, say Michael O'Reilly? Or for Hans Angel Mandraco, how about Sean Mulligan? And it's hard to imagine that Doctor Ernst Stavro Bloefeld could be substituted with Paddy Murphy? We know it just wouldn't work, villains have villainous names and there is menace and foreboding just in the sound of these names. And as for Bond, well why not Eamon or indeed Seamus?

Now imagine one of those nightmarish situations Bond found himself in.

He has rung the gauntlet of the man-eating sharks and the piranha infested pond. He's reached the heart of the wolf's liar, his position is desperate, and Scaramanga tortures him to within an inch of his life and demands he reveals his identity. To save his manhood Bond relents. "Alright, I submit, I submit. Release me. I confess. My name's Bond, Seamus Bond!"

When Scaramanga and Odd job hear this, they would surely fall about the place with laughter knowing that someone called Seamus couldn't possibly be any threat to them. Seamus is a name for poets and storytellers, not killers.

They'd throw their arms around him and plead for his forgiveness, especially for all the piranha bites and having pulled out his fingernails. And yet, while knowing that someone called Seamus couldn't possibly be a killer, they'd realise that he would not be averse to other aspects of a secret agent's work. I suppose what we could call extra-curricular activity. Later, sending Seamus happily on his way, Scaramanga would make him promise that as soon as his finger nails grew back and the shark bites healed, he'd call back and they'd have great craic torturing some genuine secret agent with a real spy's name.

This connection between a name and a personality also holds true in reality. For most of history's worst tyrants had cruel threatening names like Hitler, Attila the Hun and Genghis Khan. There's the sound of battle and suffering on a continental scale just in that name.

Now suppose he had been given a different name. I mean in that part of the world, he could have been called Tin Khan and then no-one would ever have heard of him. And then we would just laugh at his name, at least I hope we would anyway! He would have spent his entire life on the windswept steppes of Mongolia, milking goats and making cheese. What happened in reality wasn't his fault; he was just given the wrong name!

My Last Toastmaster's Speech:
(Advanced Toastmaster's Programme)
Mr Toastmaster, Ladies and Gentlemen,
All of society's laws, its customs, codes of ethics indeed its entire morality is based totally on the belief that we all have free will. That at all times and in every circumstance, with a few very rare exceptions, we are free agents.

The opposing theory is known as determinism which says that all that we are both physically and intellectually is determined by the interplay of our genes and our environment. This is what I believe and I hope my evidence will convince you also.

I stand here before you tonight ladies and gentlemen a male specimen of humanity. I'm 6ft tall when I'm wearing my very thick winter socks, all that you see, all that I am physically and much more, was determined at the moment of my conception. In that earth shattering, momentous, unparalleled instant in the history of mankind when my father's sperm encountered my mother's egg and with the throw of at least 90,000 genetic dice, I inherited half my father's genes and half my mother's. From my father I got a gene I didn't want giving me white hair at age 30 and a genetic eye defect from my mother. ON the plus side my father died in his 90th year, my mother was 87. So the chances are or I may have a long life. I say "chances" because in this incredible game of genetic dice certain traits in our parents' physical or psychological make-up need not be manifest in us. Genes may remain dormant or unexpressed for one or many generations. So you see even if you could pick your parents, to be certain of success you'd have to select just the most beneficial genes at precisely the moment of conception. And if we could do that then we really would be free.

You can see how genes hit-or-miss in families where one child may be blonde and the rest dark, the milkman is blamed. If on the other hand the odd one out is dark then that would have to be the Coalman (usually completely black from all that coal dust) but if there is a redhead then this really is sinister because we thought of travellers or the travelling community as being mainly redheads.

Now everyone is agreed that physical characteristics are genetically determined, but what about character, personality or behaviour? Large-scale studies in the USA over the past 20 years on identical twins and adopted children – has established that there is a generic component to just about every human trait and behaviour including personality, intelligence and verbal ability. The personality traits of identical twins are remarkably similar, for fraternal twins, it's given as 25 per cent and siblings that are not twins it is 11 per cent and for strangers it's zero.

Most remarkably for identical twins reared apart the studies show that as adults they are just as similar as identical twins reared in the same house. With similar religious inclinations, political leanings, and things such as enthusiasm for arts and crafts. From the twin studies perhaps the most important finding is that intelligence is the most heritable characteristic.

So the evidence is piling up that our generic inheritance is predominant in the nature versus nurture debate. In the right environment our inherited characteristics will be enhanced but without certain innate qualities the environment is of minor importance.

Now while this debate on whether or not we have free will is usually carried on in philosophical or theological circles I thought I'd read up on what psychology might have to offer. On page 446 of the most prestigious American Psychological Association's report it says that "psychology seeks to describe, explain, and predict human behaviour, and also to attempt to control it in certain circumstances".

As a body of scientists they disagree about many aspects of human nature but they all agree that every psychological event has a definite cause and will give rise to a particular effect. That the psychological state of an individual is largely determined by early childhood experiences, later by peer pressure, social conditioning and parental influences. There are over 700 pages of the most searching analysis of how exactly we all come to be as we are, that our behaviour can be explained in terms of our past history and that our characters and personalities are the product of our heredity, education and environment. Psychology also has categories for the differing personality types such as introverts and extroverts, passive, aggressive, impulsive and so on. Remember this is the science of the intellectual giants of the 20th century, the science of Freud, Jung and Adler. How can all this be reconciled with the concept of free will?

However, orthodox psychology does not concern itself with what is regarded as a philosophical question. It is just never mentioned. After all the describing, analysing, explaining, predicting and the categorising there can only be one conclusion. We are all mere pawns in a complex dance of genes and circumstances and any sense of free will we might have is just an illusion.

In the Christian tradition the concept of free will originates with St Thomas Aquinas, but he took much of what Aristotle taught to form a major part of

Christian theology. He believed that free will was implanted in us by God so we always had a choice between good and evil. But the desperate dilemma for the good St Thomas was that there was evil in the world and the source of this evil was people making evil choices. How could an omnipotent and just God bestow a gift that resulted in evil? But the alternative was even more unthinkable. If all our choices were determined by the same omnipotent and just God then there could be no individual responsibility. But this was a harsh, punishing God in the 13th century so free will became the cornerstone of Christian teaching and we would suffer in hell if we made evil choices. Since that time, this question has been the sole preserve of philosophers and the best that can be said is that they are divided and inconclusive.

Philosophers in favour of determinism are Spinoza and Schopenhauer and at the other extreme are the French existentialists Camus and Sartre who utterly and totally reject determinism. But the greatest living philosopher and linguist Noam Chomsky believes that much of what we are is innate and inherited and most importantly I haven't heard of anyone challenging him.

The present state of play is moving inexorably towards determinism. It's led by the evolutionary psychologists such as Richard Hawking, Steven Pinker and Edward O Wilson. These people say that our genes are all that we are. There isn't a choice, an attitude of mind, behaviour or personality trait that doesn't originate with our genetic makeup. And the genome research project is providing new evidence for this almost daily. The latest one is for a gene for shyness, would you believe, there it was all the time on chromosome 9 hiding behind the gene for arrogance!

In your own thoughts about this dilemma remember this, ladies and gentlemen; there are no half-measures here. Either your personal history from conception through childhood, peer pressure, social conditioning, religion, relationships, parents, teachers, neighbours, marriage, lovers and so on - all this history has left a mark or it hasn't.

Remember also that predicting human behaviour is now an industry and is led by psychologists along with economists, social scientists, advertising agents and so many others. Does anyone here believe that predicting human behaviour is compatible with the concept of free will?

Now if you believe your will is free do you think you can change your will? I don't mean leave your money to someone else! If we are free to will what we will then we could reinvent ourselves day-by-day, but we just know we can't reinvent what we inherently and intrinsically are. Our wills, ladies and gentlemen is simply the Crucible where our genes and our entire complex history meet, all that you are, everything that you do and think flows from this.

Conclusion

That was my swansong in the Toastmasters club. I attended for fifteen years and had stopped learning and contributing. It's time to move on. Writing this had been on the agenda for some time, so I made a start. And now that the moving finger is slowing down to a stop, you're thinking
"Great, thank God, at long last it's over." But just before the final stop, a grandchild may wonder –

"What's it all about, anyway? You travelled the road, did you learn anything?" Surely, no-one can live for so long and experience so much and not learn something. Well the truth is - all that I have learned or can be reasonable sure about will take up very little space indeed.

From an early age we learn relationships can be difficult. We are all unique and infinitely complex creatures, so it is impossible to imagine a relationship where all these differences can be reconciled without some difficulty. This is bad enough but now we have to factor in the peculiar trait we all have of deceiving ourselves. And guess what? Psychologists tell us the smartest among us deceive themselves most of all. Refer." Deceiving ourselves, thinking fast and slow" by Nobel laureate Daniel Kahneman. Publisher "Allen Lang." And it's much harder these days. Everyone is so well educated and supremely confident arguing their case. And we can page the Oracle, the Holy Grail of knowledge and access the fount of all wisdom with the press of a button.

We are told all the time that 'knowledge is power' so our pride takes precedence over compromise. If you want to remain sane, you must forgive - ten times, a thousand times. You can do this realising you would behave precisely the same if you were standing in the other person's shoes.

Oh wad some power the Giftie gie us
To see ourselves as others see us.
Robbie Burns

But remember, forgiving yourself is most difficult of all. I still haven't forgiven myself for all the times I passed my school teacher's home and never once called. And as an adult, those special people in my private pantheon I also ignored. I could so easily have crossed the fields when I was home and acknowledged their kindness and affection given all those years earlier. Then the inevitable sad day - mama's letter to tell me so-and-so had died and in the space of a few years, they all had. I felt such pangs of guilt, and still do. It seemed criminal that all the special things I had nurtured, thought about for so long and looked forward to saying to them were never said. It felt like a priceless debt, unpaid to someone most deserving.

Now that you have forgiven yourself, you must accept yourself. You must do this because you had no hand, act or part in deciding how handsome you are any more than you had in determining your personality. How you are and what you are is simply the hand life has dealt you-you had no choice any more than you choose to be born. So you must always accept yourself utterly, and without question. I only fully realised the importance of this fundamental truth as an old man. It's probably the only thing of value that I have learned - the only thing I am sure of. Imagine - it took me sixty years to accept such an obvious truth. Everything else is as open and questionable as the origin of the universe. This isn't. Up until the day I retired, I felt a failure. I thought everything I tried just ended up in what Father McDermott would call 'a squalid mess'. I spent all my life resenting I hadn't the gifts that would bring me great success.

It is almost always the case that people who are especially gifted in some ways can be seriously defective in others. You can accept yourself knowing that what you feel you lack in one way, you will be adequately compensated in others. And everyone has gifts. Some are not easily discovered. This is when you need patience and belief in yourself, this belief will bring your gifts to the surface so that they can blossom and grow. Maybe you didn't power your way through maths and physics? Here I'm thinking of Albert Einstein. For him, imagination was more important than knowledge. He was ridiculed by his former headmaster when his father enquired about his son's prospects. He failed several lowly teaching job interviews. After two years of failed interviews a classmate's father helped him get the humble position of "Clerk - third class" in the patent office in Berne, Switzerland.

A year later, he failed the interview for promotion to "Clerk – second class".

Still a Clerk, and a mere couple of years later, he gave the world the greatest intellectual triumph of all time - his theory of relativity – stating that quantities such as time, distance and mass are not absolute, but depend on motion. Do you dare imagine he stopped believing in himself? I say never ever stop believing in and accepting yourself. This way your heart and your conscience will be free so your imagination will guide you to doing something you love.

Finally, most importantly – this way you'll avoid the poison, the misery, and the sickness of low self-worth - having a positive, healthy regard for yourself doesn't mean self-love, just loving yourself. This way, you could end up like Narcissus – very lonely.

But if all this fails, and you are blessed with love, this most special, the ultimate gift, then as the song repeats: Love, love, love, love is indeed all you need.

What is this life if, full of care,
We have no time to stand and stare.
No time to stand beneath the boughs
And stare as long as sheep or cows.
No time to see, when woods we pass,
Where squirrels hide their nuts in grass.
No time to see, in broad daylight,
Streams full of stars, like skies at night.
No time to turn at Beauty's glance,
And watch her feet, how they can dance.
No time to wait till her mouth can
enrich that smile her eyes began.
A poor life this if, full of care,
We have no time to stand and stare.
William Henry Davies